THE NURSE AND THE NAVIGATOR
A Son's Memoir of his Parents' Battlefield Romance

BY CHARLES W. DUNN III

Copyright 2017 Charles W. Dunn III
ISBN No. 9781946022219

Dedicated to the grandchildren:

Billu, Skye, Monica, Andy, Larry, Chris and Lizzy

And to the great-grandchildren:

Rahm, Vayd , Zoe, Isaac J., Lucy, Isaac D., Emily

and especially Isabella

TABLE OF CONTENTS

A GRANDDAUGHTER REMEMBERS
By Monica Dunn Royer

As a young girl I remember thinking that my grandparents-- my Nana and Dada-- were like any anyone's. I remember listening to stories of the War often told in the abbreviated way that was necessary for a child's ear. As their only granddaughter at the time, I remember them giving me special attention. As a preschooler, I even was able to spend time alone with them in their ranch house in the Upper Peninsula of Michigan. I remember the gazebo in the back. I remember Bonnie, their toy collie. Mostly, I recall that my Nana would talk to me about who I would someday fall in love with and marry. We would head over to the local A & W Root Beer drive-in , sit inside the car and eat hamburgers while sipping root beer floats. It seemed to me that their life and their relationship were rather idyllic and that they simply existed for each other. Admittedly, I would sometimes hide in the bathroom and cry that I missed my Mom & Dad-- not realizing that this would be my only solo opportunity to be with Nana and Dada together.

Despite being very young at the time, I do remember many of their stories. Dada, for example, once told of his plane going down in the African desert and his having to walk for days back to his base. Nana talked of being a nurse and adding, laughingly, that Dada was by far her worst patient. He explained, in turn, that his towel would be thrown on the floor only when he needed to get the nurse's attention. Both spoke of having seen terrible things in the war, but also of how they had fallen in love nonetheless.

I will never forget the last time that I saw Dada. He was waving to us from the steps of my Aunt Jane's house back in Illinois, smiling as if nothing was wrong. He seemed so cheerful and so alive. He had wanted us to stay for ice cream, but we couldn't. I can still see the vest he was wearing and the twinkle in his eye as we pulled out of the driveway. Even at the age of nine, I knew that he was ill and realized that this might be his last time with us. It was. Now, as an adult looking back on it all, I realize how brave he was to put on such a cheerful face when he knew he was dying.

I think back to my own father on the morning that we found out that Grandfather had died. It was the only morning that I can remember Dad not getting out of bed. Mom informed my little brother Andy and me that Dad would talk to us later. We didn't wait, racing into our parents' bedroom to cuddle and make him feel better. I don't know that we succeeded.

After Dada's death, Nana enjoyed some lucid years during which I sometimes visited with her at the nearby retirement home to which she had relocated. Together, we would read Agatha Christie novels while sipping "7-Up." I remember trying to copy her mannerisms. I wanted the same red shade of "Clinique" lipstick that she wore as well as the white linen perfume that she always had on her dresser. We then would take a shopping cart to a local convenience store where we picked up treats for later. In the evening she would continue with her stories about the past and all its difficulties. And she would often repeat that my grandfather was the most handsome man she had ever seen. Then she would add that someday I would find a man like Grandfather and that I'd be very happy.

As the years passed, she slipped further and further away. When visiting her at the nursing home, I would sit at her bedside. Dada's uniformed WWII photograph would look down on us from her dresser shelf. Even after all of the other names-- including mine-- had been forgotten, she seemed still to be remembering him. From her I learned that, at the end, all the bad is somehow erased while only the good remains.

The night that she died, I was alone in my studio apartment in Chicago's Lincoln Park neighborhood. Being a sound sleeper, I usually make it through the night undisturbed. On this particular occasion, however, I awoke suddenly at around 3:30 AM. Listening into the night, I heard nothing. But in my heart I felt that she was gone. In the morning I called my parents for confirmation of what I already knew.

As I stood at the veterans' cemetery near Joliet on that grim February day as my grandmother was buried, I had so many regrets. I wished that Dada had lived longer so that I could have known him better. I wished that Nana had been able to continue re-telling her stories as I was growing older when I would have been better able to appreciate them. I wished now that the family could linger at the cemetery longer. But the wind ripping through the grass on that February day would not allow it. As we were leaving, I wondered what additional stories were being buried with her-- stories we would never hear.

I always knew about the trunk in the basement. When Dad opened it, I was amazed at the extent of its contents. After that I remember Dad attempting to organize its contents by laying them about on his office floor. Even then I did not fully appreciate the extent of the gift that Nana had left behind. I did not yet know that the entire story of my grandparents' relationship was available to us in their own words. My grandparents' military adventures, their wartime courtship, and everything that followed-- both good and bad-- would be reassembled one letter at a time.

AUTHOR'S NOTE

This story relies heavily on passages quoted from my parents' personal correspondence and, to a lesser extent, from the historical record. However, the verbatim passages from these two types of sources are treated somewhat differently. Passages quoted from other sources are handled in the usual way. That is, short passages are embedded within the narrative and set off by quotation marks. Lengthier passages are indented. The shorter passages quoted from my parents' letters are also embedded within the narrative while longer passages are indented. However, quotation marks do not set off their shorter passages. Instead, all of my parents' words-- whether lifted from their letters or from recollections of what they later said in my presence-- are italicized for emphasis. When any verbatim passage includes its own quote, this quote within a quote always uses single quotation marks regardless of how it appeared in the original.

In nearly all respects, I have attempted to preserve my parents' words as written. To clarify occasional ambiguity, I have sometimes added missing punctuation. Their occasional misspellings and uses of swing-era slang appear as in the original. Where a proper noun is misspelled, however, I have tried to call this to the reader's attention with a "sic" notation inside brackets appearing immediately after the misspelled word.

To this rule of calling attention to misspelled proper nouns, there is one exception. While in England, Mom's landlady was Mrs. Marjory Sims. When Mrs. Sims signed a letter, or when her husband referred to his wife in a letter of his own, they both spelled her casual name as "Marj." Mom and Dad, on the other hand, always misspelled her nickname as *Marge*. Their correspondence contains so many references to *Marge* that I have placed a [sic] notation after only the first such references in Chapters 3 and 4, respectively. All other such references to *Marge* are left unnoted.

My own occasional insertions for the purpose of clarification within verbatim passages are also by way of brackets rather than parentheses. When parentheses do appear, it is because either Mom or Dad used them in a letter. Occasional underlining within verbatim passages either appeared as such in the original or indicates an excision by military censors.

Also, this narrative includes many numbers. For military designations-- such as Army units and airplane types-- the numerals themselves are always used, e.g., the 45th Evacuation Hospital or the B-17 Flying Fortress. References to past decades in time appear as words. Beyond that, other numbers ten or less are given as words; those over ten appear as numerals. The only exception to all of this is when a number appear within a quote. Then that number appears as in the original.

For various WWII acronyms still in widespread use today-- such as ETO, RAF, USAAF, V-E Day, V-J Day, etc.-- I have generally continued to use those acronyms with an occasional, bracketed reminder of the full term being referred to. However, for various USAAF military units-- bomb groups, combat wings, air divisions-- I have written out the full names for these entities. To this last rule, there is one exception: all such references to these units within verbatim passages are preserved as in the original.

. . . in the course of working on this book I have realized how many stories still remain unknown to the larger world, confined as they are to the memories of veterans and their families . . . . [i]

Tom Brokaw
The Greatest Generation

And a . . . reason for tears tonight is one that can barely be understood now; it's for a reason far into the future, one that I've no basis for yet; but I save your letters each one because they'll be valuable someday to someone besides me. They're so like you, your personal experiences, your hopes, the war, impatience, music-- evidence of the very best? *Why yes! And all in truth. Can you understand the trend of my thoughts?*

From 1st Lt. Alva North in Belgium,
To Capt. Charles Dunn in England,
January 23, 1945

Some day I feel that your letters will mean a great deal . . .

From 1st Lt. Alva Dunn at Buchenwald,
To Capt. Charles Dunn in England,
May 6, 1945

Prologue
THE FOOTLOCKER

Going back to my earliest childhood days, my parents had always possessed an olive drab footlocker. Regardless of where we were living or how frequently we moved-- which was quite frequently-- this footlocker was always stored somewhere in the basement. White stenciling on the lid indicates that its contents belonged to

Alva G. Dunn
617 N. Waller Ave.
Chicago, Illinois

Of course I had always known that my mother was a combat nurse in WWII, that my parents married in England in 1945 wearing their officers' uniforms, that, because Mom's last name on the trunk is "Dunn" rather than her maiden name of "North," it must have been stenciled sometime after their marriage, that it was addressed to her parents' home on the west side of Chicago, and that it primarily contained their massive WWII correspondence. However, to the best of my recollection, during all the years that I lived in my parents' home, Mom had opened it in my presence only twice. On the first occasion she did so to retrieve some Army memorabilia. Since those items were not returned to the trunk, most are now lost. On the second occasion she had wanted to show me a picture of her younger brother, who had died as a newborn. Because the picture was taken after the infant had passed away, I remember thinking that my tiny uncle's lifeless image was a bit morbid to look at.

In the autumn of 1975 my wife Usha and I had been married two years. Usha was pregnant for the first time. I had just begun a sabbatical leave from my high school teaching position to meet the residency requirement for a graduate degree that I was then pursuing at Northwestern University. We knew that Dad was thinking about closing his private practice in Oak Park, Illinois, and moving back to Michigan where he had done his medical residency years before. But, to our surprise, Mom and Dad now offered to sell us their brick, split-level home in suburban Westchester. Because there soon would be full-time university tuition to pay, and because Usha was planning to take a maternity leave from her own career as a medical technician, this was not a good year for us to contemplate the purchase of our first house. However, Dad's terms were too favorable to decline. Like Don Vito Corleone, the family patriarch in the gangster movie *The Godfather,* he was making an offer that I could not refuse.

About the time that my parents were packing up and preparing to vacate the Westchester house, Mom informed us that she was leaving the footlocker behind in the home's paved crawl space. Further, she made us promise that the trunk not be opened until . . . *after we are both gone.* Except on one occasion, Usha and I did honor her request. During a later move to a different house, we did briefly open the footlocker to make sure that its contents were not suffering from mildew or insects.

The next few years in Michigan were some of the happiest of my parents' often-turbulent marriage. However, in 1981 Dad was diagnosed with leukemia. Because of his rapidly declining health, he soon retired from his position with the Michigan Department of Mental Health. In December of 1985, after considerable suffering, he passed on. Before his death, he made the request that his remains be cremated. That wish was honored, with Mom initially taking possession of his ashes.

Following Dad's death, Mom was determined to continue residing in the new home that they had built together in a remote corner of Michigan's Upper Peninsula. However, over the next two years she proved incapable of doing so. She was obliged to transfer the management of her financial affairs over to my sister Jane, Mrs. Jane Jethani, who persuaded her to move to a nursing home in Batavia, Illinois, near Jane's own Glen Ellyn residence. By 1995 Mom was suffering from dementia. She could neither remember my name nor carry on a conversation in complete sentences. In February of 2003 she also passed on.

A day or two afterward, Jane telephoned to ask if I knew Mom's Army serial number. I replied that, off hand, I had no idea but could consult the footlocker for the answer. Since our younger brother Bob, Robert N. Dunn M.D., had recently conducted considerable research on Dad's military flying career, we already had his military records. When I asked who needed to know about Mom's wartime military service, Jane's explanation was that-- since she was now in possession of Dad's ashes-- the Government would provide for the interment of both our parents at the new Abraham Lincoln National Cemetery near Joliet-- provided that we could supply documentation on Mom. So the footlocker was opened. [As it turned out, Mom's serial number was available not only on many of the envelopes contained within, it also was stenciled on an outside corner of the footlocker itself: N-771835.]

At the funeral, a small military honor guard was present. The wartime awards that had been earned by both Mom and Dad were read out. A three-gun salute was fired. And for the first time in many years, I cried a little bit. Later, Jane was told by the cemetery's caretakers that, among all the married couples buried together there, our parents were the only such couple that were both WWII veterans.

Our parents' were both gone. But I was no longer bound by the promise not to investigate the footlocker's contents. Some of the correspondence was still in the original envelopes, which were distributed randomly throughout. However, many of the multipage letters were now in loose-leaf fragments. In the months that followed, the footlocker's contents were arranged into an elaborate file system by date and topic. Care was taken to correctly reassemble as many of the multipage letters as possible. While no exact count has been made, the footlocker held perhaps 1200 letters and other family documents, of which about 900 were Mom and Dad's wartime correspondence to each other.

Mom never said that she intended for me to write a manuscript based on their wartime correspondence. Indeed, she never even said that she expected me to read the letters. Perhaps, she had passed the trunk along to me because I was the first of her three children to marry and was, in some sense, the most settled at the time. Or perhaps it was merely a matter of convenience. After all, it was easier for her to simply leave the trunk behind in the Westchester house when she and Dad moved out than to lug it elsewhere. On the other hand, I was the oldest and possessed, arguably, the clearest memories of Mom and Dad when they were younger. Moreover, unlike my siblings who both had chosen careers in the medical profession, my own academic training was in history. I would like to think that Mom saw me as being in the best position to preserve some memory of their wartime romance.

As I began reading through the letters, I observed that my parents' respective wartime handwritings were identical to what I remember of them. Mom's letters are written in a graceful hand. Dad's penmanship, in contrast, seems like notes marked on a musical staff rather than words assembled from the Latin alphabet. Learning to read his correspondence took practice. Even now, some of his words continue to elude. Nonetheless, his letters-- and Mom's-- quickly absorbed me. A new sense of obligation toward both my parents developed. In Dad's case, I was hearing from him for the first time in nearly two decades. Reconstructing who they had been during a brief but heroic time became something that I needed to do.

Anecdotes that my parents, especially Mom, had shared decades earlier now came flooding back. Previously unknown adventures came to my attention for the first time. Significant events could now be more precisely sequenced. A vision of my parents as young lovers separated by war-- rather than as middle-aged Mom and Dad-- appeared before my mind's eye. Indeed, with some of the letters it was as if-- like the Marty McFly character in the Hollywood fantasy *Back to the Future*-- I was intruding into my parents' courtship.

On March 17, 1944 Mom knew that her evacuation hospital unit was preparing to depart from England for participation in the impending invasion of Nazi occupied Europe. For his part, Dad had already survived more than a year of combat flying. On that day he wrote Mom a letter explaining why he was now being transferred to a new bomber group.

> *Dear Gina:*[ii]
>
> *One of the first instructions everyone gets in the Army is 'Eyes open-- mouth shut-- never volunteer.' It works fairly well. I could have backed out of this transfer; but the bigwigs thought I was the man for it; and I would be better off personally; but I didn't have to go if I preferred not to.*
>
> *I am going-- and it will mean combat and more. To be very honest, <u>you</u> influenced my choice. You see, it became clear that I wasn't going to do a passive job over here and have you in position of really fighting the war. So I am going to a new place. It is far better to share this all the way.*
>
> Love,
Gallagher[iii]
>
> *P.S. This above all-- to thine own self be true.*

Now I also needed to be true to myself-- by being true to them.

1
GRENIER FIELD

In later years Mom would tell the story of how she and Dad first met at Grenier Field Army Air Force [AAF] base in New Hampshire where she was a flight nurse and he was a recovering surgical patient. However, there are two conflicting accounts of how Dad initially acquired the injury that put him on the path to Mom's medical ward.

Back in August of 1942, when Dad was 2nd Lieutenant Charles W. Dunn, Jr., he had arrived in England with advance units of the United States 8th AAF, in his case with the 92nd Bomb Group at Bovingdon in Hertfordshire. The original American battle plan had been to attack targets in Nazi occupied Europe in broad daylight so that the bombs could be aimed optically. However, this strategy failed to take into account the high percentage of days during which northern Europe is hidden by cloud cover, especially during the winter months. Consequently, by 1943 the 8th AAF began work on the adaptation of British H2S airborne radar-- already in use by the Royal Air Force [RAF] in its own nocturnal bombing campaign-- for installation on American planes. On August 20, 1943 the 482nd Bomb Group was formed for the purpose of providing "pathfinding"-- that is, radar targeting-- services to the other groups within the 8th AAF. A week later Dad was transferred to this new 482nd Bomb Group, specifically to its 813th Squadron. The 482nd was located at Alconbury, a village of less than 500 people located about a half hour by car from the university town of Cambridge. No doubt he was selected for this new assignment because of his strong academic background in mathematics and the physical sciences.

At the same time, the 8th AAF had a policy that bomber crewmen must complete 25 missions to finish out a combat tour and thus become eligible for rotation back to the States. In *Untold Valor: Forgotten Stories of American Bomber Crews Over Europe in WWII*, Rob Morris reported

> In the early months of the [American bombing] war . . . the chances of a crewman completing the obligatory twenty-five missions were almost non-existent. Assuming a loss rate of four percent per mission, no aircrews would survive to complete their tours. Even at a loss rate of only two percent per mission, a man had only a fifty-fifty chance of survival. Early in 1943, aircrews over Europe were suffering losses of 8 percent per mission . . . .[iv]

At the end of a mission, the surviving flyers who returned to base could see for themselves only the extent of their own unit's losses. According to what Mom later told me, the AAF was deliberately understating overall losses in the hope of misleading the aircrews within each bomb group into believing that only they had been unlucky. If so, such a cover-up could not hide the truth indefinitely. By the autumn of 1943 the entire 8th AAF was obliged to temporarily reduce operations. Dad could do the math. Fearful for his life, he volunteered to be among the three pathfinder crews from the 482nd that were being selected to return to the States to learn more about H2X. His application was approved. However, after his request was approved, but before actually returning to the States, he broke his ankle-- badly. It is at this point in Dad's account that a discrepancy exists between his own explanation for the circumstances of his injury and what was subsequently heard from other sources. According to Dad himself, he had suffered the injury during an off-duty volleyball match. However, back in the late eighties when my brother Bob conducted his own research into Dad's military records, he exchanged correspondence with several 8th AAF veterans who had flown with Dad. At least one of these gentlemen recalled things differently. According to this alternate account, Dad had, while off duty, gotten so drunk that he inadvertently rode a bicycle off a country bridge. I am not sure what to make of this revisionist history. For one thing, I never observed him consume an excessive amount of alcohol. For another, I don't recall him denying a shortcoming when confronted by a credible accusation to that effect. So, on the one hand, the drunken bicyclist story does not seem plausible. On the other hand, war places men under such tremendous stress that they sometimes do things they otherwise would not. Perhaps the story of booze, a bicycle, and a bridge is true.

Dad was not generally inclined to volunteer information about his past. Nor was he the sort of postwar military veteran who tries to acquire personal capital by reminding others of his service. However, I did once ask how his medical treatment came to be administered in the United States for an injury incurred in the United Kingdom. On this occasion his explanation was-- by his own standard, at least-- unusually lengthy. According to Dad, if the 8th AAF in England learned of his leg injury, he would have been hospitalized there. If this were the case, he would miss the opportunity to redeploy back to the States. In consequence, he tried to hide his condition. He even admitted to me that he and the 482nd Group's flight surgeon reached an *understanding* to the effect that this leg injury would go unreported so that he not miss the opportunity to fly home.

He would later tell me that, once back in the States, he began flying training missions at an AAF base in Maryland. Meanwhile, at the Massachusetts Institute of Technology near Boston, scientists in its Radiation Laboratory were hand-building a new American version of the British air-to-ground radar technology. This American version of this radar was to be called H2X. Soon, American bombers equipped with H2X were available for flight-testing at Grenier Field AAF base, located just outside Manchester in New Hampshire. No doubt the Air Force selected this particular facility to flight test the new technology both because Manchester is only about sixty miles north of Boston, and because Grenier Field and was already being used for other training purposes. According to Bill Yenne in his *Big Week; Six Days That Changed the Course of WWII* "by the third week in September . . . the Rad[iation] Lab had installed a dozen H2X sets in a dozen Flying Fortresses [bombers] . . . ."[v] It was about this time that Dad himself was transferred from the Maryland base to Grenier Field.

At some point after his own arrival at Grenier, Dad's leg injury became so painful that he could neither walk without a cane nor climb abroad the airplane without assistance. Only then did the Air Force become aware of his injury. Once it did, he was duly admitted to Grenier's medical facility. His ankle injury was now diagnosed as a bimalleolar fracture. To repair such an injury, surgery is always required. During this procedure surgical screws are inserted to pin the anklebones back together. Dad himself described what the doctors inserted in his ankle as a *bolt*. Whatever is used to hold the ankle in place, it is removed after eight to twelve weeks. Even then, additional physical therapy will probably be needed for full recovery.

***

At the same time, Mom was 2nd Lieutenant Alva G. North of the Army Nurse Corps [ANC]. She had been assigned to the medical facility Grenier Field base beginning September 18, 1943. It was here that my parents first met. Dad was 25; Mom was 23. Because my parents' correspondence did not begin until after Mom's departure in early November for duty elsewhere, it is not clear whether they met prior to the initial surgery or only during Dad's recovery. Nonetheless, both their own reminiscences in subsequent wartime correspondence and Mom's postwar anecdotes provide peeks into this earliest stage of their relationship. In later years Mom would frequently recall that her first impression of Dad had been that of a strikingly handsome young flying officer whose arrogance made him a difficult patient. These later anecdotes add credence to a letter she wrote on February 29, 1944. In this letter she recalled . . . *This* [upcoming] *month it will be six months since I took care of certain very saucy Lieutenant at . . . Grenier.* However, like the Elizabeth Bennet character in Jane Austen's novel *Pride and Prejudice*, Mom didn't allow an initially negative impression prevent a relationship from developing with her Darcy. By the time of her later transfer away from Grenier Field, she and Dad clearly had connected.

***

From Mom's service record, I do know that on November 6, 1943 about two months before the end of Dad's convalescence, she was ordered away from Grenier Field. She now reported to Brooklyn in New York City for further assignment. This proved to be transfer to the 45th Evacuation Hospital of U.S. 1st Army, then stationed at Camp Kilmer near New Brunswick, New Jersey.

In the meantime, Dad remained a medical patient back at Grenier Field. Over the next our days he was able to maintain occasional telephone contact with Mom. After he could no longer reach her by phone, his correspondence to her began. Dad's first letter is dated November 10, 1943.

> *Dear Gina:*
>
> *Happy is the airman today for I have your address now-- and your letter. Now stay right where you are until we can get a few letters back and forth.*
>
> *Yesterday the bandage came off, and I couldn't have been better. Of course some of your 'lilac'* [perfume?] *would have stood me in good stead. Now I am wrapped up again all smiles at the prospect of being released* [from the medical ward] *Saturday.*
>
> *The first two days after you were gone were sheer gloom. My little rotund gal in the kitchen asked if I was lonely-- then-- 'Jeez, you must 'a been in love wit' her.' All in hushed tones of awe.*

The date of Dad's actual release from the surgical recovery ward is unclear. But he did continue to keep Mom updated on his medical progress. For example, in an undated letter from the base's station hospital, he reported

> *He* [Capt. Coughlin, the attending physician] *had a nice look at my leg which does look very nice. For the first time I am sans* [without] *bandage. It is beautiful. Nice and dry-- no ooze even if a bit scabby-- yet.*

13

In another undated letter written about this same time, Dad indicated that he had indeed been released from the hospital, but not yet returned to flight status. . . . *Captain Coughlin says no flying just yet . . . .* In a V-Mail to Mom dated November 19, 1943, he reported

> *'Googie'* [?] *had guessed at least three weeks for my leg to* [illegible] *itself, but in two days the goo is gone-- at last-- and very firm. All I have is a tiny square of gauze on each side held on by a piece of tape.*

By November 30 he was complaining that he still was not cleared for a return to flying status and was getting pretty bored.

> *. . . the hours pass very slowly without news or orders. Had x-rays taken the 29th & they show me to be fairly normal. I've an* [illegible] *and still have a pronounced limp. I don't dare look a flight surgeon in the eye.*

On Christmas Eve he sounded more confident of his medical status.

> *The adjutant called yesterday afternoon and told me to return* [to his duties on the Grenier Field flight line] *and with good cause. The word is at last here that I must leave, and the days between us* [before being reunited] *may not be long or many. I'm to take a flight physical when I arrive; and I am now on duty, free from the hospital and ready.*

However, a bit further on in the same letter he did admit . . . *In fact, right now it's a little sore. 'Specially in the left area* [of his injured ankle]. As late as New Year's Eve, Dad's medical status remained in doubt.

> *Today is a big one for one and all-- not the least of whom is me. To begin with, a few people, including me, have been concerned about my having an uncompromising case of osteo-- nice eh? But it is all a mistake says Capt. Coughlin. He came today. I shall have another X-ray Monday, but I guess I'll pass.*

***

From Dad's very first letter to Mom, his salutation was always *Dear Gina,* or some variation thereof. This originated from Mom's middle name of Georgina. For the rest of his life, *Gina* remained the name he called her.

For her part, during all the time I knew them, Mom always called Dad *Charles.* So it came as a surprise to read in her wartime letters that, back then, she virtually never did. Instead, most of her correspondence addresses him as either *Ricky,* or *Gallagher,* or even *Rico Gallagher.* I have no idea how the ersatz surname *Gallagher* got started. But regarding the first name of *Rico,* an undated letter that Dad drafted on stationary monogrammed as being from the "Officer's Club; Grenier Field, Manchester, N.H." does provide a clue. Dad's original ambition had been to become an operatic performer. His favorite was the great Italian tenor Enrico Caruso. Indeed, when I knew him, one of his few hobbies was collecting new releases of old Caruso recordings. In this particular letter to Mom from the officers' club at Grenier, he wrote . . . *So now I am 'Rico.' That is what Caruso's wife called him.*

***

Of all of Mom's subsequent letters to Dad-- at least among those that are in my possession-- the one that reveals the most about their time together at Grenier Field was written on December 23, 1943, about six weeks after her departure from that base.

> *Dear Gallager* [sic],
>
> *This afternoon I received your letter . . . . To think that you tried to call me the night before I left* [the U.S.], *now it's my turn to say damnation!*
>
> *It all seems so very long ago. I remember dashing like mad to the mailroom* [at Camp Kilmer] *15 minutes before we left to see if there was one last letter from you. When there was none, I thought you had reasoned that I had left already. And here is that letter now, for Christmas.*
>
> *O Gallager, even now I miss you so. I'm glad I'm not adjusting to missing you. Each day I review the time we had together so that nothing can possibly intervene; it is so sweet to be able to keep those days apart from all others. Remember--*
>
> *The day I knew you sang before you told me.*
> *The first evening I cam down to see you.*
> *The W.A.C.'s* [Women's Auxiliary Corps] *pie.*
> *Your singing in the bathroom.*
> *The whistling in the corridor which herald*[ed] *your visit. (remember when you came in daily to see Capt. Coughlin and would stop on my ward?)*
> *The evening you came to the Nurses' Quarters with cane instead of your crutches like a naughty boy-- and how very, very wonderful you looked in your uniform that night.*
> *The first morning I saw you in your overseas hat and leather jacket. It impressed me so much in your uniform I think.*
> *Our walk that first evening and our wish to see England together-- or any place else for that matter.*
> *The first night I rode in a brand new shiny, green Ford-- the Wheat Field and you!*
> *Staples* [?] *catching us on the steps.*
> *Our fried eggs as an evening snack.*
> *The movies (corny pictures), then a club, then the Wheat Field again.*
> *The afternoons we had ice cream in town.*
> *Our first and only dinner at the club one afternoon.*
> *Our only evening at the club.*
> *The first night after your 2nd surgery, you held my hand and didn't want me to go. You should have known I'd never leave you alone.*
> *Each morning the suspense about what Capt. Coughlin would say about your leg-- the knowledge that I was to blame. 'Give me strength Lord, give me strength.'*

The meaning of this last paragraph is unclear. Had Mom made some nursing error that necessitated a second surgery? Or had Dad somehow re-injured his leg while away from the hospital and together with Mom on an off-duty tryst? The two references to a *Wheat Field* do imply that they were already enjoying occasional private moments. Whatever the explanation, neither Dad nor Mom ever said anything to me about her having been responsible for aggravating his original injury. Mom's letter continues.

> *The afternoon you wrote 'may I always be as close to you as I am now,' and I tore it up because I was afraid of (or for) the future.*
> *The afternoon you gave me the wings* [from Dad's uniform].
> *The afternoon of the three pence, now do you know why I was so happy with the three pence?*
> *The afternoon your mother* [Mrs. Helen Dunn, who was visiting from nearby Massachusetts] *sat with us on the porch and I was afraid she'd see the wings. I didn't want to upset her, if only I could have known her then.*
> *The 'maple walnut' ice cream.*
> *Listening to the records-- 'If I Could Tell You,' Caruso, YOU, Crooks, Bjoerling* [three tenors who Dad admired].
> *The first night I really heard you sing. . . . Oh I was thrilled beyond expectation.*
> *Our chats--*
> *Our last day-- a hectic afternoon and a most peaceful lonely night.*
> *How could I ever forget those wonderful weeks?*
> > *I do love you so*
> > *Goodnight--*
> > *Gina*

Later in the War Dad, too, occasionally reminisced about those early days at Grenier Field. In February of 1944 he made his own reference to a second surgery. Specifically, on February 21 he wrote

> *I've been thinking about the night you sat up with me after my second ops-- I can hardly remember it. But I shall never forget your telling of it or my imagination of it.*

By November of 1944 they were moving toward considering themselves formally engaged. On November 14 Dad-- now a captain-- sent Mom the lieutenant's bars that he had worn back at Grenier Field. He then reminded her of that first occasion in which she had seen him wearing his officer's uniform, complete with those bars, rather than the hospital attire of a surgical patient.

> *These are the ones* [bars] *I wore on my* [military] *blouse . . . remember the first time you saw me in my blouse? And how we 'walked'* [Dad was on crutches] *from the nurses quarters down the road and back. It almost brings tears thinking of just that. You held my arm and it swept right over me: 'Why, this is the first time you've* [Dad himself] *ever known anything as clear and wonderful as this.' It was a brand new emotion. Somewhere I had subconsciously decided long before that*

16

girls just thought you were nice or they didn't. But this!-- I was awed-- even had to push it back to arm's length so as not to be completely dazed. And there isn't any of that that has disappeared except being more grown and full.

Did you feel that wonderful surge that night too? Can you wonder why I think myself blessed when I can remember one such evening? Do[es] all of this tell you how much I love you and that we are one?

Ricky

On November 29 Mom responded.

Yes, I remember our walk at Grenier, the way you looked in your blouse. At that time I don't know if I was conscious of love, perhaps because it wasn't like me to admit to myself recognition of love-- but remember when I did-- I was awed, too. I almost ran away, or did I? But you came to England!

On December 11 Dad again reminisced about those idyllic early days at Grenier Field.

I wish I were your patient again. Remember how you used to stand on the foot of my bed against the wall? Thinking of things like that drives away all care-- except for you.

***

During his convalescence, Dad also continued to keep track of the air war over Europe. On November 10, 1943, just three days after Mom's departure from Grenier Field, he was still confined to the base's station hospital. On that date, in his very first letter to Mom, he was already lamenting the loss of some flying colleagues. He had learned of their deaths from a magazine article.

I read an article in the Cosmopolitan today and learned of the death of my closest friends in the old group & and an enlisted man I was 'pal' to. I wonder how many more there are I know nothing about.

He understood that this temporary redeployment back to the United States-- plus the delayed return to England on account of his hospitalization-- had probably saved his life. By not being on one of those first H2X-equipped B-17s that departed for England back in September, he missed going on bombing raids in which the 8th AAF sustained some of its highest loss rates of the war. On October 2, 1944 months after he had returned to England he wrote

I didn't want to stay behind the sq[uadron] when they left Grenier [to return to England] because I was in a pretty up & coming spot at the time. I might possible be a major now. But I might equally well be a dead major . . . .

***

In his remaining days at Grenier, Dad's letters began providing hints of his impending return to duty. He ended his New Year's Eve letter with an enigmatic postscript: *Leaving Grenier Monday* [January 3, 1944]*, you ponder on that.* Regarding his return to England, it is doubtful that Dad would have been given any advance information. When Mom had boarded a troop ship New York Harbor on November 16, 1943, her unit was not informed of the ship's destination until after it sailed   Presumably, Dad now found himself in the same position.

2

BEGINNINGS

Before Mom's footlocker was opened, what little I knew about Dad's early life and military career came from anecdotes he would occasionally share, usually only when requested to do so, and from some research into his official U.S. military records that my younger brother Bob had conducted back in the eighties. Dad had grown up in Danvers, a suburb of Boston, as the only child of an older couple, Charles and Helen Dunn. He originally assumed them to be his biological parents. Though he later would say virtually nothing about his childhood years, I do know that the Dunns had been affluent enough to provide him with a private school education at the Huntington School for Boys. I also know that, at some point along the way, he had skipped a grade, finishing high school in the spring of 1934. He was not quite 17. That autumn he began attending classes at

Dad's high school graduation picture.

Harvard College in nearby Cambridge. While at Harvard he did not live on campus but rather commuted from Danvers. Perhaps this was because Mr. Dunn was in declining health. Then too, perhaps the Great Depression was taking a financial toll on the Dunn household. If so, perhaps Dad's parents could afford only his tuition but not anything additional for room and board. At Harvard Dad majored in astronomy. Years later, when I was a college undergraduate seeking fatherly advice about my own course of study, he told me the story of a particular Harvard classmate. According to Dad, he had asked this other young man to account for the particular combination of courses that he was taking, an assemblage that did not seem to lead toward any discernable goal. In response, the young man explained that the advantage of his particular course schedule was that all of his classes were located on the first floor. In any event, after two years of low grades, the academic dean informed Dad that his own presence at the college would no longer be required. [In 1960, when Sen. John F. Kennedy was running for president, I realized that he and Dad had been enrolled at Harvard at about the same time. So I asked if they had been acquainted. Dad's answer was that he had not known Sen. Kennedy himself, but had once been introduced to his maternal grandfather, "Honey Fitz" Fitzgerald, a local Boston politician.]

Regarding the next four years there is a gap in my understanding of Dad's activities. I do know that at this stage of his life his ambition was to become an operatic tenor. Toward this goal, he did take professional voice lessons, at least occasionally. He also once told me that he had for a time driven a delivery truck for his father's small shoe manufacturing business. However, in 1939 the original Charles Dunn died at the age of 80. What remained of his firm was sold off and Dad's relationship with the family business ended. Then, in July of 1941, at the age of 22 Dad enlisted in the Army Air Force, initially to train as a radio operator. He first heard the news of the Japanese attack on Pearl Harbor while lying in his bunk at an AAF training base. A week after Pearl Harbor, he was promoted to a pre-flight training program for air cadets at Maxwell Field in Alabama. Below is a photo taken sometime during these early AAF days, although it is not clear whether this particular picture was taken at Maxwell Field.

Dad is standing in the center wearing the goofy hat.

***

While Charles & Helen Dunn had raised Dad as if he was their biological child, they informed him about the time he was finishing high school that they were actually only his adoptive parents. His birth parents were, in fact, Maj. Benjamin A. Moeller, a retired Marine Corps officer, and his wife Marguerite of Fountain City, Tennessee, then an unincorporated suburb of Knoxville. Indeed, rather than being an only child, Dad was the fourth of six children born into the Moeller household. Moreover, his five siblings were all still living with their parents in Fountain City. The Dunns then handed Dad a train ticket to Knoxville and sent him off to meet his original family. Upon his arrival, he was introduced to his brothers Benjamin, Jr. and John and to his sisters Sarah, Maryon and Marguerite, nicknamed Reet.

During the War years, it seems that the one member of the Moeller family to whom Dad felt close was his older brother Benjy, who was nearly five years his senior. However, unlike Dad, who had flunked out of Harvard's undergraduate program back in

1937, Benjy was nearing graduation from the University of Tennessee Medical School in the Memphis area.

Decades later, on a Saturday in December, I was a teenager watching a football game on television when Dad casually mentioned that he and Uncle Benjy had once attended this particular game together. Because Dad normally took no interest in competitive sports, this anecdote came as something of a surprise. Presumably, he had agreed to attend this event only because it was an opportunity to spend time with the older brother he looked up to. But when had this brotherly bonding occurred? Dad provided few details. This particular game, the Blue-Gray All Star Classic, was always played in Montgomery Alabama after the regular college football season had ended. In 1941 this was on December 27. Dad had been assigned to pre-flight training at Maxwell Field near Montgomery just thirteen days earlier. At this same time, his brother Benjy was in his fourth and final year at the medical school in Memphis. Had Uncle Benjy taken advantage of his days off from school during this holiday season to drive the 300+ miles from Memphis to Montgomery to join Dad? If so, it probably was the first opportunity for the two brothers to become acquainted outside the presence of their parents.

***

From Maxwell Field, Dad was sent to the Advanced Navigator's school at Turner Field in Georgia, eventually graduating as a 2nd lieutenant. Dad's birth mother, Mrs. Marguerite Moeller, and youngest sister Reet traveled from their new home in Black Mountain, North Carolina to attend this event.

Dad at his AAF graduation, Turner Field, Georgia, May, 1942.
Courtesy of Mrs. Marguerite Elliott.

On May 23 Dad was assigned to the 92nd Bomb Group of the 8th Army Air Force. During WWII, virtually all of the AAF's operational missions were flown overseas. Yet Dad's own first such mission originated from Sarasota, Florida. This was because German submarines, popularly known as U-boats, were preying on cargo ships headed for the European Theatre of Operations-- sometimes immediately after their departure from American ports. Very briefly, Dad was assigned to fly obsolete twin-engine B-18 "Bolo" bombers that were tasked with locating and destroying U-boats operating in the

Florida area. However, according to what he later told me, his plane never made actual contact with an enemy submarine.

***

The 8th Army Air Force, the "Mighty Eighth," was soon being assembled in England for a massive strategic bombing campaign planned against Hitler's Fortress Europe. Dad's 92nd Group was among the first to launch bombing raids from England. Before deploying overseas, its B-18s were replaced with more capable four-engine B-17 Flying Fortresses. On August 18 Dad's B-17 landed at Bovingdon in Hertfordshire, England. He later told my younger brother Bob that, while with the 92nd Group, he flew at least on one of the 8th Air Force's first bombing missions over France. Its first such mission had been on August 17. Dad was in England and available for flying duties two days later.

Since Dad and Mom had not yet met, they of course exchanged no letters them during this earlier time. However, later in the war Dad would occasionally reminisce about his early days in England. On August 16, 1944 for example, he reflected on how long he had now been in a theatre of war. *Two years ago today was my first day overseas. I can remember flying out very well indeed. We were on our way to England then.* On August 27, 1944 Dad was not going on a mission himself, but nonetheless compared this new morning with how he felt two years before when flying those initial missions.

> *We were up early and went to the control tower to watch the planes take off on the mission. It is a very dramatic thing to witness. There was fog on the ground and something was in the air that made it all seem fresh and new and full of excitement & curiosity as it did in '42. The feeling has persisted all day. For instance the weather is just like spring here again. Two years ago we were so new and explorative & had lots of time. I <u>have</u> changed for the deeper side since then.*

On March 12, 1945 Dad again reminisced about these early days at Bovingdon.

> *This afternoon I had to visit two of the other groups. As I drove away from the last one, the planes were just finishing landing on return from the mission. All the English folk were standing by watching the planes land and taxi past. I thought of how it must be to them, on their Sunday stroll or bicycle ride with the curious interest of the anachronous B-17's & Americans zooping past their haystacks. The war must be pretty far in the background, it has been so long. Planes are part of the English scene rather more than two years ago. On our original field the road used to be so close to the perimeter that the wing tips went over the sidewalk, and the bicycles and prams were there.*

***

Dad could not have known at the time that those 8th AAF airmen who flew such missions from England during the 1942-43 period had only about a 35% chance of surviving the war.[vi] So it was fortunate for him that he was almost immediately reassigned to the 1/11th Combat Crew Replacement Center [1/11th CCRC], which, among other things, was tasked with providing final orientation for new 8th AAF aircrews arriving in England.

Since this latter entity was also located at Bovingdon, the transfer involved no geographic relocation-- at least initially.

Very soon after this reassignment, however, some flying personnel from both units at Bovingdon, the 92nd Bomb Group and the 1/11th Combat Crew Replacement Center were temporarily detached from their regular duties to prepare for the American invasion of North Africa.[vii] Nearly two years later, in a letter written to Mom on August 23, 1944 he reminisced about it.

> *Just think-- two years ago we were just overseas and all set to get in on the African invasion. The place we landed first was [illegible], a very muddy hole. The only place to sleep was in the plane or a hanger. The hanger was more home-- part of it had a dry floor. We had a fire in it-- and we were real comfortable. Christmas eve we were very homesick. I sang Xmas songs for an hour. I remember thinking how much the Manger might have been like that hanger.*

Dad later told me that his B-17 was sometimes required to provide navigational services to smaller, single-seat American warplanes, such as P-38s and P-39s. Dad's B-17 would lead these smaller planes in formation from the United Kingdom around both neutral Spain and Portugal to the British military base on Gibraltar where American forces were being assembled in support of the African invasion.[viii] On October 26, 1942, about the same time that Dad was guiding other planes to Gibraltar, he was promoted to 1st lieutenant.

Operation Torch, the American invasion of North Africa, actually began on November 8, 1942. That day, American forces went ashore near Casablanca on the Atlantic coast of Morocco and near Oran and Algiers on the Mediterranean coast of Algeria. Dad never spoke in specific terms about this historic event, at least to me. But he did mention having flown as navigator on a B-25 Mitchell medium bomber at some point during the North African campaign. Indeed, he later told my brother Bob that he had flown 18 combat missions there. While Dad never mentioned to me having gone on a specific number of North African combat missions, he did share two relevant anecdotes. B-25s were twin-engine airplanes with the wing mounted at mid-fuselage and spanning about 70 feet. So, too, was a *Luftwaffe* bomber, the Ju-88. Dad remembered an instance when one Ju-88, apparently lost, tried to join his formation. At about the same time both sides noticed this blunder. Machine gun fire was briefly exchanged. The German plane then flew off, apparently unharmed. Further, Dad recalled for me-- without apparent embarrassment-- an occasion when he and his crewmates had wrecked their plane well short of the runway. He never specified exactly where this had occurred, but the main American force was then in the process of making its way from Morocco through Algeria to Tunisia. He did say, however, that when he and the others in his crew had attempted to walk back to their airfield-- leaving behind all the machine guns on their wrecked plane-- they had been relieved of their valuables, including Dad's wristwatch, by armed men who Dad took to be nomadic tribesmen.

On June 1, 1945 shortly after the end of European hostilities, Dad's correspondence again reminisces about his North African experiences. On that day he happened to be visiting a military hospital in England where a fellow navigator was recovering from a nervous breakdown. While visiting this man on the hospital ward, he ran into an airman who he had apparently met during his days with the 1/11th Combat Crew Replacement Center nearly three years earlier.

> *On the same ward was a lad whom I came overseas with. He was shot down early in the game-- over France. The underground smuggled him to the border* [with Spain], *but in crossing the Pyrenees he was unfortunate and had to have a few toes amputated as a result of frostbite. The Spanish authorities sent him to Gibraltar where he was held for air transport to* [the] *UK . . . . Well, when we were in Gibraltar coming back to England they gave us news that we should have escapees for passengers. We went down to give them a cheery American word in an English world, and it turned out he was one of them. His name is Frost & he is from Detroit.*

Uncle Benjy later mentioned that his own initial overseas contact with Dad had occurred in North Africa where he was a supervisor of the Army's surgical care program on behalf of the Allied campaign to evict Germans forces from that continent. In any event, at some point the two brothers had briefly met up somewhere in northern Africa.

***

On January 6, 1943 Dad was officially returned the 92nd Bomb Group, which had in the meantime moved from its original location at Bovingdon in Hertfordshire moved to Alconbury in Cambridgeshire. Many years ago I was leafing through an illustrated history of the United States Air Force. This volume [which has long since been discarded] included a picture taken at the beginning of a mission with a row of B-17's taxiing into position for takeoff when the first plane in line suddenly exploded. I remember showing this picture to Dad. In a standard B-17 the navigator sat in front of and just below the pilots' raised flight deck, but behind the bombardier, who was positioned in the extreme nose of the plane. Because the B-17 was originally designed for the bombs to be aimed optically, its clear Plexiglas nose provided the bombardier-- and the navigator sitting immediately behind him-- with a virtually unobstructed view looking forward. Upon seeing the photograph, he explained how, at the beginning of a mission, each plane was loaded with as much fuel, ammunition, and bomb tonnage as possible. He added that his plane had been third in line. According to Dad, when the first plane unexpectedly blew up-- probably from a bomb detonating prematurely-- molten debris from this first plane had ignited the second. He described for me his horror as he peered forward and wondered whether his own plane would be next.

Back in the late eighties, shortly after Dad's passing, my brother Bob was conducting his own research into Dad's military flying career. As part of this effort, Bob contacted a number of men who had served with Dad in the 92nd Bomb Group. His research revealed an incident very similar to the account Dad had previously shared with me. According to Bob, this event had occurred

> . . . at Alconbury on May 27, 1943 . . . Dad was still with the 92nd BG. At that time Alconbury was being used by the 92nd and 95th BG's, and one of the latter exploded when being loaded with bombs. I only know about one B-17 blowing up, but at least 4 others were damaged beyond repair and a dozen more were damaged. 19 men were killed and 30 more were wounded. Small pieces of

human flesh remained stuck to fences and trees for weeks afterwards. Dad was there at the time. As to two B-17s exploding while waiting to take off, it is possible that Dad's plane could have been taxiing at the time of the explosion and the planes in front of the line were destroyed . . . . [ix]

[Bob's version of Dad's account does not quite agree with mine. Perhaps Dad had been asked to fly a mission with the 95th Group that day. Or perhaps I had misunderstood that Dad had witnessed the catastrophe from a ground position.]

***

For her part, Alva North was born in Chicago to immigrant parents, graduated from a public high school on the City's west side in 1937, graduated from the nurses' training program at West Suburban Hospital in neighboring Oak Park in May of 1941, and

Mom's nursing school graduation picture, May, 1941.

received her nurse's registry from the State of Illinois in August of that year. Upon her graduation, she secured employment as a surgical nurse at West Suburban. In April of 1943 Mom enlisted in the U.S. Army and was immediately ordered to report for duty to the military hospital at Selfridge Field AAF Base in Harrison County near Detroit, Michigan.

I later once asked Mom why she had enlisted in the military when it was still a rarity for women to do so. Her explanation was that it had been to break off a romantic relationship from which she could not otherwise extricate herself. According to Mom, she had actually been engaged to a physician on the staff of West Suburban Hospital. She had then changed her mind about any future marriage to this man. And because this physician was not intending to enlist in the military, she did. Whenever she recounted this story, she always referred to him as *John* but never included a surname. [Decades later, when I opened the footlocker, there were seven wartime letters to Mom handwritten on office stationary under the pre-printed letterhead of Dr. John_____ .]

***

Following her enlistment in the Army, Mom's first life threatening experience occurred not on some overseas battlefield but in an American city not too far from home. In the 1940's racial prejudice in America was still overt. Legalized segregation of public accommodations, a system called "Jim Crow," was rampant in the states of the former southern Confederacy. Moreover, this Jim Crow system extended to the military where African-Americans were required to serve in segregated units and confined to mostly menial jobs. By May of 1943 Mom had been in the Army for only one month. On May 5, while off duty from her nursing responsibilities on the medical ward at Selfridge Field, she happened to be in the base's officer's club. She would later described to my brother Bob what happened next.

> Mom told me after arriving at Selfridge Field . . . she was at the officers' club. An officer . . . had a few too many drinks and called the motor pool for a ride home. A car arrived that was being driven by a Negro enlisted man. The officer pulled out his .45 caliber pistol and shot the driver in the head, killing him instantly. The officer was not charged with a crime.[x]

Mom did not claim to have actually witnessed the shooting, which occurred just outside the club. And, contrary to her recollection, the shooter, base commander Col. William Coleman, did face various charges. However, he was convicted only of the careless use of a firearm. His only punishment was demotion to the rank of captain.

A month later, still in the United States, Mom's own life was endangered. In northern cities like Chicago and Detroit, local laws generally did not ban African Americans from patronizing certain businesses, traveling in the same railroad passenger cars as whites, or attending the same public schools, but social custom often prevented them from actually doing these ordinary things. The onset of the War, however, soon threatened this de facto system. With 15 million young Americans of all colors joining the military, there was now a labor shortage. Consequently, many employers who had previously declined to hire minorities were now obliged to do so. In a great migration even larger than one that had occurred during the previous world war, many African American families that had lived for generations in the South now abandoned their traditional agricultural work for new, better paying opportunities in northern factories. In particular, many southern families moved to Detroit, where automobile factories were now being converted over to the production of airplanes and tanks. This shift in demographics created new racial tensions. In particular, on Sunday, June 20, 1943 a race riot erupted in Detroit. 25 blacks and nine whites were killed.

At that time Mom was still posted to Selfridge Field near Detroit. As it happened, the Army had granted Mom her first three-day leave from duty just a day before the rioting began. She had used this leave to return to her family back home, a five-hour trip. She was in Chicago when the trouble began. On Monday, June 21, the day her leave ended, Mom planned to return to duty at Selfridge Field as scheduled. But she was not yet aware of the rioting. According to what her sister Louis later heard, as Mom was de-boarding from her journey at a Detroit depot, a policeman yelled out a warning that a race riot was in progress. Mom replied that she was a nurse who could render first aid to the injured. The officer responded that it would be most helpful to him if she would take refuge in the ladies' room!

The story Mom told me many years afterward is different from-- but not inconsistent with-- that which she shared with her younger sister at the time. According to this latter version, Mom did board a local bus for the trip from the depot to Selfridge Field. As a precaution, she took a seat in the back, hoping to mind her own business. However, a fellow passenger then walked back to her seat and threatened her with a knife. At this point the driver became aware of the disturbance in the back. He glanced up through his rear view mirror to see what was going on. When he observed the knife-wielding man standing over Mom, he had the presence of mind to reroute the bus to the nearest police station. The man who had been assaulting Mom then fled the scene.

On September 18, 1943 Mom was transferred to Grenier Field in New Hampshire.

3

ENGLAND

Mom once remarked to me that she had requested a transfer from her original military duties as a flight nurse to those of an evacuation hospital nurse because this increased the likelihood of being assigned to the European Theatre of Operations [ETO]. Of course she knew that Dad had previously served in England and was still assigned to an AAF bomb group stationed there. Further, she assumed that he would be returned to his unit in that country as soon as his surgical recovery permitted. Consequently, if she was also in the ETO, then a resumption of their relationship might be possible. However, such a transfer also increased the likelihood of finding herself in harm's way. In WWII, American flight nurses rarely faced real danger. But evacuation hospital nurses frequently did. Mom knew that.

Mom departed Grenier Field AAF base on November. 7, 1943 and was soon reassigned to the 45th Evacuation Hospital, then temporarily located at Camp Kilmer in New Jersey. Nine days later the 45th Evacuation Hospital's entire staff, including Mom, boarded the British troopship RMS *Aquitania* from Pier 90 on the Hudson River side of Manhattan Island. She was not informed prior to boarding what their destination was. To reduce the risk of being intercepted by the enemy, such information was a carefully guarded military secret. Besides, even if Mom had heard rumors that the *Aquitania's* destination was England, she would have been under strict orders not to share such information with anyone.

As it turned out, Dad was stuck at Grenier Field for another six weeks. When it was no longer possible for him to reach her by phone, his correspondence began. Since he was still officially attached to the 813rd Squadron of the 482nd Bomb Group back in England, he assumed that he would be returning to his combat flying duties there once his doctors pronounced him healed.

Mom wrote no letters from aboard the *Aquitania*, at least none that have survived. But once it began sailing eastward, its destination quickly became obvious to the passengers-- even without the captain making any official announcement to that effect. To Dad back in New Hampshire, however, Mom's location was by no means clear. So, on November 22, 1943 he made an attempt at humor-- as if her travel arrangements were discretionary.

> *The thought struck me that you might be sitting in some POE* [port of entry] *and* [still] *be in the country. If you really are off, why don't you dare think of going anywhere but England.*

Nevertheless, others of his letters assume that they both would eventually wind up in England. For example, in an undated letter drafted on the stationary of the "Officers Club, Grenier Field, Manchester New Hampshire," Dad requested that Mom

> *Send . . . your English and American phone numbers. I can make a call when I get there then. Just think, no crutches, cane or limp-- oh paradise! I decided to hang onto your Xmas present' till I got there. 'Till I can give it to you in person, I hope.*

In the meantime, Mom found herself aboard what, in peacetime, had been a luxury cruise ship operated on transatlantic routes by the Cunard Line, commercial rival to the White Star Line that had once operated the *Titanic*. With Mom and her unit's medical and support staff of several hundred included among the thousands on board, the ship now pushed toward Great Britain alone. This was because the *Aquitania* was a fast ship capable of outrunning WWII-era submarines. If it joined a convoy, it would be obliged to reduce its speed to that of the slowest ship in the group, thus becoming easier prey for enemy. [Years later, I remember Mom describing a conversation with an *Aquitania* crewman who claimed that it was a great mystery why the U-boats attacked some Allied ships while allowing others to pass through. However, most naval histories agree that the great "wolf packs" of these U-boats had been largely defeated by the spring of 1943, several months prior to Mom's passage.]

Robert Roberts, who served with the 45th Evacuation Hospital as a laboratory technician, later described some of the restrictions imposed during the voyage. In his *A Medic's Story: An Autobiography of Experiences During World War II,* he remembered

> It was . . . announced that anyone overboard, for whatever reason, would be left [behind] and there would be not attempt for a rescue since we would be a sitting duck for submarines.[xi]

Sgt. Roberts also described trying to deal with the boredom of seven days at sea in an overcrowded ship with little to do except gamble. "Our entire trip was uneventful, other than some big games of 'craps' in which I learned one soldier lost $5000 and jumped overboard never to be seen again."[xii]

On November 24 the *Aquitania* safely disembarked its remaining passengers near Glasgow in Scotland. From there, the 45th Evacuation Hospital's entire company immediately boarded a railroad train that took them 175 miles south to a place in western England called Charfield. From the depot at Charfield, motorized transport took the unit's personnel one mile further on to the community of Wotton-under-Edge, meaning located under the edge of the Cotswold Hills, in Gloucestershire. Here Mom was billeted in the home of an English couple, Reginald and Marjory Sims.

Meanwhile, Dad returned to England by air on January 3, 1944.

***

It was fortunate for the future of my parents' relationship that both were now deployed to the same theatre of war, but this did not necessarily mean that they would be seeing each other any time soon. Mom was at Wotton-under-Edge in Gloucestershire, about two hours by rail west of London. Dad was at Alconbury in Cambridgeshire, a similar distance from London, but to the north. Even after Dad arrived in Alconbury, several more weeks would go by before either knew for certain of the other's whereabouts. However, as Dad's old V-Mails from Grenier Field finally began reaching her in Wotton, Mom realized that he was now-- or soon would be-- released from the medical ward back in New Hampshire. Better still, beginning in January of 1944 these V-Mails indicated that his return address was no longer the officer's club at Grenier Field but rather the *482nd Bomb Group, APO 634*. From her previous conversations with Dad back at Grenier, she knew precisely where this unit was based.

In Britain, telegraph services were available at Government Post Offices rather than being offered by a for-profit company such as Western Union back in the United States. Moreover, the percentage British households with private telephones was lower than in the United States. Mom's hosts Reginald and Marjory Sims, for instance, did not have a phone. Further, now that Mom was familiar with Army life, she knew that Dad would not have access to a private phone either. Consequently, now that she had a pretty good idea where she could reach him, she figured that sending a telegram to be delivered by a Government messenger would be the quickest and most dramatic way to do so. So on January 14 Mom traveled from Wotton-under-Edge to the larger city of Bristol where the Post Office facility included a telegraph desk. From there she wired a message to Huntingdon, a large Cambridge town offering the nearest civilian telegraph service to Dad's AAF base.

> LT CHARLES W DUNN USARMY HUNTINGBON [sic]
> CAN YOU MEET ME IN BRISTOL   PLEASE WIRE REPLY
>   LOVE=GINA

Four days later, not yet having received a response, she wrote her first letter to him at his 482nd Bomb Group Army Post Office address [APO].

> *It seems I must be dreaming. I just received your V-mail with you're A.P.O. From your B. Gr. [Bomb Group] number; you should be renewing old acquaintances; and that is something to look forward to. Remember the many times you wondered how they were doing, and there you were at G.F. [Grenier Field] hospital? I sincerely hope there won't be too many changes or disappointments when you arrive.*

Two days later, Mom stated in a very brief letter that she was *Hoping so much to see you soon-- just can't seem to write a letter now that I know you could be back soon.* Three days after that, in an even shorter letter, she added that she was *Still to anxious to write; [I] keep wondering if you could be back here right now.* Two days after that, on January 23, she closed a letter with the admission . . . *Each morning I begin the day hoping that this will be the day. If only it be soon.*

Dad's first acknowledgement of Mom's attempts at re-establishing communications was drafted on February 1.

> *Got your letters and cable of the 14th. I haven't any days off yet, but that'll come. As soon as I get time, I'll call . . . . It's swell knowing where you are. And, having your letters, I'm writing in bed. Yes, Gina, I am here. I wonder if we'll be together in Bristol, London or Cambridge. I'm happy.*

By February 7 Dad was feeling impatient. *if I hear from you before I get leave-- I'll leave at the proper time. I think that I may start for Bristol anyway, before long.*

Two doors from where Mom was billeted with the Sims family lived Marjory Sims' brother Fred Breadman, his wife Phyllis, and their two young daughters Jean and Bernice. The older of the two, Jean, who is now Ms. Jean Ambers, kept a childhood diary. This diary helps place the date of Dad's first arrival in Wotton. Jean later wrote

I do remember when she [Mom] knew Charles was coming to England, the excitement was great; and when he actually came to Wotton, it was like a fairy-tale romance to someone like me. Your mother's delight was obvious to all when he came to stay. The first date I have recorded when he stayed with us for several days was February 10th. . . . .[xiii]

Whichever was their first actual day in England together, it definitely had occurred before February 15 because, on that day, Dad wrote to Mom that this particular letter would be . . . *the last . . . you get before I see you again.* Between February and June, Mom and Dad would rendezvous somewhere in England as frequently as possible. Wotton-under-Edge was easiest to arrange because only Dad had to be off duty, and he often enjoyed extended free periods between bombing missions. On March 31, for example, he wrote

I'd like very much to work either meeting you in London when you are off which seems quite chancy & remote or better still to meet you at Marge's [sic] [The Sims home] on a Sunday.

Again, Jean Ambers remembers ". . . he certainly came again in March and April. Sometimes just for a Sunday, sometimes longer."[xiv]

***

One of Dad's letters even describes the possibility of traveling to Wotton by plane. On April 11 he had just recently been transferred to the 96th Bomb Group in Snetterton Heath, a village of a few hundred located about 20 miles west of Norwich, the county seat of Norfolkshire in East Anglia. On that day he wrote . . .

Tomorrow I'll call Capt. [illegible]; and, if the weather promises to be good on Friday and if he has the time & I really get my pass, then-- he'll come over here; & we'll fly down to see you together. Isn't that something to look ahead to?

However, Wotton had no suitable airport. Moreover, Dad's letter mentions neither where the plane would land nor what transport might be arranged from this unnamed airfield into town.

For both of my parents, rail was really the only practical method of travel about England. While rail service to Wotton itself has never been available, it is only about 20 miles north of Bristol, a maritime and manufacturing city positioned where the River Avon empties into the Bristol Channel. To reach Bristol from London's Paddington Station requires a two hour train ride. Still, wartime trains had their inconveniences. Dad's letter on May 15 describes some of the hazards.

Things looked a bit desperate last night. The train was late at Bristol, and there wasn't enough room to stand! And little Ricky [meaning himself] holding a [illegible]! Alas.
Well, they finally tacked on the extra carriages, and then the rush was on. Just as if the darn things were full of five pound notes. We were over an hour late [to

London], *so I missed* [transferring to] *the early train but still got here* [Snetterton Heath] *in plenty of time. But, oh the differences!*

Sgt. Roberts, in his own memoir of Mom's 45th Evacuation Hospital, would later recall, "At night there was a complete blackout . . . ."[xv] He remembered-- as did Mom-- " . . . all street signs had been removed, so that enemy would have a hard time becoming oriented in the event that the enemy infiltrated or attacked."[xvi] He also opined

> The most exciting experience was traveling home by train at night . . . . Stations were unmarked, so you had to be alert to be sure you didn't miss your stop. The conductor was generally unavailable when you needed him. To make matters more difficult, the cars were sectioned off into compartments.[xvii]

***

When both my parents were able to obtain leave, they preferred to meet in London.

While Dad's service record is not specific, Mom's indicate that, during her seven months in Wotton, she was granted three official leaves of absence. Each was a two-night arrangement. Dad had not returned to England by the time of her first leave beginning on December 17. And he had not yet been able to notify her of his return by the time of her second leave that began on January 31, 1944. So, it would seem that Mom's only opportunity to rendezvous with him outside of Wotton was her third such leave, which began on March 20.

However, all other evidence contradicts this inference. For one thing, Jean Ambers reported . . . "Northie [Mom's nickname] visited London from a Sat-Wed several times. Certainly it was probably to see Charles."[xviii] For another, the letters being exchanged during this period imply that, for both of them, a London getaway was quite a routine.

The explanation for this apparent discrepancy between the official military record and their private correspondence may be that Mom was allowed to travel beyond Wotton with a day pass or even a 24-hour pass without these being noted on her official service record. For example, in a February 6 letter she mentioned . . . *I do get a few passes each month, so I may be able to visit you even though you don't have the whole day off.* Since she and Dad were both about two hours by train from London, albeit coming from different directions, it was logistically possible to meet there with only day passes.

On February 7, for example, Dad had been back in England for only about five weeks. He and Mom had not yet been reunited.

> *I don't have any days off yet, but I can get one most any time (a 48-er). So-----! If you have a regular day or days of leave, or if you have a regular interval between such days, <u>let me know</u>. <u>And</u> if on those days you visit London, tell me your usual habitats.*

By the beginning of March Dad was talking as if acquiring the necessary time off had become routine. *I'll let you know how soon my next 48 comes up.* In an undated letter, Dad advised Mom on the current availability of passes from the 8th AAF.

> *All hustle and bustle for a while, and then maybe before too long I'll have a pass coming myself. We have two 72 hour passes set up every month, and that is just fine. Just think. Not two days but three.*

In another of her letters, Mom passed along a request from a fellow nurse, whom she refers to only as *Sue,* that Dad bring along a particular AAF officer named Don Thwaites on his next trip into London. On May 7 he replied

> *. . . I don't know about coming down to see you with Don Thwaites. You see juggling pass schedules is tricky as it is (right now there are no passes for our sq.), and he may not be eligible for pass, not being operational* [flying missions].

Two days later Dad asked rhetorically: *Passes-- glorious leave! That's the subject of the hour. When?-- is the question.*

Back on March 4 Dad was contemplating his next visit to London, a city restricted by a wartime blackout.

> *Looks very much as if I should get my pass on the 10th or eleventh, too. I['ll] cable if I can meet you in London. Musn't forget to bring my torch* [flashlight].

In an undated letter probably also written in early March, he wrote

> *This should reach you, but I'll telegraph anyway. Probably tomorrow night. As far as I know I will be able to get off on the 10th or 11th. So you just go to the London Charles St. Club and* [I] *will meet you there.*

For some of these London expeditions, Mom and Dad would meet at train stations elsewhere and then complete their trip into the big city together. On February 15, just after Dad's first visit to Wotton, he already seemed to be inviting Mom to their first London date, although military censorship makes this impossible to confirm. In his letter that day, he wrote . . . *Tomorrow night I'll call again. I hope there is someone there* [in Wotton] *to answer. If I can't get through dreaming, take any train to_____. I'll be up there waiting for you.* Unfortunately, at the point in the letter where Dad had written the name of the place where they should meet, there is literally a hole in the paper where in the paper where the military censor had excised the forbidden word.

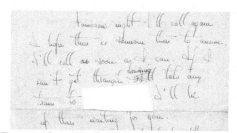

Excerpt from Dad's February 15, 1944 letter

In subsequent letters, however, Dad was allowed to name a preliminary meeting place. Peterborough, for example, is both an old cathedral city and a modern railroad hub located about 85 miles north of London. While it is located in Cambridgeshire, the same county as Dad's old base at Alconbury, it is also relatively close to Snetterton Heath in Norfolkshire where the 96th Bomb Group operated. On March 19 Dad was transferred to the 96th. Perhaps because of this transfer, the logistics of a London visit needed to be revised. In an undated letter he now wrote

> *New plans. Come to Peterborough instead of Huntingdon. You go to King's Cross just the same. I'll meet you there* [at Peterborough] *and it's a much easier place to get to London from.*

Soon, Peterborough became something of a destination in itself. On May 17 Dad wrote

> *I thought of how much we have done. Can you remember one night in Peterboro* [sic] *when you sprained your ankle? Or our enchanted moment at dinner . . . ? When I am 'with' you all is timeless. All our moments together add to eternity, seeming to be and having been always.*

On November 18, Dad sent Mom his original first lieutenant's bars as a memento. *These are the ones I wore on my blouse all the times in the States & in Wotton & Peterboro* [sic] *and London . . . .*   On March 24, 1945 Mom remembered the . . . *magic minutes at Peterborough . . . I thought sitting across from you then was perfect-- Remember?*

***

Not only did Mom travel to London more frequently than her official service record would suggest, she also visited Dad at his AAF bases: first at Alconbury and later at Snetterton Heath. On February 24, 1944, for example, while he was still at Alconbury, Dad described arrangements he made for her arrival. In particular, he . . . *just walked down to the place you are staying to let them know it will be Sat. night.* But just because Mom would be arriving in Alconbury did not necessarily mean that they would have the opportunity to socialize. The next day he added . . . *Most of my worries are about whether I'll get any days off, and how you'll like it when you get here & when I'll get a chance to see you.*

As with most of my parents' wartime photographs, there is no information about when and where the below snapshot was taken. However, it is an image of contrasting moods. If taken during Mom's visit to the 482nd Bomb Group at Alconbury, Dad's apparent grumpiness might be explained by his inability to get enough time off from his military duties while Mom's cheerfulness reflects the freedom she was enjoying that weekend.

Dad and Mom in contrasting moods.

Subsequent letters make clear that, once Dad had transferred to the 96th Bomb Group at Snetterton Heath on March 19, Mom also visited him at this latter location.   In his letter from Snetterton on April 25, for instance, he asked: *Remember the colonel who chewed us out when you were here? . . . well, he's among the missing. Remind me to tell you something about him.* Moreover, during one of such visit to the 96th Bomb Group, Dad even took Mom up for an unauthorized ride in his B-17. On June 20 he asked if she remembered . . . *the day we went up? Boy that was a swell ride. Just think how hard a time we would have had trying to do that at Grenier Field.* [Taking one's girlfriend for a joy ride on a front-line combat plane is a serious violation of military regulations and may explain why they had been *chewed out* by that unnamed colonel.]

Dad was proud of the good impression which Mom was making among his fellow airmen. In an undated letter he reported . . . *Everyone here thinks you're just grand.* Also for example, on March 31, just two weeks after his transfer to Snetterton Heath, he added

> *One of the mess-boys* [kitchen workers] *came to me this noon and asked for you and when you would be here again. You should have seen his eyes light up. 'You know, she's the first nurse I've ever been able to talk to.' His very words. When you come again, I'll have to beat competitors off with a stick. He's the one who fixed you breakfast & drove you to the train.*

Together on a tennis court.

Mom on a tennis court, probably at an AAF base.

On July 14, about a month after being geographically separated by the departure of Mom's unit for the Continent, Dad reminisced about an occasion at Snetterton where Mom was mistaken for a member of the Women's Army Auxiliary Corps, or WACs. At a time when the political concept of "equal opportunity" had not yet affected military policy, WACs were young women who volunteered for the Army knowing that they would be performing only clerical or housekeeping roles, thus freeing up more men for combat duty. Most WACs achieved only enlisted rank, unlike nurses who were always junior officers. Why had Mom been mistaken for a WAC? It was because, though an officer herself, she had served drinks to enlisted men.

> *Remember the time you served the enlisted men in the sergeant's room and they thought you were a WAC? Well Foxie* [a friend of Dad] *was reminiscing on your democratic attitude, and I asked him if he knew about that. He was quite emphatic in* [answering] *'yes'* . . . .

On November 25, Dad, still stationed at Snetterton Heath, reminisced about the day of Mom's B-17 ride. *Remember the place we lolled in the sun before the plane we later had a ride in?* On February 4, 1945 he recalled that ride yet again.

> *I went up* [today] *for a short local flight. The weather was bumpy. We flew over the same general area where 'we' flew that time. I remember your surprise at how your voice sounded over the interphone.*

By March 13, 1945 Mom's unit had long since departed for the Continent, but Dad was still at the Snetterton Heath AAF base. On that particular day, he was reminded of one of Mom's previous visits.

> *After supper I took a nice leisurely meditative walk. Remember our lane in the forest where we were with our bicycle. And how I got your feet wet? Well I went there. It was early twilight, the air was still, the moss was springy, two or three children were playing near the houses on the way.*
> *Then I came to the gate & the barbed wire where we sat and talked. The spot seems exactly the same. Thru the path (all the birds were tattling on me) and the jump across the tiny brook. It got my feet wet, too. And remember the open space . . . & the wonderful lane on the opposite side? A big pheasant went off with a rush and & startled the living daylights out of me. Down the lane I went very musingly and met, surprisingly, two little boys. I was really looking for you, but they somehow made it very nice. And then I had it all over again on the back just as we came back. I can't begin to tell you how 'whole' I feel.*

About a month later, on April 17, Dad again recalled off-duty time with Mom near his Snetterton base.

> *I've been to the show (The Thin Man) and taken an unhurried walk. Remember when we rode our bicycles to a very steep bridge over a brook and walked up on*

the crest of the bridge and talked for awhile? I went there. Why is it, do you suppose, that whenever I take a walk or a pass I am always going some place in quest of you?

4
WOTTON-UNDER-EDGE

Wotton-under-Edge itself is a picturesque town of several thousand located in the Gloucestershire area of western England. Hyman Lebson, a logistical officer with the unit, later wrote an unpublished account entitled "The Forty Fifth Evacuation Hospital in World War II, 1942-1945." In it he described Wotton-under-Edge as

> . . . one of the many English villages being affected by the current . . . 'invasion.' We were informed by a local historian that we were the first foreign troops to be billeted in the town since William the Conqueror in 1066. We fully realized that our presence disrupted the routine of the inhabitants, but we felt accepted without too much obvious resentment.[xix]

As previously noted, the unit's officers, including all the physicians and nurses, were assigned to private homes in Wotton where extra rooms were available. The hospital's enlisted men were provided only with barracks.

> Most of the nurses and officers moved in with private families two or three per home in widely scattered parts of town. It is easy to see that after some two hundred enlisted men and some eighty officers and nurses had been settled, the Forty Fifth had infiltrated every nook and cranny of Wotton. Eventually there was no section of the town that was not affected by our presence.[xx]

As previously mentioned, for Mom this meant that she would be living with Reginald and Marjory Sims. They were a childless couple about ten years older than Mom who lived in the back of a storefront at 46 Long Street. Perhaps because the Sims' living quarters were modest in size, she was the only American assigned to live in their home.

A casual image of Reg and Marj Sims from about the time that Mom knew them.
Courtesy of Mr. Jason Ambers.

Mom would later remember that Reg ran a bicycle shop in the front of the family's apartment. However, Jean Ambers, who was both Marjory's niece and the Sims' neighbor, recently informed me that, to the best of her recollection, during much of the

War Reg worked six miles away at a nearby aviation factory and did not take over operation of a bicycle shop business from a neighbor until near the very end of the War. According to her account, the space in the Sims home that later became the bicycle storefront was then used as . . . "a big front room in which we sat on Sundays."[xxi] Marj herself was then employed as a clerk at a local grocery. On April 21 Mom found herself the object of Marj's boss' attentions, a man whom Jean Ambers would later recall being " . . . a bit odd."[xxii] However, Mom herself was not too concerned.

> *Marge*[sic] *and I have been laughing ever since I got in because her boss asked her to ask me to go to the cinema with him at my convenience. He's about 40, a bachelor and Marge's boss-- that* [is] *really putting her on the spot. Tact! If you could only see him you'd know how funny the situation is. Thinks he's Adonis. If you ever met him on the street, it'll be hard to keep from laughing, and I'm sure I'll never visit the place Marge works in again.*

***

Mom soon bonded with the Sims. Judging from the letters that have survived, their initial relationship toward Mom seemed to be that of playful older siblings. Mom's letter on February 29, 1944 offers an example. *Pardon the interruption, but Reg is strutting around here with my bars* [lieutenant's insignia] *and teasing me so that I'll never get this letter finished.* Also, in an undated letter, she wrote

> *Reg just came in, and we're beginning to fight. . . . he keeps insisting that I'm not a Yank and you are. Gosh darn, I like the English, but if you're a Yank I 'wanta' be one too. I'm not English, am I?*

Further, on March 15 on Mom described an attempt to do her washing in the Sims' household.

> *I just put on my seersucker uniform to do my washing. This is the first time that Reg has seen me in a dress, and I'm taking another verbal beating. Seems that he didn't know I was a female before, and I'm being called 'a bit of a fluff.' Why don't I wear this when Charles comes down? etc., etc. What a tease! Give me strength, Lord, give me strength.*

Decades later Reg's niece Jean Ambers would remember . . . "Uncle Reg was always a 'tease.'"[xxiii]

***

Soon, some of the letters begin to suggest that the Sims were assuming the additional role of surrogate parents protecting the virtue of an eligible daughter. Happily for my parents' ongoing courtship, once Reg and Marj had the opportunity to evaluate Dad's worthiness, they found him to be acceptable. For instance, Mom closed her letter of April 3 with the explanation that she had to stop writing because Marj, like a good mother, would actually tuck her in bed. She . . . *is about to tuck Charles* [apparently a photograph of Dad] *into my bed; its time for a Goodnight.* Also like a good mother, Mother comforted Mom when circumstances called for it. On April 25

39

Marge just called up to say that a cup of tea was on the way up. Lately I've been spoiled with their attentions, all because I cried that Sunday morning [when Dad returned to his AAF base from Wotton] like a big baby and made everyone feel badly.

The very next day, Reg added his own fatherly advice.

Reg had a little confidential chat with me this evening. When it was over I couldn't help but think of the mental conflicts each one has, and of the obstacles to overcome each day. Also, of the necessities of beliefs to <u>maintain</u> our zest for the 'right' goal.

***

Beyond all of this, Reg and Marj occasionally even assumed the roles of rival suitors. For example, in that same April 25 letter, Mom hinted as much regarding Marjory's possible attraction toward Dad.

Marge has that gleam in her eye. (Just told her what I wrote. She said to tell you that the next time you come, she'll have the love light in her eyes.) (Now she's saying you'd better cross all that out.)

***

By this time Dad had already visited Mom in Wotton frequently enough to be on his own familiar terms with the Sims. For example, on April 26 he asked Mom . . . *to tell Reg that I still have his* [pipe] *tobacco . . .* which he had recently purchased but not yet had the opportunity to deliver. Dad then added, rather impishly, that Reg need not worry about the condition of this tobacco because . . . *the mice much prefer chocolate.*

***

Soon it would appear that Mom, Dad and the Sims were functioning together as an extended family. As preparations for the invasion of Europe were nearing completion. Mom knew that her time in Wotton was growing short. With that in mind, on May 5, she asked Dad for a favor.

She [Marjory Sims] *will write to my mom* [in Chicago], *which will be a big help. If you ever have time, would you write to the Sims 'cause they have been so very kind-- I think they'd appreciate hearing from you.*

At 7 AM on May 25, Mom reported . . . *Last night because of a cold I was tucked in very early, given a drink of whiskey and ordered to go to sleep by yours truly, Marge and Reg.*

***

Another factor causing Mom to make common cause with the Sims was the possibility of an enemy air raid. The likelihood of an intentional German air raid on a sleepy village in western England like Wotton was remote. At the same time, however, nocturnal bombings in WWII were notoriously inaccurate. Perhaps it was for this reason that the Sims household suffered a scare on May 14, 1944.

> *Last night just as I fell asleep Reg awakened me 'cause the air raid* [siren] *was 'going to town.' The house had been so shaken that the blackout* [curtain over the window] *fell down. But did I hear it-- nope. Marge and Reg made me come downstairs, but after a few minutes I was back up in bed again.*

***

Mom, Dad and the Sims even began observing milestones in each other's lives. On May 24, Dad wrote: *Still haven't been to the P-X* [canteen] *and Reg is still sans* [without] *present. Tell him my happy birthday for me though.* Meanwhile, back in Chicago, Mom's little sister Louise would be celebrating her 13th birthday. So, on the evening of May 25, Mom reported having on preparations for that occasion.

> *I had some necklaces made for Louise and my mother. Thought your mother* [Dad's adoptive mother Helen Dunn] *might like one too, so am sending it for you to send to her* if you like. *It will be accompanied by some candy-- yum, yum.*
> *Louise's birthday is June 6th so she should get her package before then. Reg helped me pack it up tonight, they* [he and Marj] *seemed to get as much a kick' out of it as I did.*

On June 2 Dad was preparing to mail a birthday gift for Reg.

> *Had Reg's package all set to mail yesterday. Now I'll have to rip it open & put in a special slip* [birthday message?], *and get more Scotch tape to do it up again.*

***

Now that Mom and Dad were both living in England, they could ring each other up on the phone for the first time since Mom had boarded the *Aquitania* back in New York. The Sims possessed no telephone in their modest living quarters on Long Street. But their neighbors two doors away did. These were Fred and Phyllis Breadman and their two young daughters. Not coincidentally, Fred Breadman was Marj Sims' older brother. By January 20, although Mom had not seen Dad yet, she knew he was in England. On that day she wrote that she was

> *Hoping so much to see you soon-- just can't seem to write a letter now that I know you could be back soon. You could leave a phone message with Mrs. Breadman's number: Wotton-under-Edge 65 (Gloucestershire).*

Mom's routine during these Wotton months was to participate in her medical unit's field maneuvers out in the countryside during the day and return to the Sims household each evening for dinner. She then would walk over to the Breadman home afterward in the hope that Dad would be placing a call to her from his AAF base. When bedtime came for the Breadman children, Mom would excuse herself and return to the Sims. On March 17 the Breadman phone came to Dad's rescue. On that occasion, he wanted to notify Mom about his impending transfer from the AAF base at Alconbury near Cambridge to the one at Snetterton Heath near Norwich. He was clearly apprehensive about the more frequent combat flying he anticipated would come with the new assignment. Nevertheless, he sought to reassure Mom that he was not unnerved by this change in circumstances. However, by the time that he placed his call that evening, she had already returned to the Sims' quarters. *Just missed on the phone again. At least Mrs. Breadman has the message for you-- bless her. She's very nice about it.*

Dad's letter of May 9 describes an adventure when he again tried to communicate with Mom via the Breadman's phone.

> *Made a call to the Breadman's and got quite a kick out of it. During the course of things I got locked in the phone booth (which is solid except for a plexiglass [sic] window). No doorknob inside or outside either. Got rescued by the flight surgeon.*
> *Now I'm writing at a little table loaded with glasses and glasses, waiting for the phone to ring for me . . . .*
> *This is the very hour when the operator said she could put thru my second call to you. Mrs. Breadman said she expected you would call . . . .*
> *I shall hound the telephone now that we have one. It's quite recent. Some drunk ripped the other from the wall-- but the phone company has renewed faith.*

Both Mom and Dad lived for the evening phone calls that the Breadman family phone made possible. On May 10, 1944 Dad wrote

> *As it happened I had to attend a briefing and had just time to return to the club for the call which they promised to put thru at 9:40 PM. 'Till you spoke I did not realize how much I had been waiting and waiting.*

On the evening of May 16 Dad was again having trouble with the telephone service at his end of the line.

> *The regular phone service is out of order again, and it was quite a little while before I found out what was what & that there was another in R.C.[?] club. Well, they promised me for sure by 10:30; but 11:00 came and still the wires were jammed; so here I am writing-- 11:20.*

That same evening Mom was indeed at the Breadmans waiting for the call that Dad was unable to place.

> *Knitted all evening at Breadman's thinking you might phone tonight-- but no soap, so I came back and find Marge is preparing a late supper 'cause Reg had been at some C.D. [civil defense] meeting. Oh, boy, fish and chips.*

In an undated letter that was also probably written in the middle of May of 1944, Mom wrote that she was . . . *So peeved because I missed your phone call, and got in too late to call you back because the Breadmans are in bed.*

On May 26, because it was a Friday evening, Dad thought that there was good opportunity to catch Mom at the Breadman's.

> *Just a wee bit disappointed this noon when you weren't to be found, but didn't really hope for such luck. Mrs. Breadman said Pumpkin just smiled hugely. She was right there. It was my only chance to call.*

At 9 PM on June 5 Mom noted a change in the training routine for the medical personnel of the 45th Evacuation Hospital in Wotton-- an evening lecture.

> *Just got back from the lecture on 'shock.' Only three nurses were required to attend and <u>all</u> the rest (and there were plenty) were doctors. Felt rather foolish but was able to be attentive and benefit by what was said all because I didn't have to miss your phone call-- you called before 4:30 PM.*
> *In reference to your phoning early, Marge said, 'You sure have a good guardian angel'-- and so I have.*

***

Fred and Phyllis Breadman operated the Herrick & Gorham newsagents shop at the intersection of Long and Market Streets, just around the corner from the Sims residence. Phyllis' Breadman's mother, Florence Cossons, was co-owner. The Breadmans had two daughters. Jean was the older; Bernice was the younger. However, in their letters, Mom and Dad always referred to Bernice as *Pumpkin* rather than by her given name. To these

Jeannie and Pumpkin, courtesy of Ms. Karen Anstice.

two little girls, both Mom and Dad became very attached. For example, in a little note written on an undated Thursday evening, Mom told Dad of having left her . . . *knitting next door* [meaning at the Breadmans]. When she went back there to retrieve it, . . . *believe it or not Pumpkin gave me this honey suckle to send to you. So here it is . . . . She said 'Smell it.'* [When I first opened this particular letter in 2004, the honeysuckle was still inside, the paper around it discolored by the biological material.]

Clockwise from left: Maxine [?], Dad, Mom, Jean and Pumpkin.

By April of 1944 Mom had been living in Wotton for around four months. At that particular time, Jean Breadman had recently taken ill. In her letter of April 1, Mom noted

> *Jean is sitting up today. Played cards with her this evening. Her dad joined so we played 'hearts.' Pumpkin looked very forlorn; so after Mr. Breadman left, Pumpkin played 'war' with us. Did you ever play that card game when you were little? Pumpkin won; wish you could have seen her smiling face.*
> *Jean had a letter from Louise. Mrs. Breadman thought it nice that the letter came while Jeanie was sick.*

Two days later Mom reported that *Jeanie is better today.* Two days after that, with the Easter weekend approaching, Mom added . . . *Jeanie was outdoors for the first time. She and Pumpkin . . . had two Easter dresses, they brought them over to show us.*

Jean's father Fred had more serious health problems, perhaps accounting for his not having been called into military service. On April 23, Mom reported . . . *Fred Breadman has been quite ill with some heart condition this week. Had everyone a little worried. He's much better today.* Three days letter, a doctor looked in on Fred. *The verdict wasn't too bad. Special milk diet and bed rest.* However, according to this same letter, Jean herself was feeling confident enough about her father's condition to converse with Mom about other topics.

> *Jean was in early this afternoon. We shared an orange. I listened while she chatted on about the wonders of the farm where she had just spent a week. Suddenly she said, 'You know I like the shoes that Charles wears.' How about that! Glamour boots!*

However, by the next day Mom herself was beginning to worry. *Fred Breadman is still quite ill. Mrs. Breadman, Sr. [Fred's mother Ada Breadman] was just in, weeping-- she is quite worried about him, just like a mother.* On May 3 Mom added that now . . . *Fred Breadman has have some chest x-rays, guess it has him worried.*

From left to right: Pumpkin, Mom, Fred Breadman, Marie Williams [a friend of Jean] and Jean.
Courtesy of Ms. Karen Anstice.

Dad was soon made aware of Fred Breadman's illness. By April 27 he was . . . *sorry to hear Mr. Breadman has been ill. Give my best, and tell Jean & Pumpkin I'll bring them some Life Savers* [breath mints] *when I come.* On May 1 he did again come to Wotton. Two days after that, Dad was again inquiring about their father's health. *First of all, how's Fred Breadman?* [I] *should truly hate to see him lose the gay twinkle in his eye. Tell all of them I asked. Pumpkin too.*
On Friday, May 5, Mom took the two Breadman girls with her to church.

> *They were very good throughout the service. Could hear Jean sing, but Pumpkin is too young to follow the hymns; but when the Lord's prayer was said in unison, then Pumpkin could be heard.*
> *The children looked very sweet and colorful in the drab morning. Jean was dressed in green and Pumpkin in blue with a yellow bonnet.*

That evening Mom and another nurse named Jean Hall played cards with the Sims and the Breadmans. *We played until midnight; of course Fred and Reg were as 'daft' as ever. Jean* [Hall] *and I took our usual ribbing about Joe* [Jean's boyfriend] *and you.* On May 7 Mom described a Sunday evening in Wotton.

> *. . . after dinner the children were over. We walked up to their grandmother's, then down to the cricket field. At 5 p.m. they had tea with me. Some tea! Jean was amazed at the little American tea bags. . . . .*
> *A very happy day-- and not without you either. Even Jean said, when a plane flew over, 'wonder where Charles is now.'*

On May 8 Mom observed

> *Pumpkin was listening to the phonograph and was enthralled with some music from Snow White and the Seven Dwarfs. Wish you could have watched her-- solely for the purpose of watching the effect of music and song on a six year old.*

On that same day Dad closed his letter that day by requesting that Mom *Tell Pumpkin that I'm saving gum for her.*

The next day, while at the Breadmans hoping that Dad would call, Mom added

> *Had Pumpkin to myself the latter part of the evening. Just before I read to her she said 'I know why you like to hold me: because I'm 'cuddly.' And I like to hold you too.' We played cards with Jean a little while, a pleasant way to spend time waiting for your phone call.*

On June 3 Mom had to explain to Jean the difference in color between the blue uniforms of RAF officers and the brown over tan worn by their AAF equivalents.

> *Jean Breadman spent the afternoon knitting with me. She's making an RAF (blue) scarf. Asked if you'd like it; but, of course, I explained about the color; so she's going to dye it. What's this strange power you have over the Breadman girls?*

***

Rev. George W. Zinz was the 45th Evacuation Hospital's chaplain. He also was the first member of the unit who Mom's correspondence makes a specific reference to. On January 21, 1944 she described. . . *Playing cards tonight (for fun) with the Chaplain. A rather pleasant evening.* By March 2 she was referring to Rev. Zinz as *Chappie.* On that day, anticipating Dad's next visit to Wotton, she wrote . . . *Chappie says you're welcome to stay with him the next time. That is, if you come down here alone.* The next day she added that, in Dad's absence, social events no longer interested her.

> *Everyone has gone to the dance tonight. Remembering last Saturday night, if I had gone tonight I'd just be wishing twice as much that you were here.*
> *'Chappy' couldn't even tempt me* [meaning with a game of cards] *tonight-- so I am spending another evening at home.*

As previously noted, Dad was able to obtain both day passes and full leaves from his military duties more frequently than could Mom. In his letter dated March 31 he wondered out loud whether he should use his next pass to try to meet with up Mom in London or travel on further to visit Mom in Wotton. The implication was that, in London, he and Mom would have more privacy. In Wotton, on the other hand, he would have the opportunity to both catch up with Mom's friends and sing in the Sunday choir, as he had already been doing. Indeed, as early as March 13, Mom reported

> . . . *Mrs. Elliott* [the landlady in whose home Rev. Zinz was billeted] *told Mrs. Burnett* [?] *about hearing you Sunday morning. Her statements were full of praise. Mrs. Burnett asked the nurse staying at her home about you. So this morning the nurse asked if you sing professionally.*

In his March 31 letter Dad requested that Mom . . . *Tell Chappie that, if I can make it on Sunday, . . . I'll sing for him . . . . .* Similarly, in an undated letter that was probably written on April 19, Dad asked her to . . . *Tell Chappie that he's got to get together for a*

46

duet the next time for sure, and also it was swell to see him again. On April 5 Mom was anticipating Dad's arrival for another weekend together in Wotton. Just where Dad had boarded during his previous visits is unclear. But for this next visit, where would he stay? *Chappie is going to find out from Mrs. Elliott if you can stay with him. Of course you can, if they have no other visitors. Hope so!*

Beyond Chappie's interest in both playing cards and leading the choir, he was also beginning to emerge as counselor to my parents' relationship. On April 21, Mom wrote

> *Dear Ricky,*
>
> *Wish you could have been at Bible class; we benefited much from the lesson. After class I had a chat with Chappie. He thought you and I were much alike. I don't see that though. Said it did his heart good to see us sitting together in church Friday and Sunday-- that we were his specials.*
>
> *This afternoon, out of a clear sky, he called me into his office and gave me his picture. Had made some for his wife-- was very <u>surprised</u> that he gave one. Some day it will be in our album. What a day that will be when we thumb through it and say-- why there is Chappie, remember those wonderful days in England . . .*

Latter in the same letter, Mom added

> *Tonight Chappie said that we choose our heaven or hell on earth. It made me feel secure in the happiness we feel when together, and heaven we can choose for tomorrow.*

On May 1 Mom's thoughts returned again to Rev. Zinz.

> *In another week or so you will have another leave. I'll have to tell Chappie to save some time to practice with you; it would be nice if you two could sing together.*

On May 5 Mom attended another of Rev Zinz's Bible classes. *I had an 'old time' chat with Chappie. Gee, it felt wonderful, like finding an old friend after thinking one lost.*

With Mom's own father far away and in declining health, Rev. Zinz was clearly becoming not only a spiritual advisor, but something of a surrogate dad as well. As such, Mom now sought his approval for her budding romance with Dad. For example, on May 16 Mom reported she . . . *Had a little chat with Chappie at supper. He said nice things about you.*

***

By early June Dad was increasingly concerned that Mom's unit would soon be making its way to the Continent . So he was relieved one day when it was she who answered the Breadman phone.

> *I think the most exciting thing was talking to you. I really hesitated to call thinking you wouldn't be there and was really surprised. And wasn't the connection swell! You sounded so real.*

47

***

After the 45th Evacuation Hospital did finally depart for the Continent, Dad continued to make occasional phone calls to Wotton providing updates about Mom. In an undated letter that was probably written on October 8 he reported

> *. . . this afternoon I called the Breadmans. No one in Wotton has heard from you in weeks, and Marge hadn't written of it to me for fear that I hadn't heard either. Fred sounded well & even invited me (us I hope) there for Xmas.*

The next day Dad acknowledged receiving

> *A wonderful letter from you today with another from Reg inside. And Fred with his 'Hello Sweetheart'-- the rascal! I told him he was one over the phone, and he rather liked it.*

By October Mom had been away from Wotton for five months. But she was still thinking about all the English friends who had been so good to her and also about the upcoming holidays. On October 22 she made another request of Dad. *When you are shopping sometime, would you get a Christmas present for the* [Breadman] *children, Marge and Reg for me.* Three days later Mom added *. . . I shall send you a money order payday. . . .*

In his own letter to Mom of November 28, Reg Sims provided an update on his in-laws.

> We [the Sims and Breadmans] are posting a cake to him [Dad] in the morning. Let me tell you the sad story of the cake. Mrs. Breadman [Fred & Marj's mother] made it for us to send to you; we packed it up; and Marj took it to the post this morning only to be informed we can send no food abroad. We were very disappointed and so have decided to send it to Charles; we know that will please you as much if not more than if you had received it yourself.

Americans military personnel, unlike British civilians, were not restricted from shipping food internationally. So after receiving the parcel from Wotton, Dad duly forwarded it to Mom in Belgium, although it did not reach her there until February 19. Upon finally receiving the cake, Mom was under the misimpression that it had originated with Marjory Sims rather than Mrs. Breadman. But she could say that it was still *. . . in good condition. It was moist and tasted good.*

Dad, date unknown.

5

A HERO

On April 14, 1944 Mom reported that a certain *Captain M.* was giving lectures to the personnel of the 45th Evacuation Hospital, then still stationed in Wotton-under-Edge, about the activities of the 8th AAF. She admitted that, while the overall presentation was interesting enough, she . . . *didn't enjoy hearing about the dangers of a mission.* That evening she attended the local cinema along with some other off-duty nurses to see the movie *Sweet Rosie O'Grady* and happened to run into this same *Captain M.*

> *Of course the conversation drifted around to you. He said you were the best navigator he'd ever had. The kids* [other nurses] *began to razz me a little, but I didn't respond (was afraid to with him there) and remained distant-- as much as within me lies. Hope you don't suffer any delayed teasing . . . .*

Similarly, on May 1 Mom described another conversation with someone from the AAF who also spoke highly of Dad.

> *On the train I sat with Sgt. Wenander from the 413th* [Squadron within the 96th Bomb Group]. *He said some very nice things about you. Told that you really put in some long hours but stayed cheerful. 'Kinda' nice to have those kind of admirers.*

Two days later she added that this Sgt. Wenander had said that Dad was . . . *the most important personage of the 413th.*

***

As previously mentioned, on August 27, 1943 Dad was transferred from his original 92nd Bomb Group to the 482nd and, in particular, to its 813th Squadron. According to John J. O'Neil in Thixton, et. al. in *Bombs Away: By Pathfinders of the Eighth Air Force,* this newly formed Group-- sometimes referred to as the Pathfinder Force [or PFF]-- was tasked with leading " . . . combat missions over Europe by means of radar and other electronic navigational devices."[xxiv] On a mission the radar-equipped B-17s of the 482nd Bomb Group did not fly together. Rather, each plane was assigned to provide pathfinding services for one of the other groups, or perhaps for an entire bomb wing. As described in Donald Miller's *Masters of the Air: American Bomber Boys Who Fought the Air War Against Nazi Germany,* The pathfinder plane with its Mickey [radar] navigator led all others within a given formation.

> When the target was sighted, the Pathfinder Planes dropped sky marker flares for the rest of the bomber stream. 'All eyes are on the Mickey ship when we are over the target,' a navigator described the procedure. 'When Mickey drops his bombs, we drop ours.'[xxv]

However, being in the lead plane was regarded as particularly dangerous because that was the part of the formation that the Luftwaffe preferred to first attack. This tactic was partly attributable to the fact that early models of the B-17 lacked a power-operated machine gun turret in the nose to protect the plane from frontal attack. But it also may have been that the pilots of *Luftwaffe* interceptors understood that taking out the pathfinder plane could blind an entire formation. In an undated letter to Mom, Dad tried to make light of his pathfinder status by describing how, when the destination during a training flight had been left up to him, he directed the entire formation to Wotton-under-Edge.

> *I was flying on the lead plane in the lead flight in the lead squadron in the lead group in the lead wing in the leading* [illegible] *air force. Guess where I led everyone. It shouldn't be too hard.*

***

On March 9, 1944 the 8th AAF was ordered to attack Berlin, among other targets. Dad's H2X-equipped B-17, piloted by a Capt. Hamilton, was pathfinding for the 40th Combat Wing that day. This meant that, well before dawn, Dad's PFF plane took off from the 482nd Bomb Group's own base at Alconbury to one of the 40th Wing's three bases, probably its headquarters at Thurleigh. While on the ground at this facility, Dad's PFF plane took on an additional passenger, the Wing's Executive Officer, Lt. Col. Andre R. Brousseau. It then took off again, this time headed for Germany, with the 40th's entire force of three bomb groups-- perhaps 60 planes-- following. Among all the combat wings attacking Berlin a few planes, as usual, aborted the mission due to various mechanical problems. Beyond this, six additional B-17s and one P-38 escort fighter were destroyed by enemy action along the way. 43 air crewmen were listed as missing in action. 339 B-17s actually made it all the way to the Berlin. Among those planes returning to their English bases afterward, an additional ten crewmen were found dead and six wounded.

Two days later Col. Brousseau wrote a memo lauding Dad's contribution that day.

HEADQUARTERS
AAF STATION 109
AP0 634

SUBJECT: Commendation of PFF Crew.

TO: Commanding Officer, 482 Bomb Gp. (P), APO 634.

THRU: Commanding Officer, 40th Combat Wing, APO 634.

1. The undersigned acting as Air Commander of the 40th Combat Wing, which led the Division on operational mission 9 March, 1944, rode with Captain Hamilton and crew. This was definitely a well disciplined . . . team that fully understood the importance of their job. On the whole trip each individual performed his duty in an excellent manor. The pilot, navigator and radio operator were especially outstanding in their performance. The pilot, Captain Hamilton, was thoroughly familiar with all of his duties as lead pilot and carried each out perfectly. The Mickey Navigator, Lt. Dunn, gave the D.R. [?] lead navigator perfect cooperation over enemy territory where there was a solid overcast and wind changes that caused the formation to be forty-five minutes late at the target. Without Lt. Dunn's work the completion of the mission would have been hopeless. He cannot be given too much credit for his assistance in navigation and bombing of the target . . . .

2. The Undersigned cannot give too much praise for this crew. It is one of the best. They are a credit to the Air Forces and should be cited for their outstanding performance.

s/g Andre R. Brousseau
ANDRE R. BROUSSEAU
Lt. Colonel, AC,
Air Executive

In recognition of his competence and bravery on this particular mission, Mickey navigator Lt. Dunn-- my Dad-- was soon informed that he would be awarded the Distinguished Flying Cross, the highest award that the Air Force can issue. [Only the Medal of Honor is more prestigious. But this highest of all American military awards is granted by an act of Congress, not by the military itself.]

***

On March 17 Dad reported . . . *I am definitely being transferred to another field, and I'll definitely go back on ops* [operations, *i.e.,* flying combat missions] *too.* Further, in this Friday letter Dad also reveals how much their relationship now meant to him, especially under these extraordinarily stressful circumstances.

Dear Gina:

One of the first instructions everyone gets in the Army is 'Eyes open-- mouth shut--- never volunteer.' It works fairly well. I could have backed out of this transfer but the bigwigs thought I was the man for it; and I would be better off personally; but I didn't have to go if I preferred not to.

I am going-- and it will mean combat and more. To be very honest, you influenced my choice. You see it became clear that I wasn't going to do a passive job over here and have you in position of really fighting the war. So I am going to a new place. It is far better to share this all the way.

Love,

Gallagher

P.S. This above all-- to thine own self be true.

Dad had heard that The 482ⁿᵈ Group itself was now being broken up. Following the Group's last mission, its flying personnel were given the choice of remaining at Alconbury in a training capacity or transferring to other units to complete their combat flying tours.[xxvi] Dad took the latter option. On March 19 he was indeed reassigned to the 96th Bomb Group at Snetterton Heath, specifically to its 413th Squadron. A month later, on April 26, Dad wrote a letter implying that he had volunteered for a return to combat flying because he would he also be entitled to regular leaves only if he were doing so. And he could visit Mom in Wotton only if he could obtain leave.

I'm happy thinking of how well I shall sing for you when I come again [to Wotton]; *and how you will listen with pride & love; and how roguish I can be. Aren't we fortunate that I am in combat, for how else should I be able to visit you?*

***

In their later history of Dad's new unit, *Snetterton Falcons: The 96th Bomb Group in World War II,* Robert E. Doherty and Geoffrey D. Ward explain that, in the effort to disseminate pathfinding technology throughout the 8th AAF, every effort had been made

... to call out men who had some special academic background in physics. Fortunately for the project, an unrelenting contributor was Captain Charles Dunn. At Harvard, Dunn had studied astrophysics. At the 94th [actually the 92ⁿᵈ] Bomb Group he had flown many missions as lead navigator. He transferred to [the 482ⁿᵈ Bomb Group at] Alconbury as a charter member of the project and now he was on detached service to the 413th PFF effort .... (Eventually, Captain Dunn would transfer ... into the 96th ....)[xxvii]

As previously mentioned, the 8th AAF's aircrew personnel policy was that all bomber crewman was required to complete 25 missions before being rotated back to the States. While this policy applied equally to Mickey navigators, it is clear from Dad's correspondence that he, at least, was not required to fly into combat as frequently as most other airmen. Perhaps this was because the Mickey navigators flew the lead planes in each formation, the planes that often were the first to be attacked. Perhaps, too, there was a general policy to use each Mickey navigator sparingly because they were harder to replace.

Moreover, PFF crews faced an additional danger not shared with other most 8th AAF personnel. By the end of the war, both sides had developed very effective "intruder" tactics. These tactics involved sending a twin-engine plane, which had been reconfigured for night fighting, to an enemy airfield after dark. This intruder would circle the enemy airfield as if it were in the landing pattern, thus mimicking a friendly plane waiting its turn to land. When an actual friendly plane either came in to land or had just cleared the runway on takeoff, the intruder opened fire. Because the friendly plane was flying too slowly for evasive action and too low to bailout, its crew was frequently doomed. Since RAF Bomber Command conducted virtually all operations at night, its planes were under constant threat of being interdicted by nocturnal intruders. In the 8th AAF, on the other hand, most operations were carried out during daylight hours and thus spared from such attack-- except for its PFF planes, many of which were required to take off from their own airfields before dawn to lead formations that would be originating from elsewhere.

One of Dad's letters hints at this routine. His 96th Bomb Group was part of the 45th Bomb Wing, which was, in turn, part of the 3rd Air Division. Within the 96th Group itself there were four squadrons. Among these, only Dad's squadron, the 413th, was tasked with pathfinding. Its B-17s flew as lead aircraft for the three other squadrons within the Group However, some of the PFF crews of the 96th Bomb Group would also lead other groups within the 45th Bomb Wing, or in other wings within its 3rd Division. Consequently, all PFF planes from Dad's 413th Squadron at Snetterton that were assigned to pathfind elsewhere were obliged to depart before dawn for that other group within the Wing or that of another wing within in the Division. On May 28, though limited by censorship, Dad wrote that he was . . . *up at 1:30 again, then on the job at 4:30* . . . .

From Dad's perspective the danger from enemy intruders was very, very real. In a letter written on March 4, just prior to his departure from 482nd Bomb Group at Alconbury, he mentioned having just witnessed such an intruder-style attack. *One of the crews was waylaid by 'bandits' last night with tragic results. I hope I have the time to visit them* [in the hospital] *soon.*

Similarly, on April 13, shortly after his transfer to the 96th Bomb Group at Snetterton Heath, his navigational colleague Lt. Jack Croul noted in his diary "Last night a PFF ship of ours was on the final approach at another field when an enemy intruder hit it-- navigator, bombardier and radio operator are dead."[xxviii] Further, my brother Bob remembers Dad once telling him that the pathfinder squadron within the 96th Group went on to lose a total of five planes in this manner. " . . . all were shot down by German intruders at night while flying from Snetterton to one of the other 3rd Division groups."[xxix]

***

Whether or not the added risks of being a Mickey navigator contributed to Dad's relatively low frequency of combat flying, his expanding job description certainly did. Because of his experience in this field, he was now being called upon to deliver lectures on pathfinding to novice airmen. Judging from a letter which Dad wrote on April 12, classroom instruction had become, at least for the time being, his . . . *regular job* . . . .

> *Since the last Berlin raid, I've been used in pretty much of an advisory & instructive capacity. Which is just fine except that I feel guilty, or very*

responsible, at least when these boys that I've tried to teach everything to have been [bombing Germany] *without me. As soon as they prove themselves, then I'll have to start again myself.*

On April 25 he described what these instructional duties were like.

Today I had to ride 40 miles & back to give a lecture that was pretty much a flop because I was practically out [from flu-like symptoms] *when I got there & had no backboard and stuff.*

***

A number of the bombing missions that Dad did go on are not mentioned in any of his letters. These include those that he had flown with the 92nd Bomb Group over Europe and with the 1/11th Combat Crew Replacement Center in North Africa, all prior to meeting Mom. But, even after their correspondence begins, there were other missions that his surviving letters make no mention of. In the case of the attack on an oil refinery at Zwickau in Czechoslovakia on May 12, this omission may have been because this day was a particularly costly-- at least for the 96th Bomb Group. On that day more than 900 8th AAF bombers attacked Zwickau and other targets. Of these, Dad's 96th Group contributed 26 planes. On this occasion Dad's Group happened to suffer a much higher loss ratio that day than did the 8th AAF as a whole. From the overall attacking force of 900 bombers, the 8th AAF lost a total of 46. But, of the 26 B-17s contributed by the 96th Group, 12 planes did not return to Snetterton Heath that evening. Dad wrote no letters to Mom that night or even the next day. Perhaps he was so saddened by the losses that he could not bring himself to write Mom even a censured letter about other subjects.

Mom at Camp Kilmer NJ, November, 1943.

6

A HEROINE

For an American woman to volunteer for the military and thus place herself in harm's way was, during World War II, still quite exceptional. Nonetheless, judging from her letters, Mom never regretted having done so. Indeed, she viewed the War as an opportunity for personal liberation. On April 13, 1944, as the U.S. Army's preparations for the invasion of the Continent were accelerating, Mom wrote a letter in which she sounded both a like a young woman in love, which she was, and a feminist, which she was not quite.

> *I'm ashamed of my thoughts today. They've been exceedingly ungrateful. Instead of being satisfied having just seen you a few days ago, I'm constantly longing for things I can't have yet-- such as you here.*
>
> *I deserve a good swift kick-- you know I'm one of the most privileged girls in the U.S. to belong to profession that can really experience and be part of this event. You know it's the only profession in which women have so active a part. If I had been a 'hen' medic I shouldn't be eligible to be here-- more important I shouldn't have met you.*

The very next day, however, she assured Dad that their love provided her the strength to face what was surely coming. *With the 'sacred' moments in our very 'sacred' place in Marge's passageway to remember, I do have courage for the future in every possible respect.*

On May 6 Dad received a letter [which has not survived] from Mom accusing him of having done something hurtful during her visit to his AAF base at Snetterton Heath the previous weekend. In his reply. the specific nature of Dad's offense is not mentioned. But the tone of his response is both regretful and apprehensive. However, the source of this apprehension was not the possibility that Mom might "dump him," but rather fear that Mom's unit would soon be participating in the impending invasion of France. If so, Dad might not see her again-- at least not anytime soon-- and consequently be unable to apologize in person for his gaffe.

> *Since you were here, I have thought with shame in my imagination that, if I were not to get a pass in time to see you again, then I would be doubly lost. Lost in that I asked too much & lost in that I now had that much less-- am that much less.*
> *. . . Now here alone I know that for ever shall I be reminded of the ways that were better. It is the light of beauty that makes of lesser thoughts a shadow.*

He closed this letter of apology by asking if she could

> *'------------------. Remember the very sacred place in the passageway? The door is open------.' Isn't there a wealth of meaning in that?*
> *Somehow I feel more like that evening now than any time since, and in my heart (and in this letter I hope) there is more 'being with you' than some moments you were here.*
> *The door is open. It is always so in your letters as in your heart.*
> > *A penitent*
> > *Ricky*

By the next day, Mom was steeling herself for what she knew was coming.

> *Dear Ricky;*
> *After much debating I decided to send you my Scofield Bible 'cause maybe you'll have more time to use it than I. It will make reading the Old Testament easier and more interesting. It will be the first time since July of 1937 that I haven't had it with me.*

Since disembarking from the troop ship *RMS Aquitania* the previous November, Mom really had not been in any more danger than an ordinary English civilian. But she was aware that this was about to change. While the specific day and destination for Operation Overlord were carefully guarded military secrets, the preparations for it were now manifestly visible throughout southern England. There is a long military tradition of not telling soldiers more about the strategic situation than they need to know in order to perform their individual duties. Indeed, as they wrote their letters, both Mom & Dad frequently knew less about the strategic situation than even a casual student of the World War II would today. By early May of 1944, however, both knew that Mom would soon be entering a real battlefield. Clearly, Dad was worried. In a letter written on May 8 he begged her to *Please stay 'put' for a little longer.*

Moreover, to the extent that either of them knew the specifics of what was about to happen, wartime censorship constrained them from mentioning this information-- at least in their correspondence. In his letter of June 15, Dad joked about the restrictions.

I bet that we're both wishing that we could write down stuff about what we are doing that would get by the censor 'cause, if your activities are shaping up the way mine are, it would make a lot of interesting reading.

Nevertheless, despite this censorship, their mutual correspondence now increasingly alluded to their mutual foreboding that Mom would soon be shipped out. For example:

31 May 1944
Wednesday evening

Dearest Gina:

It was hell waiting for that call to go thru this afternoon knowing that you might be leaving just as it came in. And then you were there and sounded so cheerful.

Truly, you have given more to me than I have returned. You see I get a boost, too.

Tonight I think of our first parting [at Grenier Field]. We had so little comparatively. And yet, we met because--------well, I guess we were trying. Shan't we try even harder this time?

And shall we be afraid? Yes. And yet when you realize that you can carry the fear of the others, you sort of glory in the knowledge that you are strong enough. 'Night.

Love you,
Ricky

7

D-DAY

Operation Overlord actually began in the early morning of June 6, 1944, a date that shall forever be remembered as "D-Day." It was the largest amphibious assault in military history. On that first day more than 150,000 Allied soldiers landed at five beaches along the Normandy coast of France. On D-Day itself Mom was still safe in Wotton-under-Edge. And even though she heard the news as it was unfolding, her letter that day makes no specific mention of it

> *Since early this morning, my thoughts have been of you and of home alternatively. Today is Louise's* [her sister's] *13th birthday, and the news of the day will have clouded the day at home; but I suppose there are many children with birthdays today who have brothers in the thick of things and with very anxious parents. If my parents are anxious, it will be for nothing 'cause here I am more than comfortable writing to you; if only they could know so that Louise would have her usual gay birthday. Poor mothers and fathers, the trouble their children do cause.*

✱✱✱

For the 8th AAF, the Normandy Invasion meant a temporary change in job description. For the past year or more it had specialized in long-range, high altitude attacks against strategic targets in Germany and elsewhere in Central Europe. The medium and low altitude bombing of tactical targets in France was normally left to the AAF's 9th Air Force and to the RAF's 2nd Tactical Air Force. Now, however, the 8th AAF was called upon to temporarily assist in the bombing of enemy forces in and around Normandy. To Dad's way of thinking, this change had both plusses and minuses. On the one hand, a successful blow against the German occupation of France would bring about a more prompt end to the war. On the other hand, he would be required to suspend his current instructional duties and resume flying combat missions.

On the evening of June 6, Jack Croul, wrote in his diary

> We took off around 0200 this morning. I was flying with Captain Bowman-- Captain Abel was navigator, I was his assistant-- Col. Travis flew and Captain Dunn was the mickey navigator; we were flying a PFF ship.[xxx]

Because Lt. Croul was merely making entries in an uncensored private diary, he was more candid about ongoing military activities than could either Mom or Dad when posting letters to each other. His D-Day entry even identifies that morning's target as St. Aubin-Sur-Mer. He then claimed that his flight "Dropped our bombs on the invasion coast just 6 minutes before our boys landed; '0' hr. was at 0725." [xxxi] Significantly, neither Lt. Croul's diary entry of June 6 nor Dad's letter to Mom the next evening make mention of any attempt by the *Luftwaffe* to intercept these attacks, most of its remaining planes having previously been pulled back to Germany in effort to protect the Fatherland.

Dad wrote no letter to Mom on D-Day. His letter on the next implies that it had taken him a while to grasp the enormity of what was unfolding beneath the wings of his plane. He now observed that it was

> *Kinda fun to pick up the S&S to find out what's been going on all about. And to think that the invasion has actually begun! Wow! How casually we thought of it before.*

This letter then goes on to say that the bombing missions which the AAF was now flying over France would reduce the burden for those other military personnel-- such as Mom herself who would soon be going ashore with the invasion.

> *You have no idea how the Air Force is fighting for the ground force. The crews* [are] *keyed up to put their very best efforts into the job at hand. Fighting together.*

For a time, Dad was called upon to fly missions more frequently, even twice in a single day. In his same June 6 diary entry, Lt. Croul noted

> After the [initial] mission [I] got into bed and was called out for another raid [at Pont l'Eveque just south of LaHavre] which I led alone with Dunn again as the mickey navigator . . . . [xxxii]

In Dad's own letter to Mom at eight the next evening, he described himself as

> *. . . sleepy as a cat. Surprising feeling 'cause I was still in bed at one o'clock (got in bed at two before). In the last few days I went on everything there was to go on.*

On June 11, in effort to prevent the Germans from sending reinforcements to the Normandy area, a small force of B-17s was sent to destroy a railroad bridge at a place in northern France called Pontaubault. For this mission Dad was ordered to fill in for the navigator on a different plane.

> *At the last moment they decided to send me, and I was put on in another navigator's place who filled in on* [yet] *another crew. It seemed like a queer swap looking back, but here I am writing to you-- the other crew? We seem to be watched over, don't we?*

The pathfinder plane that he normally would have been on that day was had been shot down with the loss of all but one crewmen.

This increased level of activity soon became a source of grumbling among some of Dad's fellow airmen. On June 9-- three days after the invasion had begun, but still seven days, as it turned out, before Mom's actual arrival in Normandy-- Dad asserted the others would not be complaining if they had a loved one who was on the ground in France. Normally, 8th AAF formations conducted their attacks from at least 20,000 feet of altitude to avoid small arms fire from the ground. Now he wrote

All of the boys are griping about the number of missions they are required to go on. . . . I guess the bunch of squawkers just don't know anyone on the other side [of the English Channel]. *Those that do would go over there at 1000 feet anywhere if they could do the job better that way.*

***

By this stage in the war Dad had been encountering the enemy for nearly two years. Mom's letters up until now had been offering Dad assurances that God was watching over him. Now, however, it was she who needed reassurance. Her June 9 letter expresses something close to guilt about this role reversal. She found herself

. . . wishing I was with you rather than waiting, but then you'd have double trouble with me along on a 'trip' [bombing mission]. *In addition to your job you'd be <u>anxious unnecessarily</u> about me, as I am about you.*

Now I need to practice what I preach; forgive me if I seem to lack Faith <u>at the moment</u>, but it's only because I'm very selfishly in love with you, that I push God's ways in the background. All I need is take out our verse 'Trust in the Lord' and apply it.

Am writing just as the thoughts come to me, and I feel better. [I] *find that the gremlins (doubts) are losing ground but fast if I only will keep my thoughts in the proper channels.*

Now who's introspective tonight?

Instead of the encouragement you should be getting, I will use your letter [probably one written on May 31] *to soothe out my ruffled feelings.*

On June 13, while her own unit was being marshaled for Normandy, Mom closed a very brief, unspecific letter with . . . *Take good care of yourself for me, won't you? Believe me dear, I have more than all in you-- being loved and loving you always . . . .* Two days after that, on June 15, she tried to assure him. . . . *all I need in your letter-- please don't worry-- We have faith.*

***

Also on June 13, that the 45th Evacuation Hospital actually departed Wotton-under-Edge bound for France. In his letter that evening, Dad noted that he had talked with Phyllis Breadman earlier that day. She, in turn, reported having seen Mom the day before . . . *and believed that you* [Mom] *had left in good spirits. That was a lot.*

On June 15th, Mom's 45th Evacuation Hospital arrived in the English harbor city of Southhampton. The next day its personnel were ordered to embark for Normandy. Mom would later say that her unit went ashore on June 14. But all sources agree that the 45th Evacuation Hospital did so on June 16. Transport was provided by the HMS *Glenearn,* a 10,000 ton British freighter that had been converted into a Landing Ship Infantry, or LSI. Given its maximum speed of only 16 knots, it must have taken the *Glenearn* several hours to reach its designated landing point. Robert Roberts, a medical lab technician with the 45th, later described what he saw from the deck of the ship.

. . . the view was mind boggling to the point where it was almost unbelievable.

As far as you could see, in all directions, were ships of all descriptions each flying a barrage balloon from its deck. It was difficult to count the number of ships, there were so many.[xxxiii]

Hyman Lebson described his impressions as the *Glenearn* approached the beach.

By noon, we were able to catch a glimpse of the shores of France and to observe modern warfare at close range. The entire coast was a beehive of activity, with more ships in this Normandy 'harbor' than we thought possible. Our planes were constantly overhead with only occasional unwelcome visitors. It was an impressive sight, complete with the sound of ack-ack [anti-aircraft] fire and booming naval activity.[xxxiv]

Lt. Lebson did concede, however, that *Luftwaffe* would sometimes send their planes as "unwelcome visitors" to bomb and strafe the invasion force. In Glucoft and Fleischmann's booklet *Medical Service in Combat: The 45th Evacuation Hospital D+10 to V-E Day,* a Major Wagner corroborated this danger.

'Considerable air activity occurred over the Omaha beach as our personnel and equipment awaited debarkation . . .. The greatest risk to personnel was ack-ack fragments, unexploded AA shells, and low level firing of .50 caliber machine guns. The intense noise of this activity caused more apprehension than the falling fragments, which fortunately caused no casualties . . . . '[xxxv]

At around two in the afternoon, still well short off Omaha Beach, the *Glenearn* dropped anchor. On its deck were 24 smaller landing craft that would actually transfer its human cargo to the beach. Davits now lowered these landing craft into the water, much as a cruise ship would deploy life boats in the event of an emergency. Sgt. Roberts described how

We disembarked by rope over the side into a Landing Craft Infantry (LCI) at a point about a half-mile from shore. The sea was rough enough to make it difficult to make the transfer. We were instructed that the LCI would try to run ashore as close to land as possible. We were cautioned that there could be deep spots left by bomb craters and not to panic.[xxxvi]

Along with all the other passengers, the doctors and nurses of the 45th now climbed down rope netting deployed along the *Glenearn*'s hull into the LCIs. Mom would later tell the story-- with some amusement-- that, just she and as the nurses were climbing down the netting, an air raid siren sounded. According to Mom, one of the nurses became so frightened that she clung to the net, refusing to either continue down into the landing craft or back up onto the deck o the *Glenearn*, despite all pleas for her to do one or the other. Again according to Sgt. Roberts "We hit the beach where the water was waist high and all made it one way or another."[xxxvii]

After coming ashore, the personnel of the 45th Evacuation Hospital initially took shelter in foxholes near the beach. Trucks then transported everyone several miles along the beach to the commune [township] of La Cambe.

Mom herself would later boast that she was among the first 100 American nurses to go ashore at Omaha Beach. Because there were about 40 nurses in each unit, this meant at that at least one other Evacuation Hospital must have preceded hers. If Mom's claim is accurate, then perhaps the medical unit arriving beforehand was the 24th Evacuation Hospital. In any event, the 45th now learned that much of their medical equipment had not been delivered. So, in the chaos of the moment, Mom's unit got to work by assisting that medical staff of the 24th. As the 45th's own gear began arriving, its support staff began installing its own medical equipment and supplies in more than 20 large tents erected in an open field bordered by ancient hedgerows. Some of these tents were large enough to accommodate as many as 40 medical patients. Soon the 45th began admitting its own patients.

In some ways, a WWII evacuation hospital functioned much like modern emergency room does today. However, unlike an emergency room, an evacuation hospital was mobile, continually moving to stay within 30 miles of the battle. [Mom would later tell me that the 45th was always within 17 miles of the front.] Moreover, unlike a modern emergency room, an evacuation hospital could not simple transfer seriously injured patients to the surgical department upstairs. Urgent surgeries had to be performed on site. Indeed, perhaps 80% of the 45th's incoming patients required surgery. Overall, an evacuation hospital like the 45th was capable of treating up to 400 patients at a time. Those soldiers who had suffered only minor wounds would be returned to their combat units. Those requiring a longer recovery period were transferred, circumstances permitting, to a permanent station hospital further back. At La Cambe, so close to the beach, this often meant shipping these patients back to England.

***

Mom now found herself the midst of a hellish 20th century battlefield. There were many, many trauma patients to treat. Her first letter from France was written on her second day on the ground. But only a brief fragment has survived. However, her second letter, written the next day, does hint at the danger.

18 June 1944

Dear Rick—
   When you say your prayers say them with a double thanksgiving, and [I] *will tell you why someday--*
   Am very well and glad to be here, except for missing you--
Love you,
Gina

Her letter the day after that is nearly as brief.

France   *19 June 1944*

Dear Ricky,
   Not much time to write letters; so when they contain only a few lines; don't feel neglected; it just can't be helped.
   Last night we had a few hours sleep-- two nurses per cot. The most I can say for the arrangement was the warmth.

Jean [nurse Jean J. Hall] says 'Hello.'

Remembering so much of the time we spent together in England, become more thankful for those days each day.

> *I love you so---*
> *Gina*

Mom's battlefield duties continued at such a high level of intensity that her next three letters each contained fewer than 100 words.

By the end of the month Allied forces had secured the beaches themselves. However, German defenders elsewhere in the Cherbourg Peninsula continued to fire from behind local farm hedgerows in an effort to keep Allied forces contained. If the Allies broke free of the Peninsula, then Paris could be liberated and all German forces swept from France. With so much at stake the fighting was intense, especially around a place called St. Lo.

On July 25 the 45th Evacuation Hospital relocated to Airel, less than a mile from St. Lo. As Mom's battlefield experience grew, her religious faith was renewed. As early as June 29 she reminded Dad of an earlier letter.

> *Remember in 'the' letter you wrote where you said 'And better to see his Stature'? Well, I think I do a little more in this respect. How, within a few inches some soldiers' escape, and the one next to them won't. It seems each one of us fits into a divine pattern.*

After her nerves settled, Mom became more expansive about her observations, even offering journalistic-style commentary.

> *28 June 44--*
> *France*
>
> *Dearest—*
>
> *I just received eleven letters and <u>six</u> from you. Now they will hold me until the next batch comes in. <u>And</u> each of your letters seem so full of wonderful thoughts that, even while I am busy, I can think of one at a time and in some way pass it on to one of my patients. My admiration for the American soldier has been boosted to the skies. In shock, of course, we get the most seriously injured, and I have yet to hear a complaint. Each man seems to look around and realize that the one next to him is just a little worse off than he is. The P.O.W.s aren't nearly so courageous, perhaps it's because they are apprehensive and frightened of the treatment they are to receive.*
>
> *Some of the girls are wishing that they were flight nurses. More glory and most important is that they get to France [on an ambulance plane] and back to England where there is peace and quiet. But most of us realize that this is the experience of our lives and wouldn't trade it for anything.*
>
> *I know now what you mean by 'flak happy,' and I see very little . . . compared to what you must go through on a mission <u>but</u>---*
>
> *I'm <u>happy</u>, <u>proud of you and</u> confident for the future. [I] Am no longer the least bit afraid.*
>
> *Always my love,*
> *Gina*

In a postscript to this same letter, Mom added . . .

Oh, one more thing. Heard one nurse say, 'Hell, I'm not sorry to be here, we're not in the least bit better than one of these boys.' I liked her for that.

The next day she described the unity of purpose that had developed within unit.

From some of this letter, I'm afraid you may think there is nothing but sorrow and illness about; but that is not true. For the most part the patients are cheerful, relieved to be resting in a quieter place . . . . The nurses love it too; the doctors are happier working. So between patients, doctors and nurses there is harmony, glorious harmony.

Eventually, German resistance at St. Lo was overcome. The Allies were able to expand their area of control beyond the Cherbourg Peninsula. As a result, the 45th Evacuation Hospital moved forward to St. Sever on August 9 and Senonches on August 22. While Mom's unit did not itself enter Paris, the French capital was liberated from German occupation on August 25.

***

The letters that Reg and Marj wrote to Mom after her unit's departure from Wotton provided an additional source of moral support beyond that which Mom was already receiving from Dad, her colleagues in the 45th Evacuation Hospital, and her parents back in Chicago. On the evening of June 14, for example, only a day after Mom had departed Wotton for the Continent, Reg was already sounding like a concerned father-- and jealous rival suitor.

Dear Northie,
Supper is over and Marj is busy sewing, and I have privilege of being first to write you, fully realizing that I shall take my place at the end of the long list of men from whom you receive letters.
Of course we are both wondering where you are and what you are going to do, where you are going, and when. All this of course must remain a mystery until that happy day when you can come and tell us all about it.
Sorry we couldn't see you off. We kept a look out until we were sure you must be gone and then returned to our sorrow and lon[e]liness.
Yes, we were really sorry you had to go; and it seems strange without you; but it just had to be; and we couldn't do anything about it. All we hope now is that it will all be soon over; then you can return home to that happy future which lies ahead.
Charles rang up [the Breadmans] on Tuesday and is going to do so occasionally just to see if we know anything about you . . . .
I hope you receive this letter on a day when you get no other mail, I shall then know it will at least receive just a glance.
Cheerio for now, take great care of yourself and lots and lots of love from us both.

A month later he again wrote to Mom.

>Dear Northy,
>Once again, my turn to write. We have not heard from you yet this week, but no doubt you are very busy, and really we have had a lovely lot of letters from you.
>You know by know that Charles rang us up last Saturday. We were so pleased he was O.K; we could not understand why we had not heard from him.

He closed this letter again sounding like a father concerned for his daughter's safety.

>As I think by now you will have thrown away this letter away, seeing it is only a lot of tripe. I had better pack up.
>We both send you lots of love, and the usual instructions, take great care of yourself and be a good girl.
>>Yours very sincerely,
>>Reg

The next day, Marj herself also wrote to Mom.

>Dear Northie:
>I am in the middle of washing the breakfast things & the postman has just been. He brought two letters from you, one from 'the lovely boy' [Dad] & two others of not much interest. I was so pleased to get the first three, I could have cried; so I thought I would drop you a line. Reg posted one to you last night. Hope you have heard from Charles by now. In case you haven't yet had the letter I posted last week. He is well and you should hear from him any day now.

Dad, too, continued to receive strength from the Sims. On the evening of July 24, he about the support he was receiving from Reg in Mom's absence.

>*Reg sent a letter welcoming me at any time and saying he wished I'd write or call more often because then he would have something of more real interest to tell [write to] you.*

A week later, on July 30, Mom expressed gratitude that Marj had even written to Mom's parents, apparently in an effort to reassure them about Mom's safety and vouch for Dad's good character.

Judging from the brevity of her recent letters to Dad, Mom's battlefield nursing duties were keeping her extremely busy. Consequently, she was regretting that her obligation to others, especially Reg and Marj, was being neglected. Late in the evening of August 4 she wrote

>*Almost too dark to write-- if you write to Marjory and Reg, say 'hello' for me. You're the only one (and, of course, home occasionally) while I'm working that I manage to write to.*

On October 6, in a letter to Dad, she lamented that she had not . . . *written to the Sims in ever so long, not even home for more than a week, but our hours are so long that it's hard to find time.*

For their part, the Sims family continued making every effort to stay in touch. On October 6, Mom noted . . . *this stationary came today from the Sims; wasn't that nice? And ever so luxurious to have it very available, no searching tonight.* Similarly, on October 31, Mom again . . . *Received a package from Marjory Sims . . . and guess what was in it? Shampoo, a book, stationary and vitamins.*

But Mom was not always reciprocating. On October 23 Dad received a letter from the Sims indicating that they were worried about not having received any letters from her in nearly two months. *Had a letter from Reg & Marge. They're quite concerned about you & said so in about so many words.* On November 13 Dad had received yet another letter from the Sims. *Did I tell you I had another letter from Reg & Marge? They sent the snap of the puppies-- scamps!*

On November 17, a battlefield-weary Mom finally responded to Dad's letter from October 23.

> *About letters to Wotton, I've answered each of the Sims letters as they arrived, very scanty letters. Maybe the English post didn't think they were worth delivering-- although, during the lull period we just had, I wrote Marjory a 'newsy,' gossipy' letter about the girls she knew* [among Mom's nursing colleagues]. *Of course the Sims have been very busy; so their letters have been few; my answers late beside; so the interval in exchange has been long. In one letter I explained that undoubtedly you were keeping them informed that I am alright; because for a long time I just didn't get in the mood to write, even my home* [her family in Chicago] *was neglected. So I am a very negligent person, not much repentant either-- I hope they understand; it isn't that I've forgotten nor am unappreciative.*

Some of the letters Reg and Marj wrote directly to Mom also have not survived. However, Reg's rather chatty letter of November 28 is available. In it he assured Mom that he and Marj had extended an invitation for Dad to join them at Christmas time, if his military duties would allow. In this same letter, Reg also seemed to revert back to his occasional role of jealous rival suitor. First, he opened by saying . . . "If I start by writing about Charles, that may be some temptation for you to read the whole letter." Then he rejected a previous assertion by Mom that he could be persuaded to attend a future wedding only if champagne were served at the reception. "Fancy you thinking I needed tempting to pay a visit to my little treasure. (Hope this little bit gets past Marj when she censors the letter.)" Finally, after remembering that Mom had first joined into the Sims household almost exactly a year earlier, Reg expressed regret regarding an omission he had made during the previous Christmas season. "I should have kissed you under the mistletoe last year. I won't get the opportunity this."

8
TRYING TO RENDEZVOUS

When my parents first met on medical ward at Grenier Field AAF base in New Hampshire, they were seeing each other nearly every day.   When later reunited in England, they continued seeing each other as frequently as one or the other could obtain leave. This was not often enough to suit Mom. On April 25, 1944 she wrote

> *Am in such a rebellious mood I've isolated myself from the civilized world by going to bed. . . .*
>
> *Feel as though I'm wasting these glorious spring days doing nothing when I could be enjoying a leave. But this is the army, Mr. Gallagher-- hurry up and wait. . . .*
>
> *What ails me is that since . . . the first time I saw you* [in England], *to our last visit this has been the longest interval between our meetings; and I don't like it one bit.*

But things would only get worse. The Allied invasion of northern Europe in June completely disrupted the logistics of their courtship.   For the next ten months Mom was on the Continent while Dad remained in England. Within a month Dad was admitting that the separation was causing him feelings of depression. On July 14 he asked

> *Have you a cure for me? I'm generally thinking of one subject that I can't seem to get my mind from and hardly want to. Drug symptoms-- and . . . visionary dreams and moments of depression and exultation.*

By late July, after having been bottled up by enemy resistance near the Normandy beaches for several weeks, the Allied armies broke loose from their beachhead by capturing the town of St. Lo. Within a month Paris was liberated. Once the Allies controlled this northern portion of France, USAAF and RAF planes returning from their bombing raids had a new option. Those suffering from battle damage, experiencing mechanical trouble, or simply running low on fuel were no longer obliged to limp all the way back to England. These airplanes now could simply cross over to western side of the front lines and land at the nearest friendly airstrip. Dad grumbled, jealously, that some aircrews were actually faking such emergencies as an excuse to visit the City of Lights. On October 4 he reported

> *One of our planes that landed in France is back with stories of beautiful women and steaks. I sort of hoped they'd pick the place near the 45th, but they 'managed' to land just outside of Paris.*

He then added, dryly, that this was an example . . . *of the strange tricks that navigation will play on you.* On October 23 he reported to Mom

> *They are making it rough . . . on indiscreet & unofficial visits to the 'far shore'*

now. I guess that the amount of it reached such a high level that they had to lay it on. It's been quite a favorite trick to run out of gas around Brussels & then stagger on to Paris. . . . Last week they drew the line on that, too.

Nonetheless, high ranking AAF officers, men who did not normally fly combat missions, were soon finding excuses to travel to those areas of France already under Allied control. For example, on November 1 Dad complained

> *. . . one of the officers at wing* [headquarters] *had me green with envy. He's been to France four times over the last eight weeks-- on orders of course. I think he wound up in Paris each time.*

On November 24 he again grumbled

> *Maj. Jerges, whose wife has been and still is with the 3rd Army, left to look for her a week ago. The ground exec is with him and I seriously doubt if the colonel will ever allow such luxury to anyone else. And when your letters tell of engagements and dates, the war seems so unimportant . . . and the barriers between us so trivial; and yet you are there; and I am here. It seems to be so simple to overcome. Could you see the longing in my heart?*
>
>

*I just want to
see you so,
<u>Ricky</u>*

Nonetheless, when this Maj. Jerges returned the next day after having succeeded in locating his wife, Dad did not begrudge him his success.

> *Maj. Jerges came back today. He is going home now or very soon for R&R* [Rest & Recuperation] *. . . and none of us really expect him to return. He and the colonel had quite a time (I only heard a bit of the whole), but he found his wife & said she is fixed up in a grand spot near Nancy. They were free-lancing it without orders and had to do a considerable amount of bluffing here and there. A swell guy. I hate to see him leave.*

***

Eventually, the U.S. Army's position on the Continent was secure enough to permit the AAF to begin transferring entire squadrons of warplanes from English to French bases, thus reducing flying distances to targets. However, the possibility of being redeployed to France did not apply equally to all units. In England the American bombing effort against Hitler's Fortress Europe had been divided between the 8th and 9th Army Air Forces. The Mighty 8th, to which Dad belonged, was tasked with the long-range strategic bombing from high altitude of Germany itself. In contrast, the 9th AAF was assigned with the shorter-range tactical bombing from medium and low altitudes of targets in France and the Low Countries. As a result, once the USAAF began shifting some of its operations to newly liberated airports on the Continent, that privilege usually went to 9th Air Force units. There was little likelihood that any such redeployment applied to Dad's 96th Bombardment Group. Indeed, once Mom was on the battlefield, she quickly became aware of the distinction between American airplanes based nearby and those that Dad was likely to be on. But even if Dad's bomb group was never redeployed to France, and even if Dad himself was not reassigned to the 9th AAF, there remained the possibility that he might be able to hitch a ride on some 9th AAF plane that would be landing near Mom's tent hospital. In Mom's letter on July 19 she described a conversation with Rev. Zinz in which the feasibility of such a scheme was discussed. *Chappie and I have been putting our heads together, and this is the result. You could make friends with the 9th AAF.* Of course Mom was fully aware that it would be risky for Dad to attempt such a venture-- both to his military standing and to his personal safety. So she concluded this letter by cautioning . . . *If you can't do it without difficulty, don't try 'cause I don't want to get you in trouble.* Her next missive retreated even further.

> *In my very 'suggestive' letter, which I imagine you received, don't do anything rash. I'm almost a little sorry I wrote it; the trip would be too risky. Chappie and I let our imaginations run away.*

However, even before Mom wrote the letter describing the above conversation with Rev. Zinz, Dad himself was thinking along similar lines. As early as July 14, he was wondering aloud whether such a visit was possible. [I] *Also seem to think that a furlough to the Normandy front might cure it all for a while. Of course that is absurd. Ha!* Nonetheless, by July 27 he was taking a hard look at the logistics of such an attempt.

> *Strange that I should have been 'casing' the possibilities of spending a pass in Normandy. It may yet come to pass. The biggest job is finding where to go to get a ride across.*

By the middle of August, my parents had been apart for three months. On August 22 Dad spoke more boldly of a possible rendezvous.

> *How long do you suppose it will be before we will be together?* [I am] *Thinking about that meeting so many times-- dreaming up all kinds of possibilities of places & circumstances.*

By August 25 he was claiming

> *I can get a seven-day leave just about any time, and I doubt if I'd have much difficulty getting across the Channel. Let's see: mess kit, toothbrush, socks, field jacket-- h'm; s'pose Chappie could put me up? What a way to spend seven days! What a thought!*

From Dad's point of view, the real obstacle was not his unwillingness to be party to a fake air emergency, nor his lack of more senior rank, nor the unlikelihood of his being redeployed to France, nor-- as it turned out-- any lack of opportunity to catch a lift on some local flight. Rather, it was that he could never be certain where Mom's unit was located at any given moment. When they both had been stationed in England, this restriction had not really been an issue. During her seven months in that country Mom's unit always remained at the same location; Dad was transferred only once. There were frequent opportunities to visit each other.   And between these visits, it was relatively easy to maintain immediate contact using the Breadman's phone.   Any impending change in circumstances could be verbally communicated.   However, once Mom came ashore at Omaha Beach in Normandy, her unit would relocate at least 17 times.   Since there was virtually no possibility of making a telephone connection, it was difficult for Dad to keep up with where she might be at any given time.

Not long after her arrival in France, Mom did attempt to phone Dad a few times, albeit unsuccessfully.   On August 10, for instance, Dad thought that Mom was again trying to reach him by phone, mentioning a . . . *mysterious telephone call . . .* the previous evening. It had him

> *. . . agog. I haven't found out who it was from . . . .   Naturally, when I was told it was long distance, I scrambled out of bed for the orderly room; but, just as I started to say 'hello!,' the sq. CO unwittingly cut in from the extension in his quarters & I had 'had it.'*

***

With Mom no longer in England, and with cross channel calls virtually impossible to place, that left the mail as the only readily available medium of communication.   But letters sent through the Army Post Office [APO] routinely took at least one week to be delivered, sometimes far longer-- especially during military crises.   Sometimes, this extended delay was intentional.   For example, Hyman Lebson reported that, on the eve of the Normandy invasion, " . . . mail was temporarily impounded, and we later learned that ever since April, all of our mail had already been subjected to a routine automatic ten day delay."[xxxviii]   Dad was fully aware of this policy.   On June 16 he received . . . *Four, 4, IV (count 'em!) letters from you today. I have them with me now. The censor has been holding them up for two weeks.*   Any delay resulting from the Army's intentional policy was really a form of censorship.   If mail was not posted until after a military operation was underway, it could not leak out to the enemy beforehand.   Moreover, the letters themselves were also censured.   A military censor within each unit-- such as Mom's 45th Evacuation Hospital or Dad's 96th Bomb Group-- screened the contents of each letter before it was actually posted.   Any information deemed potentially useful to the enemy-- such as the unit's location-- was excised from the letter prior to delivery.   If a letter contained too much inappropriate information, it was simply not delivered.   In an undated letter that was probably written in March of 1944, Dad reported

> *. . . one of my letters to you was returned to me with appropriate remarks by the adjutant. It seems that the censor didn't relish my putting such a complete train schedule as it gives away the location* [of their respective units in England].

In an undated letter probably written on April 23, 1944 Dad described in almost Biblical terms how he felt while waiting to see if that day's courier mail included a new letter from Mom.

> *Happy!*

> *Dear Gina:*

I should say so! You see there once was a fella who looked happy, but only he knew that he was quite sad. And then one day a messenger came bringing him news. Now messengers come to him nearly every day from far-off places in distant lands, but he had been waiting for this one, and there was anxiety in his heart . . . for he had to pass many times thru the land belonging to the savage Censors.

In a letter written on May 18, 1944 Dad again made light of the censor's intervention. This time he was reacting to four letters from Mom that all arriving on the same day.

Three of the four letters were censored, and one of those had two deletions. I haven't yet decided whether practically all mail is being checked now or if the censor enjoys reading your letters and quotations . . . .

Every letter was at risk. Mom would now sometimes write *Somewhere in France,* or simply *Belgium,* in the upper right corner of her letter's first page where the return address normally appears. Moreover, in the body of the letter she might be able to mention where the 45th Evacuation Hospital had been. However, if she named its current location or where it might be moving to next, such details would have been physically excised. This being the case, Dad was soon complaining that rapid American advances from the initial invasion beachhead were making it even harder for him to surmise exactly where Mom's unit might be located. Needless to say, this lack of transparency made any rendezvous attempt more difficult to plan. As early as August 14 Dad described

. . . speculating [with two other duty airmen] *on whether the 45th will stay where they are or move up with the advances. One of the other fellows . . . and I are conniving & plotting for the future. But of course we're all bewildered by the big advances.*

On August 17 he added

I know that you're reasonably safe where you are, but I feel my chances of a Normandy trip slipping away as you move up. How I would like to know where *& how you are . . . .*

Dad's letter three days later continue his speculations about the possibility of hitching a ride on some AAF plane that would be landing near Mom's tent hospital.

Nearly had a seven-day leave myself, but couldn't use it now. Can't you give me a precise hint as to where you are or even what sector? Is there a landing strip nearby? I want to be well prepared when my time rolls around.

***

On August 28 Mom proposed, circumspectly, a scheme by which Dad might be able to locate her after his arrival in France-- assuming he could first hitch a ride on a medical evacuation flight originating from England.

71

If you should come here, come to the landing strip farthest from each coast [of the Cherbourg Peninsula]*; the airfield that is farthest inland is one that evacuates by air our patients. Then call Surgeon's Office 1st Army Headquarters. Col. Snyder at that office visits here frequently and is well acquainted with our group.*

Here Mom's letter is misleading. It implies that the 45th Evacuation Hospital is still near the Normandy beachhead when in fact it had now moved to Senonches, in the Loire Valley. Perhaps she had lost track of her true location. Later in this same letter, Mom also cautioned

If you should come, be very, very careful-- won't you. It seems almost impossible; and I haven't sincerely thought of seeing you until the war is over; but then I never dreamed of being with you in England.

In an undated fragment that must have been written about the same time, she added some more practical advise on how to locate her specific unit.

If you can come to the most forward Evacuation Hospital Transport Landing Strip, the Ambulance Service to and from our hospital could help you locate this hospital.

She also offered Dad some advice about how to stay alive when he would so close to the battle lines: *If it* [a rendezvous] *should materialize, glorious dream-- bring your helmet and gas mask-- and I'm not just kidding.*

***

Three days later, Dad could not yet have received these most recent letters from Mom. Nevertheless, on that day he made his final preparations. Perhaps fearing that the authorities might disapprove of his plan, his letter was deliberately vague.

If ever a man was excited, it's me. Last night we didn't have any flights for our site, and I spent the evening packing and getting ready. I just wore myself out last night hoping and imagining, so I didn't get much sound sleep. I have a plane ride cooked up for the first half of the trip. Ha! The second half is still in the dark.

For the next few days, Dad wrote no letters. When his correspondence did resume on September 4, it describes quite an adventure.

Long before my leave came through, I had tried every way I could think of to see if I could locate the 45th. No one on our field could help at all; and I switched . . . [in the] afternoon to visit nearby hospitals; but they didn't know of their [1st Army Surgeon's Office] *Hqs. Nor could any of the patients give me any help. Still, I made progress.*
It turned out that our base is a stop for the 'blood plane' that runs a collection trip and delivers it . . . [to] a place that looked promising for us. I was all set to go on that; but it was scrubbed because of weather; but instead I stumbled on a

72

pilot who was going to a London 'drome [aerodrome, i.e., airport]. We were off. I felt as if I were perhaps better off than if I went there by train but still disappointed.

Where we landed [near London] was a jumping off point for the far side [of the English Channel]; and, although I met a classmate of mine working in ops.[operational headquarters] there; he couldn't help me out 'cause I didn't have any orders; and security was absolute. Time was getting on, and I went to London to get a 'sack' for the evening. They have a billeting office there.

I thought I should look into all of the air possibilities, too, instead of by sea as I had originally planned. I got billeted but . . . couldn't make any real progress and was further advised that I wouldn't be able to go by sea either.

Then Dad did find a way to sneak over to France.

Just as I was packing off to bed, another bus from the field pulled in, and who should be on it but a pilot I flew to Africa with a long time ago. His name is Bob Grant, and was he surprised. More than I 'cause he had heard I was done away with long ago. He'd just come in from Scotland and was to go to France the next day. But he had no crew-- I signed on as copilot-- elated?

When Dad enlisted in the AAF back in 1941, he had hoped to become a pilot. But his eyesight had been judge as marginal for that role. Consequently, they had made him a navigator instead. He was hardly qualified to fly as copilot on a twin-engine military transport. Perhaps this lack of credentials was part of the reason for his adding, in this same letter, that, after having made this plan for the next morning with his old friend Bob Grant, he now

. . . hardly slept. At about eight (the next morning) [September 1] we piled into our 'clunk' and were off.

One of the first raids I was ever on was to bomb a certain airfield in France, and we flew [now] right over [the] thing at 1,000 ft. instead of 25,000 ft. I marvelled at it. It just didn't seem real. I felt like decoy down too low.

I wish we might tell names so I might know where I was closest to you. Every field we landed at I'd pop out and collar someone-- 'Ever hear of the 45th-- 'Nope.' And so it went.

The next to the last place [we] went to there was a G.I. waiting for us. He knew where you were '-- only a few miles from here-- only a few days ago.' But he knew that you'd moved, too. For a few minutes while we were loading up, I gambled with the thought of getting out right there and thumbing it. I had on OD's [?], field jacket, mess gear & stuff. The odds against finding you & getting out crossing the Channel & making home base all in six days were too great.

But just think. There I was. I'd flown over lots of tents with red crosses & seen lots of ambulances on the roads. Were you here or here? Had you seen us fly over and looked up and not known? Were you only a few miles away . . . ? It was tantalizing, but we didn't know anything for certain except that I couldn't wander around France on foot without sticking my foot in it sooner or later . . . . I was so close to you. Can't you see me there looking for you?

We had covered Normandy and were close to Paris then. Soon we had to leave and fly to Brittany. Six of us flew in formation. Six transports heading west-- did you see us? It was getting on in the afternoon [of] September 1st.

We got back to England after dark having flown over most American-held territory and carried all sorts of loads including wounded. We were working together. I liked that thought.

We didn't finish up until nearly two AM, and it was nearly dawn before we tucked ourselves in again. We slept most of the [following] day.

Back at Snetterton Heath, Dad's friends AAF were amazed that, given the current wartime situation, he had found a way to first of all reach the battle zone in France and then gotten back to England without any negative consequences. In a letter written on September 5, he told Mom

Now that I am back I'm besieged with questions. 'Ya really got to France [and] back? Hoja do it? Boy, that's fer me!' Etc. I've been talking myself silly. I hadn't realized just what the odds were against getting there at all.

***

On September 8, a week after his failed attempt to meet Mom in France, Dad received three letters from her written before his failed rendezvous attempt, including the one written on August 28 that had provided advice on locating the 45th Evacuation Hospital once he arrived in France. His reaction was introspective.

Dearest Gina:

Tonight I am a very considering, thoughtful, philosophical wondering young man; and I wouldn't be fibbing if said I was just a bit on the sad side too.

You see three letters came from you today. I checked the mail room at noon and there wasn't a one-- they said it had already been checked. Then I went to the hut [his barracks in a Quonset hut]; but there wasn't a single letter on my bed; so I thought I'd 'had it.' I flew this afternoon with some new boys; and, when I started back for the ops [operations] office after the flight, Steve [?] was holding one of your letters; & his nose was against the window with a devilish grin on his face. I was too pleased and absorbed in that area to notice the other two lying right on the desk . . . .

After this outburst of happiness, you're wondering what I could possibly be sad about-- you must be. You see, it was what was in them. And that was the directions you gave to get to the 45th.

Now I'm balancing what I did against what I might have done. I'm wondering if I should have taken my leave later than I did, feeling sure that you wouldn't move up in the meantime. Then could I have managed a ride to the right airstrip? (Do you suppose I was at the right one?) Or could I have even wrangled a ride? I remember so well the wounded we flew out and how close I felt to you as we took them on. I don't feel bitterly disappointed, but I do feel as though I perhaps let you down even though I might not have gotten over at all.

And then I think of all those here who are so far away. How I would have loved to surprise you. I had it all dreamed out. Happy? I was sleepless.

I guess you'd better have a consolation chat with Chappie. 'Member the time we were in his office.

> *All my love*
> *Ricky*

P.S. I forgot to bring my helmet.

The next day, in his postscript to another letter, Dad tried to reassure Mom that his risky search for her in France had not motivated by any impending redeployed to the Far East.
.

> *I am not trying to cleverly tell you something. Neither was I [n]or am I anxious to be with you because I am expecting something of the sort* [i.e., reassignment to the war against Japan]. *My Normandy sortie was pure longing and nothing else.*

On September 17 Mom received the first letters written by Dad following his return to England. She finally learned that he had been in France. Ironically enough, she had just arrived in Belgium at a place called Baelen.

> *Darling,*
> *Received twenty letters last night, ten from you. Wasn't very busy last night and couldn't wait until this morning to read them. Learned that you were here on this side of the channel; read them with mixed emotions: happy because of your letters, sad because you couldn't find me <u>and when</u> I read in your last letter 'P.S. I forgot to bring my helmet.'*
> *I cried on the ward; [I] could picture your disappointment; and then I lost myself in mine.*
> *And on this Sunday morning, I'm striving to find consolation by writing to you-- could never sleep if I didn't. More and more I turn and find just what I need being alone with you, as now.*
> *You can probably well imagine where we have been situated, and* [that] *my cautious reminders weren't overdone, and* [that] *<u>hints</u> were impossible* [because of the mail censorship]. *Although, until now, for the past few weeks everything has been quiet. For some very good reason, not given for us to understand, you were prevented from coming all the way; but you are safely back in England; and for that I am thankful.*

As late as September 29, Dad was still expressing his frustration at not having been able to locate Mom.

> *You are reading the letter of a Ricky who is downcast tonight. I can picture your disappointment . . . not having seen me, learning that I was in France. Would that I could hold you and hear your cares and lull you. [B]ut I can only put my love out to you. It has wings-- they enfold your heart.*

It was not until October 6 that Dad received the first letters that Mom had written after her learning of his failed rendezvous effort. Because these letters were adding her own frustrations to his mix, he again attempted to clarify exactly what occurred.

And remembering your breaking out in tears in ward at my P.S. 'I forgot my helmet.' You know the reason why I couldn't find you-- or rather stay in France to keep looking for you-- wasn't because I didn't have a helmet, but because I didn't have any way of getting back to [the] UK except smuggling out by air; & that meant getting to an air-strip and catching a quickie. There wasn't time to go back any other way. . . . If only someone had known where the 45th had moved to. I didn't have a helmet in Russia either.

In the meantime, on September 28, as part of the Allies' rapid advance into Belgium, the 45th Evacuation Hospital arrived in the town of Eupen. Here it took occupancy of an abandoned high school. While in France the 45th had mostly bivouacked in tents. From now on it would mostly occupy more permanent structures. While Mom couldn't mention her current location, she was free to describe for Dad where she had previously been. On October 8 she wrote

Now for our tour, (the most recent set-ups of course can't be mentioned). La Cambe, Ariel, St. Sever de Calvados, Senonches, and La Capelle. We were at La Capelle at the time of your visit, a long way from Normandy.

Perhaps because Dad's own letters describing his rendezvous attempt had been less than precise, Mom was still inaccurate about where she had been that day. Her unit did not actually relocate to La Capelle until September 5, four days after Dad's effort.

Not for another month did Dad finally receive Mom's letter of October 8.

Friday evening
10 November 1944

Hello dear:

It's after ten; and I'm in the orderly room writing to you-- today has been very full. To begin with-- or rather this afternoon-- two letters came from you. They're older by weeks than some I already have, but you have to forgive the mail for such as these.

One of them gave the places you had been, and it wasn't until seven and after the returning mission was settled that I could go to the war room and locate them. That was both an exciting and wistful job. Yes, there was something wistful about it.

Then there was the question: and where now? That was worst & best of all. I had all the places plotted and stood before the map lost in reliving . . . my trip to France and remembering t[w]o times where I must have passed over not far away. Each place and pas[s] took on a living meaning.

***

Mom did not give up. She kept searching for a way to inform Dad of her exact location without running afoul of the censors. If she could find someone who routinely traveled back and forth between the Continent and England, perhaps such a person would agree to pass along messages. On September 14 the 45th Evacuation Hospital was still located at La Capelle in France but preparing to cross over into Belgium. On that day she prevailed on a Lt. Smith to deliver a message to Dad. Her request must have been the result of a brief and unexpected meeting because she provided the young officer with no written note of her own. Indeed, probably because the 45th Evacuation Hospital was again in transit, she wrote no letters to Dad at all on either that day or the next. However. Lt. Smith's note to Dad has been preserved.

> England
> September 16, 1944
>
> Capt. Dunn,
>
> While at an advanced base in France day before yesterday, a Nurse asked me to deliver a message upon my return to England. Her name was Alva North and her message was that she is being moved from her last base to one in Belgium, past Brussels, but she doesn't know the place by name or much of anything about it. It seems that she was expecting you to look her up when you get a leave, and she wanted you to know that she had moved.
>
> I hope this information will be of some value to you.
>
> Sincerely,
> J. M. Smith
> 2nd Lt. A.C.

Dad actually received Lt. Smith's message on September 22.

> *Dearest,*
>
> *A letter came today (small miracle) from a Lt. Smith in T.C.C.* [Troop Carrier Command]. *and has the news of your present general whereabouts. It's the first time I've heard anything at all since your letter dated the 2nd. I could kiss him, and I told him so* [presumably in a written 'thank you' note].

Later that month, Mom found a second AAF officer who might be able to aid them in circumventing military censorship.

> *18 October 1944*
>
> *Dear Ricky,*
>
> *Tonight the 45th Evac. Hosp. is having a party for our new C.O. I came escorted by both my boss and Capt. Egli* [a physician], *and who should I find but a Lt. from the 8th Air Force.*
>
> *I'm sure he thinks I am quite out of my senses; but when I learned that he is stationed near you; I could have wept out loud and laughed at the same time. He will be able to tell you where I am, but he couldn't possibly know how much I love you.*

Mom's letter of October 18 fails to mention this lieutenant's name. But subsequent correspondence from Dad make reference to a *Lt. Vinson*, whose flying duties required that he travel between his AAF base somewhere near Dad's Norfolkshire area of England and Mom's current position on the Continent-- perhaps piloting one of the 'blood planes.' Dad's first mention of him came on October 26. *...I... called Lt. Vinson, but he was out to some hospital, but they said he'll be back tomorrow, and then-- I'll know where you are.* By November 2 Lt. Vinson had finally reached Dad. In his acknowledgement to Mom of this, Dad letter observes that her two most recent letters included the word *Belgium* in the upper right hand corner of the first page.

> . . . *both are from Belgium, and the last one is only one day older than the one you gave Lt. Vinson, & he told me where you were near which wasn't Flemish at all.*

In the very next sentence, Dad's letter implies that Mom was being less than honest about her true position: *Now don't fib.* What was really happening here was that Dad suspected Mom-- in an attempt to minimize his concern for her safety-- of deliberately misrepresenting the 45th position as being further from back the front lines than it really was. By November 8 he was trying to obtain updated information through this Lt. Vinson.

> *Today I tried to call Lt. Vinson again, but he was over at some hospital and wouldn't be back until late. I wanted to see if there was anything else he might tell me about your location. That's just in case the opportunity presents itself to get across. In the* [illegible] *moments of day dreaming, I think of being with you somehow at Xmas time. Sounds remote, doesn't it-- and yet, when I think of you, I'm with you and very close-- very glowing.*

A day later, Dad was becoming annoyed that he had not been able to reach Lt. Vinson. *Tried to call Lt. Vinson again today-- same results.* By now he suspected that Mom's unit had already crossed the border from Belgium into Germany. *Why, should he tell me you were in Naziland? You must be very close.* However, contrary to his suspicions, the 45th Evacuation Hospital was not in Germany at all. Rather, it was still at Eupen in Belgium where it had been since late September, and where it would remain until the end of the year.

Mom herself first mentioned Lt. Vinson by name on November 17. [I am] *So glad you will be able to talk to Lt. Vinson to know our location-- now I am getting hopeful about a visit again.* On November 29 she finally received Dad's accusatory letter from November 2. The inside address in the upper right hand corner of her response reads: *Somewhere in Belgium, 'Honest.'* In the body of the letter, she defended her actions.

> *About Lt. Vinson, I only talked to him a few minutes-- the atmosphere was confusion . . . I don't know what kind of a person he is, except that he was feeling rather gay; so I shouldn't have been surprised if he'd have forgotten . . . . But he didn't; and if you talk to him again, thank him for me. About fibbing-- I haven't; you pen some strange words at times.*

Then, in the very same paragraph, Mom proposed taking advantage of this Lt. Vinson's services by inventing a code that would enable her to more specifically inform Dad about her future whereabouts.

> *Why not list the towns about the location he gave you, number them, and I will send back the correct one. You pen to me, okay? Does all this sound sense? It should!*

In other words, Mom was assuming that her unit would next be repositioned somewhere relatively close to its current location. If Dad made a numbered list of nearby locations, kept a copy for himself, and sent the original with Lt. Vinson on his next trip into Mom's area, then a subsequent letter from her would provide the specific code number for her unit's new location. Obviously, she was assuming that the censor would take no notice of a stray number in an otherwise innocuous letter. However, nothing came of this scheme.

Dad, too, was employing every available resource in the search for Mom's most recent address. On October 24 he noted that his own unit, the 96th Bomb Group, had just

> . . . sent some crews over to Belgium this morning to pick up some of our stranded planes over there; but I couldn't go; & I've been moaning all day long. They're back now, but the lad who promised to see what he could find about the 45th hasn't put in an appearance yet. I wish I were looking there myself.

Two days later, he still could not hide his disappointment. *The fellows who were over in Brussels . . . forgot to ask where the 45th is. What a letdown.*

In the meantime, on November 21 Mom thought that perhaps she had found a yet another potential courier.

> . . . Major Haynes, a neurosurgeon who has been with us, is going to be stationed in England. As soon as he learns his address, I shall send it to you, and I shall get in touch with him. He is familiar with our (the 45th's) situation here and where we shall be (if we move this winter). In fact, he is the second chief neurosurgical consultant (or something) in the ETO; so he'll be very informative as to our location. ALSO, HE'S FROM CHICAGO.

However, this Major Haynes' name does not reappear in any subsequent correspondence.

On December 11 Mom sent Dad a typewritten letter. While the contents of this particular letter are otherwise of little significance, the return address in the upper right hand corner was. *. . . Belgium, You'll never guess where . . . .* By December 15, it had not yet been delivered to Dad. But by now he realized that his previous communications from Lt. Vinson had been misleading.

> I am really ashamed of scolding you for 'fibbing' about being in Belgium. Here is how it came about. Lt. Vinson mailed your letter on the 24th, I think. You dated it the 18th of Oct. He said you were at Stotberg (E. of Aachen) [both in Germany] when I called, even though Aachen had not been taken on the 18th. I felt miserable thinking of you with the [enemy] forces encircling Aachen. Then I waited for your letters to say Somewhere in Deutschland; but they kept saying Belgium; and I thought-- shame on her for holding back. I would go to the situation map and make plans and surmises and reason where you must be, but I was never sure.

Ten days later Dad finally received Mom's letter from December 11. *What did you mean by the heading . . . 'Belgium-- you'll never guess where'?*

9

SHUTTLE MISSIONS

Meanwhile, elsewhere in Europe, back in January of 1943 the German Army had suffered a monumental defeat at Stalingrad. After their humiliating surrender in that Soviet city, the Germans found themselves being pushing back all along the Eastern Front. In the meantime, in September of 1943 Italy's Fascist regime capitulated. And while German forces on the Italian peninsula continued to resist, Anglo-American armies were slowly evicting them from there as well. And now, beginning with the Normandy landings in June of 1944, France was being liberated. The dimensions of Hitler's Fortress Europe were shrinking. Bombing missions coordinated among these three fronts were now feasible. The first such "shuttle mission," code named "Frantic-1," was initiated by the 15th AAF in Italy on June 2, 1944, bound for Ukraine in the Soviet Union, bombing a target in Hungary along the way. Operation Frantic-1 was completed nine days later when this same 15th AAF formation returned to Italy, bombing a target in Romania on its way back.

On June 21, 1944 the 8th AAF in England dispatched 1,234 heavy bombers and 1,170 smaller escorts to attack various German targets. Among the bombers, 163 were tasked with carrying out Operation Frantic-2, the first shuttle mission to be launched from England.   Dad's own 96th Bomb Group was a major component of this shuttle force. The initial objective was to bomb the synthetic oil refineries at Ruhland near Berlin and then continue on to landings at Mirgorod, Piryatin, and Poltava-- all located in what was then the Soviet Ukraine-- rather than return directly to England. It was hoped that this would confuse the *Luftwaffe*, which normally anticipated laying in wait for the Americans on their way back to England. Such an ambitious operation required the expertise of the 8th AAF's most experienced flying officers. Consequently, Dad found himself included as a PFF navigator for the mission.

He later provided me an account of how the day got started. According to Dad, everyone at the 96th had gone to bed the night before as usual without knowing whether a mission would be mounted the next day. The next morning, also as usual, they had been aroused well before dawn and assembled for breakfast. Dad had long since learned that, if there was to be no mission, breakfast included a powdered egg. If, on the other hand, an operation was being mounted, a fresh egg was served. On this particular morning, however, each man was offered two fresh eggs! Following breakfast, the pilots, navigators and bombardiers duly reported to their respective briefings. The navigators' briefing was always held in a room with a large map of Europe hidden behind a curtain on the back wall. It always began with a briefing officer drawing open this curtain from left to right, thus exposing the map. A red line on this map delineated the route to be taken to the day's target. On this particular morning-- as the curtain was drawn open-- Dad remembered thinking that this red line seemed never to end.

All did not go as planned. While the Ruhland refinery was successfully bombed, a single *Luftwaffe* plane shadowed the American formation to determine where the B-17 heavy bombers and their P-51 escorts would be landing. When the Luftwaffe realized that many of the American planes would be landing at Poltava [in what is now Ukraine], it launched a nighttime counterattack there. A fuel dump at this airfield exploded, igniting many of B-17s parked nearby. At least 70 American planes had been parked at

Poltava including 21 from the 96th Bomb Group. Most were either completely destroyed or so badly damaged that they could be flown back to England only after extensive repairs. Moreover, in the midst of the resulting inferno, dozens of Allied military personnel, mostly Soviets, were killed or wounded. Dad would later tell me that only one of the 96th Group's planes parked at Poltava that night survived unscathed. Doherty and Ward come close to confirming his account, reporting that only two B-17s remained flyable.xxxix Further, I remember Dad adding that, since he was the most senior navigator on the mission, he had the privilege of flying out the next morning on the only airworthy plane.

When he was allowed to resume his correspondence, his first letter described-- to the extent that censorship would allow-- what had happened.

> *Hi!*   *8 June* [he meant July] *1944*
>   *Saturday evening*
>
> *Dearest Gina:*
>   *Back to England-- home-- land of letters & letter writing-- closer to you. It has been a combination of total war and unforgettable experiences-- this trip.*
>   *Nearly three weeks now since we left England for Russia* [Ukraine]*, and plenty has happened. Russia* [the Soviet Union] *is quite secret; but by an unexpected quirk I was separated from the rest, and with a different crew we made the trip back on our own.*

Of course the *unexpected quirk* was Dad's reference to being assigned to one of the few American planes available the morning after the German counterattack.

Dad later told me of having been obliged to return to England on this undamaged B-17 via an indirect route from the Soviet Union through the Middle East and North Africa to avoid any further interference from the *Luftwaffe*. This, too, is rather eloquently corroborated in his July 8th letter.

> *First of all Persia or Iran, then Egypt, Libya, Algeria, Moroco* [sic] *& good old U.K. We've slept in holes and dined in style.* [I have] *Really flown over Jerusalem & Bethlehem & been to the Sphinx & the Pyramids on a camel.*

This same letter also hints that the AAF was trying to cover up what had really occurred.

> *Started to write this day by day & then found that we couldn't write that; & then they wouldn't mail it for us; & later everything was confiscated anyway . . .*

Mom no doubt understood that the very fact that all letters written during the mission had been confiscated must have meant that it had gone badly. Indeed, the rambling manner in which his July 8th letter closes suggests that Dad's nerves were still shaking. *Lost my pen-- this one is lousy. This is like coming to life-- writing to you again. Aren't we blessed. With love, Ricky.* While his own return from the Soviet Union had not been delayed by the destruction of the other American planes parked at Poltava, this did not mean that the B-17 he flew home on had survived the ordeal. On July 10 he conceded that, among other omissions from his previous letters, he . . . *didn't tell . . . about 'cracking up' either. Well, the latter turned out to be not so serious, but it certainly ruined a perfectly good plane.*

Nearly two weeks later, on July 22, Dad noted that a sanitized account of the first shuttle mission from England had just appeared in *Yank* magazine. *The picture of the Russian KP's* ["kitchen police," i.e. cafeteria workers] *was taken where I was. They looked almost cute when they had shoes on.*

***

On July 12, less than a week after his return from the Soviet Union, Dad returned to the subject of how infrequently he was flying. He could view his situation as a glass either "half empty or half full."

> *Discontent seems to be the fruit of too much optimism here. Everywhere there is talk of going home. It seems that to return to the States is the most glorious thing ever and that to be stuck in the ETO over three or four months altogether is to be buried alive. A couple of the fellows (mere children) said they felt a bit sorry for me tied up with a regular job and not much of a chance of finishing my missions quickly. I was a bit amused. Shall have to remember the race is not always to the swift.*

On July 14 he expanded on the advantages of his assignment. For one thing, there was little danger that he would finish his current combat tour any time soon. *You may just as well discuss absurd notions of my returning the States when I finish missions, because I don't hardly go on any . . . .* In other words, as long as he remained in England, a future rendezvous with Mom, who was then in France, remained feasible. And he further rationalized that his long tour of duty in the ETO was actually making a better person of him.

> *You know I don't mind being here for each day it is . . . more possible here to grow up and be more sensitive & loving and aware to living than anywhere else . . . .*

On August 4 he added

> *In one of them* [her most recent letters] *you spoke of comparing notes. I'm afraid I should be on the shameful side.*
>
> *You see, I haven't been on a raid since the 18th of last month. They want me to give my time toward training the others; and since there are quite a few others just beginning who need experience, I shan't get many opportunities unless something important comes up.*
>
> *I've been taking the philosophical attitude 'Oh well, I might just as well consider myself as having finished but available for special occasions.' That works just fine when you watch these kids come in & zip-- all the way through.*

***

On August 6 the 96th Bomb Group was sent to destroy a tank engine factory in Berlin.[xl] *Had a long one today-- nine hours. Expect to be out tomorrow.* While a long range

82

mission to Berlin hardly qualified, Dad now seemed almost eager to go on any mission that might take him over Normandy and thus into close proximity to Mom. Two days later his plane was over France, on this occasion to bomb a German Army battalion headquarters at Caen.

I actually might have flown over your head today for I covered the full sweep of Normandy. Really was excited about going today just on account of the possibility. Did you see me?

Similarly, on August 13 he noted that his Bomb Group, on its way to bomb targets near Paris, had traveled

Over Normandy again today-- did I fly over you? You know the reception we had from our Aryan hosts was extremely warm but quite lacking in cordiality. And that is putting it mildly.

***

Fear of military censorship continued to limit what Dad dared mention in his correspondence. Nevertheless, his letter of August 15 strongly hints that he would soon be on another mission in which he would not be returning directly to England. *'Member now-- If you don't have any letters from for a spell, it'll most likely be 'cause I'm in another theatre for a week or two. Keep well.* On September 11, 1944 another such shuttle mission to the Soviet Union was indeed flown. 1,131 heavy bombers and 440 escort planes set out from England to bomb various synthetic oil installations throughout Germany. Of these, 75 planes were assigned to bomb the oil facilities at Chemnitz. They were then to continue on to the Soviet Union-- in the case of Dad's 96th Group, specifically to Mirgorod, which, like Poltava, is located in Ukraine.

Ultimately, Dad's experience on this latter shuttle proved to be far less traumatic than before. As it turned out, the Germans did not retaliate after the Americans had landed. For their part, the Russians took more precautions to protect their guests, billeting the Americans several miles from the airfield to reduce the danger to them should another *Luftwaffe* counterattack occur. And, happily for the sake of my parents' correspondence, there was no military cover up afterward. In particular, AAF intelligence officers did not confiscate the letters that Dad had written to Mom during his time away from England as had been the case following Poltava.

12 September, 1944
Tuesday Evening

Dearest Gina:

Here I am in the place again, Russia! Only it is different this time. Let me tell you.

Last night we had to go through a few hours of interrogation and milling around before they'd fix us up for eating and sleeping, and we did bathe very eagerly. Today we had fun.

No bombs last night, and anyway we're about five miles or so from the field. Gee-- you can't imagine how quiet it is here. Absolutely nothing doing. There

has been only one plane to look at all day long. And of course we can't hear the planes at the field from here.

The lights just went out, and I am . . . writing under a blanket like a tent within a tent. We have a huge barracks here and what a luxury.

The Russians gave us a concert this afternoon that had some swell pantomime in it and some excellent voices.

The town here is in pretty fair condition, and the main attraction is the market place where you can see some of the darndest things for sale and a grand assortment of costumes. Most everyone wears boots including the women. I suppose they're more concerned about the mud than their sex appeal.

Because, unlike at Poltava, the American force was still intact the morning after, it was able to bomb a second target, the steel works at Diosgyor in Hungary, on the way back. Moreover, because the Nazi occupied area of Europe was shrinking, the return trip back to England now included one extended layover in Italy, rather than multiple stops in Iran, the Middle East and North Africa.

Dad wrote four letters from Foggia in Italy beginning on the evening of September 13. As with his correspondence following the Poltava mission, much of what he drafted in Italy digresses into travelogue. On September 14, for example, he noted what he considered to be . . . *complete differences in cultural development-- Russia, Italy & England. I'll be quite an educated person when this keeps up.* And, as with his two visits to the Soviet Union, he could not resist again commenting on the appearance of the local women.

Many of the men are very handsome, and the Italian girls have huge brown eyes and are either very attractive or homely as sin. They don't look a thing like Americans, but have a sort of old-world expression-- Mona Lisa style.

Two days after, while still in Italy, he and his fellow airmen even went for a swim.

Two trucks took us to the Gulf of Manfredonia [on Italy's Adriatic coast] *where we went swimming. It was like something you read about. The sky & mountains & air and beach. Say, the Adriatic is really great for swimming.*

Two American planes made fools of them by launching a mock strafing attack. *A P-38 and an A-20 buzzed us while we went flat on our faces.*

Months later, on December 5, Dad again contrasted his first and second shuttle mission experiences after hearing that Mom had just seen a particular Hollywood film.

And you saw 'Johnny Vagabond'-- I did to-- in Russia. Did I tell you about it? They used one (the only) wall of a building for the screen, and we waited for the stars to come out. Strictly open air-- no roof or anything. That was the first time [back in the Soviet Union] *after the horror* [of Poltava].

***

In letter of September 21, Dad again sounded envious of other airmen with less seniority than him who were completing their required missions and returning home.

One of my closest buddies is leaving in a day or two. Which leaves one other fellow and myself who were in the sq. last March. The rest of the flying personnel have come and gone.

Two days later Dad went so far as to concede . . . *This afternoon I felt like a real good bawl. I suppose it's because just about everyone I liked around here is gone.* His letter of October 5 laments further on the burden of having to carry on while younger flyers came and went. However, he added an observation about the effect this rapid turnover was having on morale.

The old boys are leaving and we have a batch of new one . . . . It's odd watching the change in them as they go thru their missions. Most of them develop a little swagger and lose a little youth. Some of them are married-- most are very young trying to look more tough & cynical than they can quite get away with.

Near the end of September, Dad was sent on three consecutive bombing missions over Germany: on September 25 probably to Ludwigshafen, on September 26 to Bremen, and on September 27 probably to Mainz. [xli] Among these, Doherty and Ward specifically mention Dad's role on the Bremen mission, thus confirming that, on this occasion at least, he was involved in the attack on the 96th Group's assigned target. Unfortunately, malfunctioning radar equipment marred his role on the Bremen operation.

The 96th arrived at the target at 15:30 hours. Since cloud and smokescreen hid the target, PFF was exercised. But while 40 miles from the target, the B Group's PFF failed. Even so, these planes bombed on the markers of A Group. But, as luck would have it, the PFF equipment in this group was weak and the Mickey Operator, Captain Charles Dunn, had difficulty picking up the target. The C Group had more luck. With well-operating equipment this group correctly identified the target while still some 40 miles away. Their bombs were on target. [xlii]

On September 29, amid this increased combat activity, Dad again wondered if Mom ever saw his plane overhead. *The other day we came back over Belgium alone and a little on the low side.* He then asked: *Did you see us?* The next day the 96th Group bombed railroad marshaling yards at Bielefeld in Germany. That night Dad again wondered: *Did you see all planes today? I was in the very first one, which is not too bad a place to be. We did a good job, or so they say.*

On October 3 Dad flew what turned out to be his final mission, to Nuremburg.

10

THE BATTLE OF THE BULGE

On October 8, 1944 Mom was given a battlefield promotion from 2nd to 1st lieutenant. But it was another week before she learned of it. Now operating from an abandoned high school in the Belgian town of Eupen, she described on October 25 the informal manner in which the good news actually reached her.

> *The evening before last Capt. Sachs* [a surgeon who Mom admired] *and I were chatting in the corridor when along came one of the MAC's* [?] *and congratulated me on my promotion. Naturally I was surprised . . . .*

However, that honor did not automatically go to everyone. According to a "SPECIAL ORDERS . . . EXTRACT" from Headquarters on October 18, 1944, 55 nurses were being promoted from 2nd to 1st lieutenant. Most of these women were from other evacuation hospitals scattered throughout 1st Army. On this list, however, Mom's was one of only three names from the 45th. Consequently, Mom expressed concern about hurt feelings among those who had been with unit longer than she but had not yet been promoted. Beyond that, Mom regarded the nursing efforts of several of these women as at least equal to her own.

> *. . . I'm* [relatively] *new to the unit and had missed maneuvers in the States. Johnny* [fellow nurse Johnnie E. Sellers] *was more pleased than I about the promotion; and she works with me-- Johnny has no aspiration to be a 1st Lt. either; and at first I thought she'd heckle me about mine; but she genuinely seems pleased; in fact she knew I was getting it all the time. Johnny is a good nurse; but she exerts a little independence, not exactly G.I.-- knowing this, it doesn't seem fair that I have one and she doesn't.*

Actually, Nurse Sellers' name is listed on the same October 18 document that announced Mom's promotion. Perhaps this Nurse Sellers' military superiors agreed with Mom's assessment that she was too independent-minded, in which case they may have informally punished her by delaying news of her promotion. In any event, Mom seemed genuinely relieved to report on October 31

> *Some more kids received their 1st Looies, and now its rumored that Evac* [Evacuation] *nurses will have them 100%. That would be most fair because all the girls work equally as hard.*

Because of the usual mail delivery delays, it was more than two weeks before Dad learned of Mom's promotion.

> *14 November 1944*
> *Tuesday evening*

Dearest Gina:

You should see me-- one big grin. Congratulations Mrs. '1st Lt.' Gallagher!
I'm getting more pride and pleasure from your promotion than my own, and that
was something-- remember? I'm not a bit ashamed to [con]fess this. I looked to
see if any of your other letters have been signed 1st Lt. and, sure enough, there it
was. You see, some of your older letters had been all mixed up chronologically--
today there were four spread out over nine days-- and I've been diving into them
without looking at the envelope very much-- forgive me.

By November 11, the human carnage that Mom and been witnessing for the past half
year seemed to be getting to her.

Tonight Johnny and I are back at our old job of [treating patients for] shock.
For the past three nights I've been on the post-operative wards. For some reason
it's making me nauseated to see the traumatic fresh injuries-- mostly blast
injuries. Although we've only five patients all in condition for surgery, I'm too
mindful of the nights and days this ward was full. Strange, but on the post-op
wards the patients' injuries seem remotely related to the war, but here they seem
too closely related. If only each soldier has some one to help them overcome the
handicaps they face when they get back.

On November 20, a Sunday evening, Mom had time to write from her ward while on
duty.

We're busy tonight, and both Johnny and I are a little depressed; we've had
some very tragic admissions. In fact Johnny has been crying; and from
appearances she seems so indifferent to life; but underneath she's 'chicken
hearted.' And I know she's crying over something she said to a patient not
knowing his condition until later-- because he'll never see again. It sort of gives
one that 'hard to swallow feeling.'

***

By the late autumn of 1944, Mom was actually in greater danger than Dad whose combat
flying was being phased out in favor of administrative duties. Meanwhile, Mom's 1st
Army was now in Belgium poised -- or so it was thought-- for the invasion of central
Germany. But the military situation was again intensifying. On December 12 Mom
wrote to assure Dad that the evacuation hospital accidently bombed by the Germans was
not the 45th. Four days later, at 7:15 PM, she admitted . . . *We had a very busy night last*
night and some excitement, too. The first in a long time . . . . By 6:30 AM the next
morning, the military situation had deteriorated further.

Would you believe it, that this is being written in the operating room. A nurse
asleep on one operating table, a doctor on another, and a patient is being
operated on the third table. He had some shrapnel removed from his abdomen,
and they're almost through. The patient is a Jerry [German soldier]. Strange.

What Mom did not yet realize was that the Battle of the Bulge-- the costliest
confrontation of WWII in terms of American casualties-- had just begun. Indeed, it

started on December 16 with a massive German offensive of half a million men, their last remaining reserves. This German force attempted to drive a wedge-- or "bulge"-- between the American and British armies on the western front. Moreover, this German offensive was deliberately launched amidst a winter snowstorm that Hitler hoped would keep bombing planes from both sides grounded, thus neutralizing the Allies' airpower advantage. At this point even Hitler realized that a German military victory over the Allies was no longer possible. But he was a gambler who was hoping that an effective counterattack would bluff the Allies into negotiated armistice, that is, a ceasefire sparing Germany itself from invasion.

Mom's 45th Evacuation Hospital soon found itself in a precarious position. A Maj. Wagner described the scene.

> 'With news of the offensive, our prisoners of war were evacuated and all personnel restricted to the hospital area. At 5:30 hours, 16 December 1944, the town of Eupen came under intense enemy artillery fire, presumably from 88 mm weapons. One shell burst about 10 yards from the building, which housed our shock and pre-operative wards. An intervening stone wall fortunately caught most of the blast and fragments. No damage resulted to the hospital. At 23:30, 17 December 1944, a gasoline dump to our immediate east was hit by a stick of 'fire' bombs falling from 150 to 180 yards of our hospital. High explosive bombs then fell within 60 yards of the northwest corner of the hospital. The concussion was severe. All windows were blown out; the lighting system was disrupted; and corridors, ward floors, and beds were littered with debris.'[xliii]

Despite the peril she now faced, Mom's letter the next day attempted to reassure Dad that-- contrary to what he might be hearing on BBC radio back in England-- everything was going to be okay. Her note on December 18 is only 52 words long. But it includes her . . . *hope* [that] *you're not too alarmed at the activity here 'cause it's not bad at all.* But the 45th's situation really was perilous. Censorship prevented Mom from describing her experiences in the battle or, indeed, even mentioning that she was in the midst of one. However, her letter of December 21 does concede that she had been unable to write for several days. Moreover, in this same letter, she let it slip out that the 45th also had not actually been treating any new patients during these same days. She then promised Dad: *All . . .[will] be told when I see you.* None of her subsequent letters add anything specific about events during this desperate battle that would eventually cost America 81,000 casualties, including 19,000 killed.

During my own childhood, Mom frequently repeated the same account of what had occurred. According to Mom, when the battle started her unit was stationed in western Germany at a place called Aachen. They then received a warning that a German counterattack was imminent. She said that this warning was accompanied by orders to evacuate the entire hospital back toward the west. A convoy of trucks duly arrived and evacuated the patients.[xliv] But before the medical staff could also be pulled out in a second convoy, somebody yelled out that German paratroopers were descending on the far side of the town. At that point-- according to Mom-- she, the doctors and other nurses hid in the basement of the abandoned high school hoping their presence would go undetected by the enemy.[xlv] Those among them who were Jewish now rid themselves of their dog tags [military identification] so that, in the event of capture by the fanatical

Waffen SS, their religious affiliation would not result in their being treated worse than the rest. At times she could see German military traffic on the streets through the basement windows of the school they were hiding in. Then, after four days of hiding in that basement, they were able to re-emerge as the Germans withdraw.

Further, Mom remembered with some amusement that, while everyone else in the unit was more than a little concerned about the possibility of being taken prisoner by the enemy, one nurse was preoccupied by the discovery that her scalp was infected with lice. Mom's letter of December 21 does to some extent confirm her later recollections. For example, it includes the same anecdote about the nurse and her lice.

> *The strangest thing that happened, the most humorous I should say, was that Jane* [nurse Jane Kreitz] *acquired those little crawling animals, which infest the human head, especially kids' heads. What a dilemma! That came when in the course of events* [where] *she had to sleep on used blankets. I fortunately had none of my own. Nothing could be done for poor Jane until today when we had something to work with, namely water. Of course we are all suffering from 'the itch,' all imaginative, I hope.*

Never during Mom' previous six months in a combat zone had her letters complain about an absence of wounded soldiers to treat, nor of unhygienic blankets, nor of a shortage of potable water. These indicate that there had been a great disruption to her routine. She rather ambiguously concluded by saying . . . *This probably seems a strange letter; but if you'll understand that I don't want you to be worried; it isn't necessary at all.* Other letters she wrote over the next days are equally enigmatic. The postscript to her letter dated December 30 says . . . *Lately, my letters must seem brainless, but I think you know why.*

Eventually, the bad weather cleared. Both the AAF and RAF were then able to resume their bombing of German positions. Within 10 days of the initial German attack, the Allied armies regained the upper hand. The Germans were obliged to pull back. And the 45th Evacuation Hospital was able to re-emerge.

***

On January 4, 1945 Dad received his first letter from Mom in weeks. In it she reassured him that she had, in fact, survived this particularly bloody recent battle. He immediately called Wotton to pass along the good news. Two days later, he described a telephone conversation. *Reg suggested that the nurses might be changed people when come back here. I told him that they would probably be deepened-- he thought it more apt, too.* On January 23 Dad added . . . *Reg sent a letter this afternoon with a reassuring, friendly part to it.*

***

[Contrary to Mom's account, all historical sources[xlvi] agree that the 45th Evacuation Hospital's "Bulge" experience occurred at Eupen in Belgium rather than at Aachen in Germany, 14 miles away. Perhaps the reason for her later confusion on this point is that her medical unit did later pass through Aachen.

Mom is second from the right in this photograph taken along the road to Aachen, February, 1945.

In all Mom's letters, the only one in which she referred to the Battle of the Bulge by name came six months later, on May 20, 1945. *Our unit got the Meritorious Service Plaque; fancy that. It must have been for the bulge 'cause the notice posted stated for the time of Dec. to Jan 1st.*]

***

After their failure at The Bulge, the Germans no longer possessed the means to launch further attacks. Their only remaining hope was to deny the Allies access into central Germany. If this entry could be prevented, then an armistice might be negotiated in which the Nazi political regime would be permitted to survive. At least that was Hitler's hope when he ordered all bridges spanning the Rhine River be detonated. In theory, this would make it impossible for the western Allies to access central Germany. By March 7, 1945 all of the Rhine's bridges had been demolished by the Germans themselves-- except for the Ludendorff railroad bridge at Remagen, south of Bonn. At the last possible moment, American soldiers were able to seize control of this bridge intact. Immediately, Allied ground forces began crossing over the Rhine into the heart of the Fatherland. Ten days later, the Ludendorff Bridge, having been weakened by repeated *Luftwaffe* bombings, collapsed. But by then it no longer mattered. U.S. Army military engineers had constructed a pontoon bridge in parallel, rendering the original structure redundant.

On March 24 Mom's 45th Evacuation Hospital moved up to near the Rhine River at a place called Bad Neuenahr. There the 45th was ordered to prepare a local building for medical use. However, the very next day-- before these preparations could be completed-- a second order was received to repack and advance eastward yet again. According to Sgt. Roberts

> This [further relocation] was difficult to take until we learned we were to cross the Rhine River at Remagen and become the first Evacuation Hospital in our armies to cross. The mood was rapidly changed to elation and welcome. On the road to Remagen we passed truck after truck with German prisoners being transported to the rear.[xlvii]

As the 45th's trucks approached the river's edge, Lt. Lebson described the scene-- and the potential danger.

> The scattered sections of our convoys began crossing the Rhine during the latter part of the morning . . . , using the Engineer constructed pontoon bridges which were now spanning the River. We could see the remains of the Remagen Bridge as we crossed below it. There was a great volume of traffic and the roadside cautions to remain 50 feet apart were no idle warning. The Nazis made the Bridge a prime target as soon as it was captured and concentrated all the firepower they could muster at it.[xlviii]

However, there was little opportunity to relish the moment.

> We had taken part in what at the moment was considered an important 'first', the first evacuation hospital in the Allied Forces to cross the Rhine River. It was felt that the additional effort expended was worth it all.
> We were proud of the accomplishment although we were not given much time to dwell on it.[xlix]

Both sources agree that by the day after that, March 25, the 45th began admitting patients at a place called Bad Honnef, about five miles north of the Remagen bridge. According to Sgt. Roberts . . . "The level of casualties [now being treating] was extremely high because we were the only Evacuation Hospital that side of the Rhine River."[l]

In her first evening east of the Rhine, Mom found time to write Dad two letters. In neither of these did she bother to describe what she had seen that day. Moreover, unlike those drafted during the battles at Normandy and The Bulge, the two March 24 letters give no indication either that she was under great stress or that censorship was preventing her from describing her experience. Perhaps in anticipation of a heavy medical workload ahead, her second letter that evening did caution Dad . . . *You'll miss a letter tomorrow, but I shall pen you as soon as the opportunity presents itself.*

11
NEARER TO VICTORY

On September 20 Dad noted that he had just heard another rumor, this one about a transfer to 96th Group headquarters which were also located at Snetterton Heath. . . . *It looks as if I should soon be leaving the 413th. Ah then-- tut, tut. I shan't be going anywhere actually. I'll simply be assigned to Group instead.* Such a reassignment would not simply be a matter of Dad's seniority. The entire pathfinder program was becoming the victim of its own success. Now that more aircrews were becoming familiar with radar, there was less reason to maintain specialized pathfinder units-- as the entire 482nd Group had once been for the entire 8th AAF and the 413th Squadron within the 96th Bomb Group had more recently been for the 3rd Air Division. Now each squadron within each group within each wing within each division had its own pathfinder crews. Dad's letter of October 29 expands on his upcoming change in job descriptions.

> *Knock on wood ever so lightly, but I may not have to fly any more missions. I'll be instructing for a while, and cussing because lecturing & singing don't go well together. I know two that do.*
>
> Love & always
> Rick

What Dad's letter does not say is that he was actually requesting the new posting. After all, most 8th AAF flyers were sent home immediately after completing their required missions. Dad had completed his missions. By asking to stay on in the ETO, albeit in a non-flying capacity, his motive was to remain in close proximity to Mom. On Christmas Eve, his transfer came through. He was officially kicked upstairs to 96th Bomb Group headquarters. On New Year's Day he was transferred again, this time to 45th Combat Wing headquarters-- all the while remaining at Snetterton Heath. On that day he wrote a letter to Mom that began with the news that a *Mrs. Miller*, who played the piano at the base's Red Cross lounge and with whom Mom was also acquainted, was returning home because of a medical issue. He then added

> *I am leaving myself. Now-now! I'm only leaving the [413th] squadron and the [96th] group. My address will be the 45th Wing, or something like that, with the same APO. Actually the place is just across the street, and I will move on paper only. Just think-- I will be in a '45th,' too.*

On February 3, 1945 he attempted to explain for a somewhat bewildered Mom, without violating censorship restrictions, as to just what it was that a Combat Wing did.

> *I think it corresponds more nearly to a brigade than anything else. There aren't any [flying] crews involved-- it's just a headquarters-- a more direct connection to the groups than a division could be. The commanding officer is a B.G. [brigadier general], and each wing is meant to operate as a tactical unit. Now a wing (formation) is merely two or three groups with a common leader-- which is all one guy can direct, and administratively it acts in a supervisory capacity over*

the groups. A combat wing does not have all the power it might have-- division hq. having a large share for unity in so large an air force. I think a normal wing is a bombardment wing. My job here is advisory, training and stuff.

While undated, this photograph may have been taken just after
Dad's reassignment to headquarters.

***

Because Mom thought that little Bernice Breadman looked a good deal like Dad, she occasionally began her letters with the salutation *Dear Pumpkin Sr.* instead of her usual *Dear Ricky.* On February 3, Dad reported that this had inadvertently created the impression among his fellow airmen that he was a parent.

Mac-- one of the S-2's [intelligence officers] *was reading over my shoulder, &, if I'm not 'Pumpkin Sr.' all over the base by tomorrow, it will be a wonder. The fiend! I guess if Pumpkin herself were here and they all jumped to conclusions-- alas. Heck no. That would really be fun!*

***

Meanwhile, Following German defeat at The Bulge, Mom found increasing opportunity to travel beyond the immediate security of her hospital. On January 8 she described an excursion through the Belgian town of Jodoigne.

Yesterday afternoon, Shirley [fellow nurse Helen G. Shirley], *Chappie and I went for a walk first through town, then off limits through the woods, we kidded ourselves about land mines but we had a serious thought about them, too.*

During this time, one of Mom's letters describes a landscape equivalent to what one might expect to see in a newly liberated concentration camp. It was written at suppertime on March 24, the same day her unit had crossed at Remagen and first arrived in Bad Honnef.

Today we went for a walk in this ghost town. Not a building intact and every now and then an atrocious odor indicating a cadaver in the vicinity. Very desolate.

On March 30 Mom let it slip out that she had been off on another such excursion, this time in Bad Honnef.

> *Managed a few hours off duty and Major* [William] *Birch took me for a walk.*
> *We walked through the town, shakily, too 'cause we kept thinking about snipers and remembering patients, sniper victims. Although none had been reported around here, else we would have been kept in. It was a strange feeling to know you were actually roaming around a German city and a long, long way from Belgium.*
> *Five truck loads of German prisoners passed through, and many of the German women broke down into tears. Needless to say, we were glad to get back to the hospital with little desire to go out again.*

***

On October 18, shortly after the 45th Evacuation Hospital had moved forward from France into Belgium, Mom first mentioned that civilians, including children, who now among the patients being treated.

> *We've had quite a few civilian patients, but little time to use the art of sign language. It's fun to have a child on the ward and watch one eat jam on crackers, etc. And do the GIs fuss over them!*

Judging from her letters, Mom was seldom unnerved when treating wounded soldiers. But, when wounded children were brought to her ward, she found this unsettling. On October 12 she described one experience.

> *Today we admitted the sweetest little Belgian (?) boy of about four; the poor child had his fingers blown off. After he became assured that we wouldn't hurt him, I stood him on the table and put a large G.I. pajama top on him. He grinned at his attire and then smiled at me 'cause he was taller than I. I carried him over to another ward to visit a little Belgian girl, 3 years old. She was pleased to see him, but he didn't seem to approve of her and wanted to hurry back to our ward-- just like a little boy.*

Thee next day she added

> *My little* [Belgian] *boy was transferred to another ward, the same ward the little girl is on. He is no more enthused about her today; he'd like to come back to a 'he-man' ward like shock. The activities here fascinate him more.*

Two days after that she was still talking about him.

> *Visited my little Belgian boy, we do have difficulty understanding one another but get along very well in spite of the language handicap. For such a little mite he certainly is courageous.*

On October 29 Mom reported on a second such child who had been harmed by war, this time German.

> *Last night among the patients was a child 12 years old. Permanently hurt, so hard to understand <u>why</u> to some one so young. What a tragic Christmas season in that German home.*

On November 9 came yet another child who had been grievously harmed.

> *Stopped in the ward to see a boy with both legs amputated. He is an Italian boy whose first name is Charlie, and as good as gold. Promised him one of your chocolate bars, so I'll take it down later. Abdominal and chest wounds are most times more serious and more painful, but amputations touch me so much more. It's an awful war.*

In a letter written at 2 AM on November 11, on duty and with her patients sleeping, Mom talked of a 12-year-old German patient, perhaps a more specific description of the same little boy she had mentioned on October 29.

> *On the cot just in front of my desk is a little German 12 yr. old boy, a brain case; he stirred, opened his eyes but decided to fall back again. Earlier in the evening I drew pictures with him, and we became quite chummy.*

In a later paragraph, Mom resumed the topic of collateral damage, although in this case the injured non-combatant was not a child.

> *These thoughts shouldn't be written, but they began early this morning. We have a German Catholic priest with a skull fracture, semi-conscious, who roused when I spoke to him. He stroked my hair, smiled kindly and seemed so at peace that I wanted to cry. The war seemed impossible to comprehend; why a priest, children, women, too, should be a part of it-- the padre seemed so alone.*
> *To have you whole seems like everything tonight. Am humbly filled with gratitude.*

In her letter on November 22, Mom offered an anecdote that expanded on her theme that this war included so many innocent people. By this stage of hostilities, Germany was running out of able-bodied men.   In its desperation, the Nazi regime began enlisting both the elderly and the very young.

> *Our German POWs are mere babes. There are four of them in line* [to receive some minor medical treatment] *with a blonde 'GI' in the middle. They thought he was German too-- don't know who was the most surprised when they tried to converse. Some GIs would be rather angry to be taken for a Jerry, but he was amused.*

***

By the early spring of 1945 Germany was being cut in two. The Soviet Army was rolling back all opposition in the East. British and American Armies were doing likewise from the West. Standard historical narratives report that the American and Soviet armies first linked up on April 25 at Torgau on the Elbe River. But Mom's own first contact with the Russians was back on March 6 when American forces liberated foreigners from a slave labor camp, probably near the German town of Eschweiler.

> *Dearest,*
> *Overslept, but it's always that way after a first night. We were rather busy but had no serious cases; even had Russian women (3) from a labor battalion. The women only had moderately severe wounds. Naturally, the G.I.s had fun; those who spoke Polish could speak to the Russians.*

As late as March 3, Mom was still reporting injuries to non-combatants.

> *This morning I relieved in the wards and had a little German boy, six years old, to care for. He has a head injury and as yet has been unable to speak. We had fun looking at pictures, eating candy, etc. He was good for my morale. Here's hoping I work there tomorrow. Children are universally nice.*

By April 4 Mom's 45th Evacuation Hospital had moved forward again, this time setting up operations at an abandoned resort hotel in the town of Bad Wildungen.

> *The patients poured in, not too seriously wounded, many Germans. We had some German medical students assisting in surgery. It seems strange to see their black boots in contrast to our operating room.*

***

Writing in November 28, 1944 from Eupen, Mom described an amusing scene. *One evening at dusk some heavy artillery came our way and one of our Lt. Col.(s) and a Major jumped into the garbage pit. A sight to behold!* On January 25, 1945 Mom again managed to find humor in what was happening around her, although this time she was laughing at herself. By then, the 45th Evacuation Hospital was operating in a converted horse stable at an old Belgian Army cavalry facility near the resort town of Spa.

> *I took an awful teasing 'cause one time when we were blitzed [attacked by low flying German aircraft] & most people were running down stairs, I ran upstairs to get your pictures-- that's something I will never live it down.*

***

Back in the First Word War, Germany had been the first to use poison gas as a military weapon. Now there was concern that they might do so again. In anticipation of this possibility, the personnel of Mom's 45th Evacuation Hospital were each issued both gas masks and skin ointment. The purpose of the latter was for topical protection against blisters and scarring. No such gas attack actually occurred, perhaps because of German fear that the Allies would retaliate in kind. Mom herself later described to me her unit's onetime proximity to a US 9th AAF airstrip where tanks of poison gas were stacked up near its P-38 planes. According to Mom's understanding, these tanks would be loaded onto the planes instead of conventional bombs should a retaliatory poison gas attack be ordered. However, what Mom more likely saw was another new chemical weapon-- napalm-- which is jellied petroleum that kills by immolating its victims. The 9th AAF first used napalm to attack German targets in France beginning in July of 1944.

Despite the absence of an actual gas attack, the 45th Evacuation Hospital was subjected to a gas alert one night. In a letter written on November 28, 1944, Mom described what happened.

> *One of the doctors jumped out of bed and began stripping. The others in his tent looked on in amazement after they had* [donned] *their gas masks and asked what he was doing. He replied, 'I don't know about the rest of you guys, but I'm putting on my protective ointment.' Burr-- and on a cold night.*

Prophetically, Mom closed this same letter by anticipating . . . *What drastic tales we can tell our young 'uns.* As it turned out, what she eventually did share with my sister, brother and me was how it came to be that her own upper back was now covered with many small, keloid-type scars. These she attributed to a skin reaction resulting from her own later application of the same ointment previously used by that panicked doctor. In all likelihood, this had occurred on the evening of January 9, 1945. For one thing, she did not write a letter that day. For another, her letter the next evening advised Dad that the chaplain . . . *said he'd write to you for me last night, and I hope he explained why.* Further, Mom wanted her children to know that she had informed Dad of this disfigurement before their marriage. However, her wartime letters make no direct mention of it.

12
STRESSES

As previously mentioned, back in 1943 Dad had been obliged to undergo orthopedic surgery to repair a bimalleolar fracture of his left ankle. Following this type of surgery, postoperative complications typically include bleeding, infection, arthritis, a permanently unstable joint, and proneness to repeated injury. On January 13, 1944, nine days after his return to flying status with the 482nd Bomb Group at Alconbury in England, he was still having trouble with his surgically rebuilt leg. On that day he rather clinically described to Mom the current status of his medical recovery.

> *So far so good. I'm still coming right along with the old ankle. Still have scabs, but no drainage and very little trouble aside from a little swelling. I guess the two*[ankles] *will never look the same size, quite though.*

Knowing how much his surgically rebuilt lower leg continued to trouble him for the remainder of his life, I might have expected the AAF to relieve Dad of any further combat flying duties. Admittedly, he could walk without noticeably favoring the other leg. But any athletic activity other than swimming was really out of the question. Parachuting behind enemy lines and evading capture-- problematic for the most physically fit airmen-- would have been even more difficult for him. On February 1, 1944 Dad did acknowledge speculation among his friends that he would be granted a Section 8, meaning reclassification as medically unfit for combat. But that did not happen. A week later, Dad was still trying to put a brave face on his predicament. *The ankle is better. Not actually, but it is beginning to scar. I guess I do have a teeny weeny bit of ortho.* By August 11, having survived another six months of combat flying status, Dad's leg still had not completely mended.

> *Dear Gina,*
> *Spent the afternoon taking 'shots' and thence to the hospital where I was x-rayed. No ortho, but I mustn't indulge in violent sports. That's a good one-- as if I could. Wearing a bandage and a slipper-- the darned thing ruptured again. Must be the hot sun.*

To some extent Dad's complaints about his chronic leg problem-- though real enough-- were related to stress levels he was experiencing at various stages of the war: first from his own actual combat flying, then from worry about the dangers that Mom was facing as a battlefield nurse, and finally from a near breakdown suffered after being relieved from his own combat flying duties. By November 7, he had not done any combat flying in a month. But that did not deter him from snapping at the physician treating his leg that day.

> *Went to the* [base] *hospital to have the doc look at my ankle which has a funny look to it; so what does he do but put some goo on it. Later I asked him out of curiosity just what good he thought it would do, and he said 'No good.' I hit the roof and practically called him a quack to his face, which is the general attitude*

toward the base M.D.s here. It made him mad at first, but he respects me for it. I was ashamed of myself afterwards, but they don't give a gosh darn about anybody here.

By April 2, 1945, however, both the war and Dad's leg were taking turns for the better. The Allies had crossed the Rhine River. German military resistance was crumbling. And Dad was feeling well enough to play baseball-- sort of.

We [desk officers at headquarters] *knocked off at four and played* [base]*ball 'till six. I felt pretty good about being in the game. I didn't have much confidence in running, but I seemed to do all right.*

***

Like a modern jet airliner, a B-17 Flying Fortress flew at extremely high altitudes, up to 30,000 feet or so. However, unlike a modern airliner, the a B-17's cabin was not pressurized. Consequently, at maximum altitude the cabin temperature might drop to 60 degrees below zero Fahrenheit. Moreover, the available oxygen level would be the same as if one had just climbed to the top of Mount Everest. 8th AAF crewmen were therefore obliged to don much special equipment. Sidney Scheinberg, also a navigator with the 96th Bomb Group, later described the required wardrobe in his *Join the Air Corps and Become a Flying Officer in the U.S. Army: A Memoir of My War Years.*

To protect ourselves from the cold, we'd wear electric warmed ski-type underwear (it didn't work always, especially if we strayed from the source of electricity), with our regular uniforms on top (necessary if we were to be shot down and captured, so that we would be identified as military airmen). Then over our uniforms, we wore sheepskin-fur lined jackets and pants, fur lined boots, leather helmets with built-in radio earphones connected to [an] interior radio system, military steel helmets (worn in flak or fighter situations), and wool gloves to be worn at all times to prevent frostbite (just touching a machine gun or any other metal object could cause frostbite). To relieve ourselves we had to urinate into our pee tubes.[li]

The loss of either the electrical heating or oxygen delivery could have fatal consequences for the bomber crewmen who were affected. Any B-17 or B-24 that broke formation over enemy territory would be singled out for special attention by the *Luftwaffe*. Consequently, it was not advisable for a plane to break formation even if the crew support systems failed. An airman who found himself disconnected from the plane's oxygen or electricity might not survive even if the plane itself returned to base intact. [Generally, the same was also true if a crewman was wounded during a mission. If the airplane remained flyable, the mission continued. Many fatalities were suffered on bombers that returned safely to base.]

Jack Croul described in his diary a mission a to Berlin on May 7, 1944.

We had a leak in our oxygen system and didn't think we'd make it, but it held out. Bombed at 25,000 feet and -42 degrees centigrade. It was quite cold to say the least.[lii]

Even training missions could be dangerous. On April 15, Lt. Croul noted that his crew

> Had a practice mission of 5 hours this morning and early afternoon. The heater was out and I didn't bring the cord to my [electrically] heated suit. Hence, at 15,000 [feet] and -12 degrees, C., I froze.[liii]

Twice in his letters to Mom, Dad himself described similar mishaps, both of which he attributed to his own carelessness. On February 21, 1944, while still with the 482nd Bomb Group at Alconbury, his plane was

> *Stooging around in the air at 25,000 feet with my oxygen disconnected accidentally. I don't know how it happened, but the first thing I knew I was getting a bit helpless. Intuition saved the day. Took all my will to get snapped on again & gave me a scare. That's what flying pay is for.*

He attributed this error to his being in love. *If I seem a bit stupid or careless, it is only because I am so richly endowed with happiness that I cannot grasp it all.* Three days later he must have still been in love, because he again made the same mistake.

> *All poohed out tonight. I went flying this afternoon at 12,000 feet for two hours, and like a d—m fool I didn't use my oxygen. Result-- my chin is draggin ' and I've a nice headache to boot.*

Because of Dad's bad leg, Mom expressed concern about the possibility that high altitude flying might pose an additional risk to his surgical recovery. On December 15 Dad reassured her that this did not exacerbate his problem.

> *Never a frown now about my leg. It is 'right as rain,' and I can run and hop about it very well. At 25,000 feet the temperature is usually at least 40 below zero, but heated boots do the trick nicely.*

[When I was in my fifties, I had the opportunity to go for a ride on a vintage B-17 that was then touring the country. With a crew of three, this plane offered brief rides for up to seven passengers. For a short flight like mine, the plane could not climb to a high enough altitude for the frigid temperatures and thin air of its unpressurized cabin to be experienced. But I came away with some strong impressions nonetheless. For one thing, despite this B-17's seeming size while parked on the tarmac, interior accommodations were surprisingly cramped. There are few places inside the fuselage where a six-footer can stand up properly. One place where I was able to do so was the radio operator's compartment. This is located behind the nose compartment for the bombardier and navigator, behind the flight deck for the two pilots, and immediately behind the flight engineer's power-operated dorsal gun turret. During the mission, the radio operator would sit at a tiny table facing a radio set. But the ceiling of this compartment also included small opening covered by a removable Plexiglas panel. Through this opening, a belt-fed 50-caliber machine gun could be fired upward to fend off *Luftwaffe* attacks. The compartment itself is less than six feet from floor to ceiling. However, for my flight, the Plexiglas panel had been removed. This permitted me to stand to my full height by sticking my head out through the roof of the plane. The dorsal turret directly in front of my face provided some protection from the wind. But the noise from the huge propeller engines just a few feet away on either side was deafening. On a real WWII mission there were four additional gunners who fired their weapons from positions behind the radio compartment. Two of these crewmen were called "waist gunners." When the plane was under attack, these two waist gunners stood with their backs to each other and fired their weapons sideways through what were-- on early models of the plane-- open windows. My excursion flight was for only about 45 minutes. I can only imagine how uncomfortable the crewman must have been on high altitude missions lasting seven or even nine hours.]

***

Mom and Dad, in their hundreds of letters, generally avoided any direct admission of the war's dangers to themselves. But a close call occasionally caused one or the other to breach the unspoken rule that the purpose of their mutual correspondence was to reassure each other rather than to alarm. One source of close calls was the new "vengeance weapons" introduced by the Germans in 1944. These were advanced technical innovations that Hitler hoped would counter the Allies numerical advantage and thus reverse the direction of the War. The first to be operationally deployed was the V-1. Today it would be called a cruise missile. Beginning in mid-1944 the first of more than 9000 V-1s were launched, predominantly against Southeastern England. British civilians referred to them as "doodlebugs." American military personnel called them "buzz bombs" because of the loud throbbing noise made by their pulse jet engines. These unmanned weapons flew at about 300 miles per hour at low altitude, about the same as the top speed as that of a WWII fighter plane. So they could be interdicted. Soon the RAF was sending up standing patrols of interceptor planes in an effort to locate them and shoot them down before they could reach a big city like London. Many V-1s were destroyed in this manner. But others got through. A V-1 fell to earth only after its pulse jet motor had run out of fuel, thus cutting off its throbbing noise. Consequently, if a buzz bomb could be heard passing overhead, there was little danger. And even when the buzzing noise suddenly cut off, there was usually time for people on the ground to take cover before the inevitable explosive impact.

When these buzz bombs began raining down on England, Mom was already in France. Being in southeastern England, Dad was at greater risk. For example, Dad's AAF squadron mate Lt. Croul, in his description of a leave spent in London in late June,` complained that

> . . . didn't get much sleep because of the buzz bombs. Saw about ten bursts around London, watching from a club window. In bed I'd hear one; it would pass overhead; the motor would stop; and I would wonder where it would land.[liv]

On the morning on October 13-- Friday the 13th-- Dad had a leave and was spending the night at the Red Cross Club in the nearby university town of Cambridge. The next morning his letter to Mom exclaimed: *Great cats! There were more buzz bombs going overhead last night than you could shake a stick at.* In an undated letter that was probably written on October 27, Dad added that a second V-1 attack had somehow made

101

him mindful of an anecdote from the 19th century American philosopher Henry David Thoreau.

> *Its odd how your stomach knots when the sirens go in the nearby town and the buzz bombs 'wump-wump' overhead. You know it has something to it that makes me think of Thoreau. The train clanking & whistling along as ever, bombs or not. There is something reassuring about it. It used to disturb Thoreau because it was noisy.*

On January 4, 1945 Dad was back in Cambridge. And again he noted the presence of these German weapons. *It rained buzz bombs last night, too.*

To a lesser extent, V-1s were a nuisance for Army personnel on the ground in Europe as well. Robert Roberts, Mom's 45th Evacuation Hospital colleague, remembers them from the autumn of 1944 when their unit was positioned in Belgium, quite near the German border.

> Flying bombs, (Buzz Bombs to us), not at all accurate, were employed as a form of harassment on the civilian population and us. Their engines sounded like a diesel train and their flight was always close to the ground just above the treetops. Buzz bombs were usually deployed in the early morning or night, especially in foggy unclear weather. The Buzz Bombers were set so they could dive or glide . . . and also fly for a predetermined time. We were in the direct path to either Liege or Verviers; there was no telling what the destination might be. Frequency varied but foggy weather or snow favored their use. After a while we learned to live with them, but of course we were always apprehensive.[lv]

The noise these weapons generated certainly caught Mom's attention. For instance, by November 3, 1944 the 45th was now functioning in the abandoned Belgian secondary school at Eupen rather than a tent. This being the case, the loud noise generated by the buzz bombs became somewhat less of a distraction. Two days later she elaborated.

> *Sometimes artillery, buzz bombs, ack-ack, seemed frightening-- especially if you couldn't fall asleep at night, but now its wonderfully quiet in this building. The buzz bombs are the topic of conversation because of their nearness . . . .*

On December 2 Dad was in Wotton-under-Edge to deliver Christmas gifts to the Sims and Breadmans. On this particular visit, the Breadmans expressed concern that these new German weapons had created an additional danger to Mom. *They heard the news a few days ago about a hospital being struck by a V1. Please send them a few lines-- they are quite concerned.*

Dad also mentioned barely escaping the destruction apparently caused by a second and even more frightening vengeance weapon, the V-2. It was an early version of the "Scud" missiles Iraq's Saddam Hussein fired against Israel in 1991. At the apex of its trajectory, a V-2 approached the reaches of outer space before descending toward its target at supersonic speed. Against such attacks there was-- during WWII, at least-- no defense, scant time for a radar warning, and virtually no audible sound until after the warhead exploded. Beginning in September of 1944, more than 3000 V-2 attacks were launched, nearly half of which were aimed against Southeastern England. On November 22 Dad happened to be at the Snetterton Heath AAF base headquarters.

> *There were a couple of very close explosions that really shook the place. Might have been anything from flak to a V-2, but it's very much of a surprise-- ordinarily there is a certain unruffled sanctity to such a higher headquarters . . .; and explosions are therefore very rude indeed.*

***

For both Mom and Dad, letters describing threats to their own safety were very much the exception. More common were expressions of concern for each another. For example, when Mom sat down at 8 AM on June 3, 1944 to write her letter of the day to Dad, she must have known that the largest amphibious invasion in history, a venture for which she and her unit had been preparing for half a year, was near at hand. Indeed, it would begin in less than 72 hours. Yet her letter that morning expressed concern only for Dad's safety.

> *Waited until 11 P.M. for your call, was a little anxious so I decided to listen to the news commentary. Which ordinarily would make me feel worse, but it so happened that all American Heavy Bombers had returned.*

By June 8, the Normandy invasion was into its third day. As far as Dad knew, Mom was still billeted in Wotton-under-Edge. Still, it was only a matter of time before her unit was sent into the battle. His letter that evening reflects his anxiety.

> *Can't help feeling anxious over this invasion, and it seems that the big brass must really be chewing their nails. You realize all at once, it seems, the possibilities of the thing.*

As previously described, Dad's first shuttle mission to the Soviet Union began on June 21. Not until his return to England on July 8 was he allowed to mail any letters describing what he had experienced. And not until another ten days after that did Mom learn that he was safe. During this interim, Mom-- who was herself now on a French battlefield and also in great danger-- grew increasingly concerned. On July 9 she wrote

> *Dear Ricky,*
> *No letters from you for ever so long; there'd better be one coming through pretty soon; or I shall feel lost. Feel sure that it's the APO mail and that you are all right.*
> *At this moment I feel very, very lonesome without you. In a few minutes I shall be so busy with my patients that the longing to see you will be suppressed-- but it's always there.*
> *But I would have it just this way for our tomorrow-- could never be sad, really sad, with that thought and hope-- nor am I alone.*
> *Love you, my darling--*
Gina

103

There's our hour each evening. Never forgotten, most times I'm able to step outside for just a moment, and you seem even closer than when I'm in the tent with my patients.

Seems God is easier reached outdoors at our hour.

On July 10, two days after his return from Poltava, Dad had not forgotten about the dangers that Mom also was facing. He asked: *Say, do you get a chance to sleep at all, and are you constantly under fire?*

Even by July 16 Mom still had not received any message from Dad written since before the Poltava mission. Consequently, in an undated letter that was probably written on July 16 from La Cambe in the Normandy Beachhead area, she reported that she . . . *Phoned you today, but the operator was unable to hold the line until you were located . . . .* The letter continues that she . . . *wasn't too disappointed; at least I learned that you were about.* So she tried to reach him through an intermediary who had reason to travel back and forth between France and England.

Dad's letter on the evening of July 16 acknowledges her effort.

> *Dear Gina:*
> *Say! Maybe you didn't give me a surprise this afternoon! I was down on the line in the ops [operations] office (you remember where you put on your coveralls that Sunday we went to fly) . . . & the phone rang. Oh yes, it was for me and a very distant voice explained he was Sergeant So & So and that [illegible] was back from Normandy with a message from Lt. Alva North. Did I know Lt. North? You bet!*
> *Well, was this really Capt. Dunn, and was there anything the matter? What a job trying to explain what 'the matter' had been and that I was quite all right. I don't think the Sergeant knows what's what, but he understood that I'm here and well now & promised to send the message back to you. I've been in super-excited state ever since. Just think, a sort of remote combat call and how slick of you! Hope my answer is relayed back pronto.*

The next day, both the sergeant and Mom's Wotton friends were finally able to confirm for her the good news.

> *18 July 44*
> *France*
> *11:30 a.m.*
>
> *Dear Ricky,*
> *Today, I'm the happiest, most thankful person alive. Late yesterday afternoon I received letters from Mrs. Breadman [Fred's mother] and Marjory both telling of your phone call. Also, I had a pilot phone you when he arrived in England Saturday. He got back last night and said he had a Sergeant phone your base and that you were alright. He came back [to France] 'bursting' with the good news.*
> *All the kids [Mom's fellow nurses] are glad you are o.k. and to tell you so-- Guess I was worried about you more than you realized.*

In a postscript to this same letter, Mom let her guard down.

This is the reason I became so alarmed about you-- The thought that persisted in my mind as I looked about me and saw so much tragedy [among her medical patients]*-- I wondered who I was to think I should escape.*

Four days later Mom was still trying to recover emotionally from the strain of not receiving any letters from Dad in nearly a month. Now she wondered out loud if, without Dad, she could have continued to perform her own battlefield duties.

Right now I wonder what I would have been like if you hadn't come back to England from the States (too afraid to think if you hadn't come back from Persia). When I left the States, I felt as though I was running away from you in a way; but you came to England; oh the difference. The difference being this: with you, how much easier I can accept all this about me.

By July 25 Dad was beginning to recognize the enormity of Mom's fright in not having been able to reach him for so long. *Ah! You really know that I'm here in England! Gee, that's fine. It hasn't really been nice being snug & safe knowing that you did not know.*

Two months later, Dad went on a second shuttle mission to the Soviet Union. This latter mission went more smoothly than the first. On this occasion, he was gone only six days. Yet he now was fully aware of the worry that the resulting delay would be causing. On Friday, September 15, while on his way back to England, he wrote: *Probably you have been counting the days from last letter as you did the last time. I hope this* [letter, when you receive it] *has been extra nice . . . .*

While Mom now lived on a battlefield, Dad-- except for bombing missions that were now being flown with decreasing frequency-- was residing in the relative safety of rural England. Almost from the moment that Mom departed for France, his letters began to express guilt about this disparity in their circumstances. As early as July 17 he was acknowledging *. . . that* [now] *you will be at war even more than I . . .* His letter of August 19 goes further.

Somehow I feel that it is almost too much for you at times and that, if there was no person who loved & knew & understood and with faith too, that it would be [too much]. *Perhaps I should have said that I wanted to suffer more* [in order] *that I be all of these things; and perhaps I vaguely felt that from such pain there would be born a* [illegible] *& a depth -- oh, Gina, I want to be with you more & more. Nor for myself.*

In her September 30 letter, Mom begged Dad to give her some forewarning before embarking on any further shuttles.

Dear Ricky,
*No letter again from you. If you ever have another long trip, could you have someone write to let me know? A letter from your base is all the indication I need
. . . .*

Wonder where you are tonight and with great concern. It's strange, but when one lacks physical 'oomph,' a mental fatigue accompanies it. If anything happened to you, there'd be little to care about.

On October 15 she again expressed fear for Dad's safety despite reassurances that his combat flying days were virtually over.

Courageous applies to you, more so than I. Sometimes I'm ashamed because I fear for you so. But with each letter comes the wonderful feeling of relief and thankfulness because you are safe.

Despite Dad's pronouncements that he was being weaned away from combat flying, Mom continued to fret. Any disruption in the arrival of his letters got her to worrying. For example, on November 25 she worried out loud.

Today brought a letter from home and one from Marjory but, alas, none from you. There should be one soon. The date on Marjory's letter is the 6th of Nov., while your last letter was date[d] Oct 28th. Oh well, it's the Christmas mail that's causing the delay-- I hope.

When the mail finally did catch up with Mom on November 29, her relief was palpable.

Dearest--
Eight wonderful letters from you after waiting so very long! They're dated from 19th [October] to the 13th Nov.-- many missing, but they'll arrive eventually.
I'm so excited I hardly know where to begin . . . .

In early December a news report circulated that an American evacuation hospital had been bombed, albeit unintentionally. As a result, it was Mom who was trying to allay Dad's concern. On December 12 she wrote

About the hospital that was bombed, as you know it wasn't we; we've been fortunate. It was one that hasn't been here very long. Quite a few of their personnel, nurses too, are resting after combat exhaustion. It must have been a surprise to a new outfit.

As previously noted, the last German offensive of the war, the Battle of the Bulge, began on December 16, 1944. Soon, Mom's unit found itself behind enemy lines. Comparing their initial correspondence during this battle with what is now known, it seems that both Mom and Dad were-- initially, at least-- completely enveloped in the "fog of war." But Dad was a keen observer of the news. Within a day he realized that the position of the American Army in Belgium had become very grave. By December 18 he was admitting

The news has been keeping me tense-- counterattack, paratroopers-- I'm anxious. The S-2 officer tried to smooth it over, but hell can't be leveled by a

phrase. Faith can be restored and a spirit deepened. '--- and he shall direct thy paths.' Oh Gina, are you alright? Is there a way I can protect you from here?
I love you so,
Ricky

Within two days, this battle was catching the attention of even the most complacent of Dad's colleagues in the 96ᵗʰ Bomb Group.

The weekly war talk and the radio are competing with each other tonight. The latest setbacks seem to have given the . . . personnel a little interest in the seriousness of the war.

By the day after that, Dad probably still did not yet know for sure where Mom actually was. Yet he was worrying that Mom might be threatened by German paratroopers at Eupen.

Kirche Eupen-- Kirche Monschau!
What dread connotations will there be for these names in tomorrow's news? And where the S & S speaks of paratroopers in Eupen, massacre of American prisoners, nurses being taken prisoner. I feel dull and drawn inside. I would be bright and brave and cheerful, yet I cannot. I can only be hopeful and patient and busy.
Not knowing how you are is to be suspended between the depths. It is hard to remember that, even tho' our hands are not joined, they are through him [the Lord].

The war crime to which Dad referred was almost certainly the infamous Malmedy Massacre back on December 17 in which 86 American soldiers-- in uniform-- surrendered honorably on a Belgian battlefield but were nonetheless summarily executed by the dreaded *Waffen SS.* By the next day, December 22, Dad had not yet received any word from Mom since the beginning of the battle nearly a week earlier. Yet he remained optimistic. Indeed, he was in a reflective enough mood to express the hope

. . . that your folks are not quite as well informed as I about your whereabouts-- it may be that you are not involved with this too deeply; and it will save them some anxiety.

Earlier in this same letter, his comments again indicate that he was keeping himself up to date on the military situation.

The news in the S&S has touched everyone, and we are chafing for good weather. This afternoon the clouds broke, and I saw the first blue sky for about a week. The Hun [Germans] *seems to have been superlatively shrewd in timing his attack.*

This same letter also describes intelligence officer trying to cheer Dad up.

The S-2 officer was very sympathetic today saying that he was sure you had been evacuated and were all right. It was good of him to say so. I'm thinking of D-Day and the eager care of those weeks. I feel like an ass-- so well and safe. There seems little to say-- much to express.

> *Wanting you-- watched over,*
> *Ricky*

Within about ten days, the Allies had regained the upper hand on the battlefield. But Dad still had heard nothing from Mom.

26 December 1944

Dearest Gina:
 Heard the news tonight for the first time in at least three days. Actually, there was practically no news about the western front at all; and that consisted of a report two days old. I like to be alone so that I can best think about you and where you are and how you are. Perhaps everything is fine except for the way you must be working; and, if so, then any extra concern probably sounds foolish from me. Yet I am worried. My God! Why was I so blithe and cocksure about going to & from combat? Yet, you must have been in hell even as I am now. Forgive me if I did not know all the depths of love.

Dad then went on to report the arrival of four letters from Mom, but all had been drafted before the onset of the battle.

About the only mail for the entire squadron were four letters from you. I opened and read them in the orderly room-- the GIs there are perfectly familiar with 'A. North-- 1st Lt ANC' and like to josh me about our torrents of mail as much as I like to have them.
 Even now it is true. I think I have learned more of love's grinding and [illegible] and sacred fire in the last 10 days than ever before.

> *Longing to see thee,*
> *Longing to hear thee,*
> *Ricky*

By December 28 some of Dad's AAF friends back at Snetterton Heath were asking about Mom's fate. *Every day there are some who ask if I have heard from you.* Perhaps Dad had told his friends that he and Mom were engaged, because those inquiring about Mom . . . *are the ones to whom I have told of my joy; & now they carry the burden of care also.*

By December 30 there was still no news that Mom had survived. But by then Dad at least knew that she was in Eupen-- or had been at the beginning of the battle.

I have read all of the papers. Once over lightly looking thru the columns for Eupen and then at the maps. Then I really read them. I wonder if you have a good map with the front's daily changes on it. Then I wonder where you are now-- and how.

Even by New Year's Day, Dad had received nothing from Mom since the battle began. Still, he was gathering as much information about the 45th Evacuation Hospital as was publicly available and trying to remain positive.

> *The days are now here when the absence of your mail has begun and has begun to tell. Now and probably for two* [more] *weeks at least the climax to your next letter will grow. . . . . I'm not afraid of what it will bring.*

On December 30 the 45th Evacuation Hospital had been pulled back to a rear area, still in Belgium but at Jodoigne. At 3 PM on January 3, 1945 Mom drafted the first of two letters to Dad that day. In the first, she pointed out that he could always get some idea about her position merely by reading the newspaper. *My general location is always with the First Army and they're always in the S&S. So you should always be able to keep up with us.* Yet she could not-- in all candor-- offer unqualified reassurances. *. . . as you know we're never way back, that's a bad characteristic of our unit. . . . Chappie may be able to take a message over there* [the nearest AAF landing strip] *for me.* At 7:15 PM, Mom wrote the second letter. In it, she promised that at the first opportunity she would again seek assistance from an AAF messenger. She was hoping that, by asking some flying officer whose plane was about to depart from Belgium to place a telephone call on her behalf as soon as he landed in England, her message would circumvent the usual mail delays. This very day, she hoped, Dad might come to learn that she had survived The Bulge.

> *The hint I planned to send you will have to wait because I'll try to get over to the air strip and send it with someone. That seems best 'cause I'll have a little idea of how long we shall be here by then . . . .*

However, Mom initially could not locate any transportation over to the local airfield. Three days later, on January 6, she finally did get that ride.

> *You'll never guess; Chappie . . . arranged it so I could get down the air strip; he went along. We went in an open jeep; it certainly was cold and snowy out. The very pleasant tingling type of day. Best of all were the very cordial* [AAF] *officers who seemed pleased to phone you.*

Mom's message to Dad undoubtedly included the specifics of the 45th's current position at Jodoigne in Belgium. In a second letter written later that evening she added

> *By this time* [hopefully] *you'll know where we were, not far from Germany at all; and at the time you were anxious it wasn't without cause. Thankfully we've recovered fairly well and without much loss.*

As it turned out, Mom's hand delivered message to the local AAF landing strip did not matter. Dad already had received the good news two day earlier. On January 4 he had been returning from a pass to used visit nearby Cambridge. On his desk in the office of the 45th Combat Wing he found six letters from Mom waiting for him. He took a . . . *deep breath before I started reading them.* The *strange* and *brainless* letters Mom had written over the past weeks had finally reached him. Dad understood that censorship had prevented Mom from actually describing the battle. But the very existence of these newest letters proved she had survived. He responded . . . *to know you are well and safe-- it's more than just wonderful.* All his previous worry was washed away. *The days you couldn't write were bridged-- zip! They all came together with your letters.*

By the next day his 96th Group friends were sharing in the good news.

> *Remember Fox-- the . . . corporal who thought so highly of you? I saw him today and told him the good news. He looks more than a little bit worn. I shouldn't be surprised if . . . all did.*

Because of ongoing delays in wartime mail delivery, it was not until January 16 that Mom knew that Dad knew she had survived. Her letter that day compared Dad's waiting for word that she had survived The Bulge to her waiting for news that he had survived Poltava.

> *. . . I am glad to know that you know we are safe-- I'm thinking of the anxiety waiting for your mail when you came back via Egypt, oh, that was dreadful waiting.*

On January 23 she added . . . *fears and prayers were not in vain because last month was one experience that I shouldn't like to live through again . . . .*

While trying to reassure Dad about her own safety, Mom continued to fear that Dad might be ordered to return to combat flying. After casually mentioning that he had recently been up in a plane, Mom wrote on February 9, 1945

> *In the one* [letter] *dated the 21st, you mentioned flying in the morning. Are you flying missions again? It made my heart sink to think you may be & I don't know about it. Somehow it's necessary* [despite the censorship of the mail] *that I know the situation, whether or not you might be in a bomber as they fly over us. Also when there is a lapse in the mail, if you're flying I think you're in Russia and it helps. I'll never forget the anxiety of your first trip to Russia and I waited six long weeks for a letter not knowing what had happened.*

In fact, Dad had been out of touch for only about four weeks. But Mom had been through so much herself since Normandy that her hyperbole is quite understandable. Her letter continues by making an indirect reference to the Battle of the Bulge in which it had been she who had been unable to notify Dad that she was unharmed. *After our experiences of December, I think you know the thankfulness and relief of knowing each other's safety.*

***

According to Morris, "Flight crews in the U.S. Army Air Corps [Force] had the highest casualty rate of any branch of the armed forces in WWII."[lvi] Regarding Dad's 8th AAF in particular, it was, by the latter stages of the war, able to mount raids by as many as 1,400 bombers escorted by perhaps 800 single-seat fighters. Because these four-engine "heavies" each carried nine or ten crewmen, , this meant that upwards of 15,000 pilots,

110

navigators, bombardiers, flight engineers, radio operators and gunners would be in the air during a single mission. By the end of the war, about 210,000 men had flown on at least one such mission with the 8th AAF. While the odds of surviving a tour improved as the war progressed, a total of 26,000 were killed in action while another 21,000 survived as POWs.[lvii]

By May of 1944, 8th AAF losses had been significantly reduced from the unacceptably high rates suffered the previous year. Still, Jack Croul, who was then stationed with Dad at Snetterton Heath, noted in his diary that, even though he had been with their 338th Squadron for less than two months, he and his B-17 crew " . . . are the next to the oldest in the squadron now . . . ."[lviii]

Dad would occasionally pass along information about friends-- some to whom Mom had been introduced-- who had either been shot down or brought back dead on damaged planes. Typical of this is a letter dated only as . . . *Tuesday evening. Some sad news. Remember the* [illegible, but apparently the nickname for a particular B-17]? *Well they lost their co-pilot and bombardier today-- two swell fellows who I liked immensely.* On March 6 Dad was less specific about the most recent loss. *The barracks is very saddened tonight and for good cause. I can tell more of this when I see you.* Because it involved the death of a crewman aboard a returning plane, Dad was able to report on March 8

> *Tomorrow I shall try to attend a funeral. Strangely enough, the passing of this friend with its attendant circumstances has made a very strong impression on me. I'll tell you of all this 'when.'*

On April 18 Dad reported on attrition among the airmen at his base as bombers came back from a mission. *The crews came back. . . . All but some of the best. The barracks are being emptied now.*

Not all of the losses affecting Dad were fatalities. Damaged planes often returned with wounded men in addition to the dead. For example, on June 19 he referred to the patients in the base hospital *Only two of our fellows* [are] *in the base hospital now. One that just came out had a jaw operation & had to be fed intravenously for a while.* On July 18, almost as an afterthought at the end of a brief letter, Dad mentioned . . . *Little Jimmie Knapp. . . is a PW* [prisoner of war].

Not all harm that befell Dad's friends was the result of enemy action. On October 2 he reported that his bombing group

> *Had a tragedy. One of the crew chiefs* [lead mechanics] *was hit in the lower leg by a fifty* [caliber machine gun] *when a careless gunner was unloading a* [B-17] *turret. The poor fellow will probably lose his leg. You've seen a stream of casualties like I'll be likely never to see but a useless one like that hurts. It seem incoherent.*

The next day, Dad returned from what proved to be his last mission, an attack on a *Luftwaffe* airfield at Nuremburg. That evening he wrote

> *It's getting later, and I'm just completely pooped out. We had a rough one today, And one of the boys*[lix] *in our ship is in a pretty bad way. So's our ship.*
> *Believe me, we were very lucky today.*

As late in the war as February 2, 1945, Dad was reporting on losses that he took personally.

The news today wasn't good. Learned that a swell guy I knew was killed in Luxembourg. It doesn't seem that he had been in the Army a year. I saw him summer before last before entering the hospital at Grenier Field.

***

On June 1, 1944 Dad attempted to provide first aid to a mechanic who had hurt his hand while making some repair on a B-17. While this was a seemingly minor incident, Dad's reaction was not.

This morning I tried to be a doctor and fix up a finger that one of the mechanics banged a bit badly. So I grabbed the flight surgeon's kit, but no scissors or mercurochrome or what I wanted. So I put iodine on straight, wiped off the excess and fixed him up. Cut myself then, too. Too eager, I guess. There was a big bottle of paregoric. . . in the hut, and its been bothering me all day long . . . . I haven't been able to figure out why.

If the resulting cut to his own hand had physically bothered him, there would be little reason to question what happened. But Dad's letter suggests that he was emotionally troubled by this otherwise insignificant event. It was as if his obligation to provide first aid-- and his inept attempt to do so-- had somehow re-opened an emotional wound. A letter from Dad on April 20, about a month after the mission for which he earned the DFC, suggests a mind teetering between euphoria and depression.

Dearest Gina:
Hardly know how to start, but I feel so swell somehow that it's very good indeed. I couldn't prop my eyelids up this morning-- I guess I've been carrying the burden of care too heavily-- so I spent all afternoon in the 'sack.'
. . . Life should always consist of beginnings, each a development of the proceeding. That is what had me feeling so low-- I really was all pooped out.

Occasionally, Dad's letters concede outbursts of inappropriate behavior he regretted immediately afterward. In an undated letter that was probably written around April 22, he confessed . . . *Today I was very bad somehow, noisy and rude and swaggering. That is not really me-- nor the way I want to be, or you to have me.* An admission such as this was very rare indeed from the father I remember in later years. The Dad that I knew was usually in control of both the situation and himself. In wartime, however, the situation, at least, cannot always be controlled. Further, Dad's letters sometimes describe ailments that he himself suspected were really not physical complaints. On April 25 he reported

I nearly wound up in the hospital today. I don't know whether I really had something or not, but I was dizzy, headaches, chills, fast breathing and an infected foot besides. The doc gave me some APC's [tablets containing aspirin, phenactin, and caffeine] *and told me to rest up a bit. I am improved already.*

112

On June 18, shortly after Mom's participation in the Normandy landings, Dad admitted to feeling depressed. *Sometime between today and yesterday lost the serenity I have had. Must get back on top. It is a very ordinary feeling to be in the trough.* In the first of two letters written on July 14, Dad begins with a description of the troubles of a childhood friend who happened to be stationed nearby. Then he moved on to an expression of sympathy for some drunken GIs with whom he had shared a compartment during his most recent rail travel. He attributed their intoxication to loneliness. In the last paragraph he expressed pity for himself.

> *Have you a cure for me? I'm generally thinking of one subject that I can't seem to get out of my mind from and hardly want to* [illegible] *symptoms-- and have visionary dreams and moments of depression & exaltation.*

Dad may have been depressed, but Mom was burdened with her own problems. Nine days later, she responded.

> *In your letter . . . you asked for a cure, naming your symptoms. I'm the wrong one to turn to 'cause I'm suffering with the same symptoms myself. The complete cure would be effected only if I could be in England for a day.*

On July 26 Dad was hospitalized for stress for the first time.

> *Just after nine o'clock and I'm writing you from (this is really rich) the hospital. Oh, there is nothing wrong except a cold and general case of 'no* [illegible];' *so Doc, good old talkative Doc, sent me down here. Last night he gave me a couple pills and insisted on a shot of bourbon that nearly finished me off. He had one, too, just to show me how a doctor takes his own medicine. In all praise, he didn't flinch a bit. I really didn't expect him to.*

By July 31 he was out of the infirmary.

> *You wouldn't know me now. I lost a few pounds in the hospital, and my hair is cut so short that it will hardly part. It makes me look very blond and young.*

On August 2 he added . . . *It's eleven* [in the evening] *now, I just couldn't write this earlier. I was homesick or just so darn low that I didn't feel very far from a weeping jag.* Four days later he admitted going to a party at the officers' club in the hope . . . *I might shake off a little bit of melancholy that seems to be sliding too close to me . . . .* However, once he arrived at the party, he changed his mind. Rather than disconnecting himself from his depression by getting drunk at the bar, . . . *I took the middle road and left.* Moreover, because he was now more often a classroom instructor than a combat flier, Dad continued to feel guilty that Mom was near the front lines and he was not. On August 4, in response to a letter from Mom, he admitted . . . *when you write '. . . maybe you flew over me,' I feel like a 4-F* [unfit for duty].

In response to this concern, on August 12 Mom provided him with a pep talk.

Dear Ricky:

Just awakened and found three letters from you, and now I am about to lecture you.

(1) Why should you feel like 4-F when you have been in this thing so long?

(2) I wasn't going to tell you this, but here goes. Remember the big raid about 2 ½ weeks ago? I watched the B-17s get it-- and then counted the ten days until your letters came to be certain you weren't in one of the unfortunate planes. When I knew you were alright, I marveled at the number of times you returned.

(3) That day we had our bit of excitement too-- you can imagine why. That incident accounted for one very philosophical letter I wrote. Deep in my heart I didn't doubt your safety but always the practical possibility of the thing com[ing] to the front.

Conclusion:

The Air Corps men are subject to as much danger; that I saw. Don't you think you've had your share? I do.

I think my motive is perhaps a little selfish, but the greater motive is try to show you how far from feeling like a 4-F you should feel. And What about the D.F.C.?

On September 19 Dad returned to the subject of what had really occurred on that June night during his first shuttle mission to the Soviet Union, this time sounding almost paranoid.

This afternoon I read a report taken from a German prisoner of war who gave in complete detail the planning and execution of a certain raid not very long ago. It was most interesting because the target was us, or rather me, as it seemed that night. And what a night. Wow!

At this point, Dad was still facing the prospect of yet more combat flying. On September 24 he

Had a long talk with the air exec. this afternoon about finishing up [this combat tour] and what after that. He didn't give me much help, so I'll just take missions in very gradually till I fill my quota. If they send me home, I should feel worse over there than without you right here-- Mrs. Gallagher.

Indeed, over the next week or so Dad experienced a temporary increase in mission frequency. Between September 25 and September 27 Dad was ordered on three missions in as many days. By this stage in the war, the *Luftwaffe*'s ability to oppose these raids had been significantly degraded, but that fact did not seem to reduce Dad's anxiety. By the evening of September 28, he seemed to be nearing what would today be diagnosed as post-traumatic stress syndrome.

Dearest:

I think it's been two days since I wrote last. They packed me out for three in a row, and between the last two I managed to pick up about one hour's sleep

between the second and third. That just about did it. I remember how broken I felt and as if I were fighting myself.

As it was, I nearly got into a fight with the mess [cafeteria] officer over some trivial thing, but it seemed serious at the time. So Doc packed me off to bed with a pill, and there I stayed for almost a day. I still feel a bit knocked out. Seems funny. I always felt that I wasn't under any stress and that combat fatigue-- Zap! But I know better now.

This increase in flying, in turn, triggered more bad memories of Poltava. In this same letter he again recalled that horrible night the Soviet Union when nearly all the American planes were destroyed on the ground.

Ever since the first Russia trip when we were blasted for three merciless screaming hours I can see where it's been piling up on me. I slept with your letters in my hand under my pillow.

On September 29 he admitted . . . *I think what I need is a good rest. The time that I was in France and Wotton was the first and only leave I've had since May.* Within a few days, Dad's combat flying days-- pending any eventual transfer to the CBI-- were finally over. But his depression was not. On December 8 he wrote . . .

Haven't been feeling over-bright all day long. I wouldn't call it a hangover, but whatever it was [was] topped off by a few 'shots' [which have left me feeling] very drowsy tonight.

On December 16 he was again hospitalized for stress.

Dear one:
In the hospital for a day. What I really needed was a few hours in the 'sack.' I hoped Doc would fix me up for a quarters confinement, but one of the station regulations says that, if you must 'sack' it, then you shall do it in the hospital, and here I am-- feeling better too. I've hardly budged all day long; just snoozed and read some of Life of Christ by Giovanni Papini [an Italian author].

Two days later he was released from the hospital but still complaining.

Left the hospital this afternoon and almost wish I hadn't. I feel lifeless as a stick and twice as woozy, but darned if I'll lie in a sack with work to do.

By January 6, 1945 Mom had gotten wind of this most recent hospitalization.

. . . your letter of the 17th puzzles me just a little. Just what are you doing in the hospital? My heart stood still for a second until I read further and discovered you couldn't be very sick 'cause you wrote in the office.

However, as was frequently the problem with their wartime communications, things often arrived out of sequence. A December 17 letter about Dad's experiences on the medical ward reached Mom on January 6, 1945. But his December 16 letter describing the circumstances of his most recent admission did not reach her until January 8. *Your letter of the 16th told why you were in the hospital, and I felt relieved it was just because you need some 'sack' time.*

In the meantime, before Mom actually received either of these December letters, Dad was in the hospital yet again. On January 14 he reported . . .

> *Doc threw me into sick quarters this morning for observation. I know what you are thinking: 'What again?'-- well it's so, here I am-- same ward. I have something that is bad with my ear. It goes snap, crackle, pop; and Doc is expecting it to do worse. You know how it is when you're really fit as a gig-- dire threats and despairing looks.*

The next day he was again released.

> *Dearest Gina:*
> *Out of the hospital. I guess my ear is miraculously better. To tell the truth I'm on orders to return to my former station* [at Alconbury] *for about a week and I pleaded my way out* [of the medical ward].

But by January 30 he was back on a medical ward with stress-related symptoms for at least the fourth time. By now he was truly embarrassed-- perhaps an indication that he was beginning to recover his equilibrium.

> *Dear Gina:*
> *Sitting here, I'm tempted not to tell you that they have me in the hospital again because it seems just short of ridiculous being here-- and yet I wouldn't be honest if I held out; & here I am.*
> *The doc couldn't find out why I should have persistent something-or-other after coming down from flying yesterday, & so I'm in a nearby station hospital for observations sans* [without] *pain, sans pajamas, sans stationary.*

By the next day, he was even beginning to feel restless.

> *Got up and dressed. Felt too good to be lying in bed. They still won't let me go. I guess they don't want to fuddle the administrative section by whisking people in & right out again.*

On February 3 he was released once and for all. *About ten minutes after getting back from the hospital this afternoon, my morale went up about 700%, which is as much as I can understate it.*

On February 18 Dad suggested . . . *those two* [previous] *paragraphs* [of the letter he was then drafting] *make me sound a little unbalanced.* In my own opinion, they do no such thing. The former paragraph concedes that he was feeling a bit *melancholy* despite the impending spring. The latter merely describes his having just reread all of Mom's letters going back to the previous April. Dad's self-analysis concludes with: *Come to think of it,* [I] *guess that I am at that. At heart, I am living an unbalanced life-- wanting to be with you.* For a young man in love, this was not an unreasonable longing. After all, on the day Dad penned this letter, he hadn't seen his beloved in eight months.

13
MILITARY LIFE

"Sad Sack" was a comic strip created by the artist George Baker. It first appeared in June of 1942 in *Yank, the* Army's weekly publication to which Sgt. Baker was then assigned. Baker's title character is an army private who finds the Army to be a humiliating experience. It was said of Sad Sack that his only lasting promotion would be to the rank of civilian. Both Mom and Dad had occasional cause to identify with Sad Sack. Mom, for instance, in an undated letter written some time during her stay in Wotton, wrote . . . *by now I'm probably 'Sad Sack's' nearest kin.*

Dad, too, was familiar with Sad Sack. In an undated letter, he described how

> *More people than a few have upbraided me today for walking around with a droopier expression than Sad Sack. They're right too. . . . but I can't seem to find out from myself just why it is, unless I'm more tired than is good for me . . . .*

Sometimes Dad reported on how the regimentation of military life was having a detrimental effect on others. On New Years Day at the beginning of 1945 he described an incident.

> *A very sad sack at the club tonight who has been completely stinko for two days chose the wrong time to pass out cold. He fell over backwards right thru a circle of five colonels who were right behind him. Poor guy-- why did he punish himself so? He must have felt terribly alone.*

***

On April 23, 1944 Mom mentioned that she was looking forward to the wedding of fellow nurse Elizabeth Dean. *Nine more days and Deanie will be married; is she ever excited. In fact the whole town* [of Wotton] *is rather excited about an American wedding here.* But sometime before their unit's departure for France-- probably just prior to the wedding-- Mom reported

> *Deanie went up to see Bob* [her fiancé, 1st Lt. Robert E. Fulton] *this week and was caught-- OhO! She's now sweating it out. As a result we had to listen to one of the articles of war. Rumors are flying about checkups on the nurses.*

Whatever sanctions the Army may have imposed on Lt. Dean for going AWOL, they couldn't have been too severe, however, because her wedding went forward as scheduled on May 2. Hyman Lebson would later remember

> The marriage of one of the nurses in the Rowland Hill Tabernacle was the social event of the month and made the headlines in the local 'Wotton-Under-Edge Gazette' [Gloucester County Gazette].[lx]

A photo of the wedding party does appear on the local newspaper. The caption beneath begins in bold letters with: "All American Wedding."

ALL-AMERICAN WEDDING. Second Lieut. Elizabeth C. Dean
and First Lieut. Robert E. Fulton, whose wedding at Rowland
Hill Tabernacle, Wotton-under-Edge, aroused much interest.

Lt. and Mrs. Robert E. Fulton with their wedding party in front of the Rowland Hill
Tabernacle Church, Wotton-under-Edge, May 2, 1944.
Courtesy of *Gazette Series*.

Rev. George Zinz, Chaplain of the 45th Evacuation Hospital, assisted the local pastor in performing the ceremony, and Hyman Lebson himself served as one of the ushers.[lxi] Mom attended the event but was not in the wedding party.

A month later, a second episode of nurses going AWOL from the 45th Evacuation Hospital in Wotton occurred-- this time involving two women, Julia Ramacciotti and Jane Kreitz. During the period that the 45th Evacuation Hospital was stationed in Wotton, these two nurses were both billeted in the Southwood home, just as Mom was with the Sims. No doubt Julia and Jane were looking for the same romantic relationship with young flying officers that Mom had already found. Apparently they did, because on May 8, in the postscript of her letter to Dad, Mom mentioned . . . *Julia & Jane met their Air Corps Friends in London last weekend-- Cupid!* Then-- according to Norah Barnes, nee Southwood, who was a little girl at the time-- Julia & Jane disappeared from her parents' household without explanation. [lxii] Apparently, these two nurses had also gone AWOL for personal reasons.

***

When Dad complained about the quality of his military experience, the essence of his grievance was what he perceived to be the absence of any correlation between talent and rank. For example, on March 3,1944-- when he himself was still only a 1st lieutenant-- he observed

> *They have me working these days as a bloody operations officer with a Lt. Colonel & a Major under me. Sure is interesting. I bet I have half the numbers in the field directory memorized already.*

119

In an undated letter probably written during the first week in April of 1944, Dad wrote rather sarcastically about a group of generals who happened to be visiting his 96th Bomb Group base at Snetterton Heath. [Some of his words were excised by the sensor.]

> *Dear Gina:*
> *Writing this from the S-2 [military intelligence] office. Big time tonight featuring Generals _____ and others with [the] good old 413 _____ of lively interest. I had to take one General along on a ride and let him see what, where, and how much-- the big picture. "It takes brains to be a----."*

On May 24 he again took a cynical view of his superiors. *Spent all day with the big-wigs at the big-wigs hangout. Didn't do much talking but more listening than you could shake a stick at.* On August 29 he again spoke irreverently of the military hierarchy.

> *New leaders to be trained-- we are up to our [illegible] in 'poop from the group for the droop'-- and of course an occasional 'fling from wing' to boot. Just so they don't take away my seven-day leave.*

On November 20 Dad was required to deliver a lecture on pathfinder navigation. His audience included the commanding general of the 8th AAF's 3rd Air Division, of which his 96th Bomb Group was part.

> *Started today with a grand flourish by appearing before the commanding general of this division. He was very nice and had me sit down while he asked me questions. I didn't think it was half the ordeal I expected, and after thirty minutes or so he thanked me, and that was all there was to it. I'm left with the curious feeling of not knowing exactly what he was really driving at and what he could have possibly learned from me. At least he really knows who I am-- he said he remembers me. Maj. Gen Partridge. I'll never forget the time the top gunner of the plane I was in one day tried to shoot him down thinking his plane was a 190 [Luftwaffe interceptor].*

On December 22 Dad related how

> *Today a squad of generals and colonels swarmed in on us (me in particular) and stayed for two hours. Every once in awhile they descend on us from their lofty roost in higher hq, and woe if all is not as it should be. . . . when major generals start asking questions, it is well to know your subject. Remember what you said to me one time at Grenier about handling the situation.*

On at least one occasion Dad criticized a superior officer not for pomposity but for ungentlemanly behavior in mixed company.

> *Big meeting at division today. One of the 'most embarrassing moments' you could ever want to see happened. Around noontime the thing got down to the discussion stage. Some major in the middle gave his opinion about certain*

matters in a manner most forthright & in words that left the rest of mere profanity in the pale. Well, inconspicuously seated in the front was a WAC stenog[rapher] who the major was blissfully ignorant about. The rest of us are sinking out of sight from shame; and this ass carries on. What a performance.

On the evening of March 20, 1945 Dad was attending a meeting of high-ranking officers that was interrupted by a crash alarm. Since this noise may have resulted from a lurking enemy intruder aircraft having just shot down an American plane coming in for a landing, precautions were taken. However, the unexpected excitement didn't prevent Dad from taking another gentle swipe at the military hierarchy.

The evening has been pretty well taken up by crash alarms and a meeting held by the general. All the big wigs were there and a few small to medium wigs like me.

***

While Dad saw the Army as being a less than perfect meritocracy, this did not prevent him from seeking higher military rank for himself. He was always looking ahead. For example, back on February 1, 1944 he complained of . . . *no promotion and no squadron navigation job. A bit to be expected. . . . and the war goes on. There'll be openings.* In a second but undated letter he added that he just experienced

. . . the nicest dream last night. It seems that the Colonel of my original group [92nd Bomb Group] *came here* [482nd Group at Alconbury] *and was so touched by my being a lieutenant so long that he immediately made me a major. It was wonderful!*

On February 7 Dad reported . . . *I think I am going to be transferred to another sq. in the group . . . .* Indeed, his official service record indicates that the previous day he was moved from the 813th to the 812th Squadron within the 482nd Group. All B-17s within the 482nd provided radar services to other groups. But every pathfinding plane carried two navigators: the pathfinder himself and a conventional navigator. With the transfer, Dad would now be flying only as the second navigator. He saw this change in job description as step in the wrong direction. Because he no longer would be pathfinding, an increase in officer's rank was, in his view, now even less likely than before. In another undated letter written about this time, he complained . . . *Since I came back* [from Grenier Field] *I lost my job here and am just another navigator, which is a bitter pill because promotion is well nigh impossible.* Moreover, if he was no longer a pathfinder, he would probably be flying his missions more frequently. In bringing all this to Mom's attention, he tried to frame his concern as peer pressure from other navigators who were being similarly reassigned.

I'm upset about it because the fellows who where in the States with me are afraid I might [illegible] *them out of their nice jobs if the Colonel who sent us back to the States starts inquiring how I got so far back in the line.*

Quite understandably Dad wanted to fly into harm's way as infrequently as possible. But he need not have worried. Only two days later, on February 9, he was returned to the

813th Squadron and reinstated to pathfinder status. As previously mentioned, On March 19 he was transferred to the 96th Group's 413th Squadron.

Dad wearing his overseas cap with captain's bars.

On May 18 he was finally promoted to captain. On May 22, four days after having learned of his new captaincy, Dad closed a letter to Mom with the observation . . . *I almost don't like being a Capt. I felt a bit humbler as a lieutenant. Teach me to be humble and loving.* But this humility did not last. He may have been contemptuous of the Army's criteria for granting promotions. However, once his came through, he could not quite silence his ego-- at least in his communications with Mom. Indeed, his letter the very next day suggests preoccupation with the new rank.

> *Had to attend a critique at another group where they passed out a few decorations first. Wore my double bars on my blouse for the first time and felt as high as a lord, as embarrassed too.*

On June 3 he was still exulting in all this. On that day he received three letters from Mom. In his acknowledgement to her, he noted . . . *One of your letters (the biggest one) was the first addressed to Capt. Ricky.*

***

Also as previously mentioned, on March 11 Dad was recommended for a commendation. Yet he feigned indifference at the prospect of being so honored. In an undated letter to Mom that was probably written around April 22 he told her . . . *My commendation hasn't been sent over yet, but I can guess how it goes-- blah, blah, etc.* Nonetheless, when the medal actually arrived on May 25, he did sound euphoric.

> *S'prise! I'll have to do it by letter instead of depending on wearing it the next*

time I get another pass. The 'it' in question is Distinguished Flying Cross. Now to get it sewn on-- wonder if I could do it all by myself.

By the next day, Mom understood from previous correspondence that he had earned this honor. She wrote that she could not . . . *begin to tell you how happy and proud I am of you, and for you.* Later in the same letter Mom noted . . . *The Breadmans and the Sims send their 'congratulations.'* A day later Mom added that *Chappie was pleased about your . . . D.F.C.*

***

Dad's correspondence implies that he valued promotions over commendations. If so, this was not because he viewed the former as more closely approximating the existence of a true meritocracy but because captaincies bring pay raises; DFCs do not. By December 7 he was hoping for a further promotion to the rank of major.

> *Christmas Bells! The C.O.* [commanding officer] *latched onto me and asked if I wouldn't join him for a drink. I said I hardly ever did, to which he replied, 'well I'm going to bawl hell out of you; so I might as well buy you a drink besides.' I took Scotch. The colonel didn't bawl me out at all, but rather insisted that I sit . . . and chat. I felt like a damn fool-- drinks appearing one after the other and stiff ones. Quite a social affair. Maybe he is going to promote me-- who knows. Anyway, Scotch is not for me-- I proved it tonight.*

If Dad was really concerned that further military promotions would make it even more difficult to keep his ego reigned in, he need not have been concerned. On January 11, 1945 he reported on . . . *Another hope dashed. It looked very hopeful for quite a while that I might become a major-- but alas. I'll have to plod along as a lowly captain.*

The seniority system may have been holding back Dad's military career. But if so, he was not alone. For example, fellow flying officer Jack Croul once wrote in his diary about having just been transferred from the 338th to Dad's 413th squadron within the 96th Bomb Group. Given this new posting, Lt. Croul believed that he now had " . . . no chance of promotion as Capt. Dunn, mickey navigator, holds the T.O.[?] rank."[lxiii]

***

On December 12, 1944 Dad's past heroism was again recognized. On that day an oak leaf was added to his original Distinguished Flying Cross. At this point Dad was still holding out hope for promotion to major. Perhaps, by awarding him this second DFC, the brass was offering a consolation prize because no further promotions in rank were in the offing. His performance during the two shuttle missions to the Soviet Union may have been deserving of an additional commendation. But, if so, the timing of this latter award was a little off. After all, it had been nearly six months since Poltava. His reaction was rather bemused.

> *Tonight I was told to attend an awards ceremony and turned out to be #1 on the list. The general presented me with an oak leaf cluster to the DFC. The PRO* [Public Relations Office] *took some pictures of the ceremony. I'll send some . . . .*

Three days later he elaborated on what had occurred at this awards ceremony.

The general [Archie Old, who presided] *has a reputation for profound profanity. I can bear it out. He is a* tartar *when he lets go. . . . The ceremony was held in the NCO club-- the lounge. Straight ahead o*[n] *my right was the bar well draped with GIs, and as I stood looking over the General's head as they read the citation, I though I'd never keep a straight face.*

Gen. Achie Old congratulates Dad, December 12, 1944.
Courtesy of Ms. Marilyn Mason.

By January 25, 1945 Mom knew of the oak leaf, although her initial reaction had been to assume that Dad's bomb group had been awarded a unit citation rather than that he had been given an individual award. *I thought your squadron was awarded a presidential citation. Just like a woman!* Mom then went on to imply that Dad had never shared with her the circumstances of his original Distinguished Flying Cross the previous year.

. . . it's not too much my fault 'cause I don't even know the story of the D.F.C., let alone the additional citation. I suppose the reasons for your awards will be told at our fireside, hmm-- but apart from my stupidity, you know how very proud I am of you.

Despite these honors, Dad's overall view of military life remained essentially negative. On November 24, 1944 he described a conversation with an enlisted man at Snetterton.

Yesterday one of the operations sergeants and I were confiding our woes to each other, *and we both agreed that what was really desired was to emerge from the Army without being stunted spiritually or mentally.*

14
MOM'S ARMY FRIENDS

As I remember my parents in their later years, Dad was usually quite reserved, standoffish even. Mom was by far the more extraverted of the two. So it was not surprising to observe that in Dad's letters a particular acquaintance is usually mentioned only once or twice. In Mom's, on the other hand, she repeatedly comes back to the same circle of friends. To be fair, Mom was assigned to the same military unit, the 45th Evacuation Hospital, throughout her entire tour of duty in the ETO. This being the case, she was with the same group of people for the duration of her wartime experience. Consequently, she had considerable opportunity to develop interpersonal relationships. Dad, on the other hand, was assigned at one time or another to eight different AAF entities. Moreover, medical personnel in the ETO were rarely killed by the enemy, and then only unintentionally. In the case of Mom's medical unit-- while there were some close calls-- no fatalities were actually suffered. In contrast, among 8th AAF bomber crewmen the casualty rates were appallingly high. [Many decades later, while attending a reunion of Dad's 96th Bomb Group, I heard one speaker mention that this unit alone had lost 960 airmen.] Therefore, not only was there less opportunity for Dad to form long lasting friendships with his peers, it may have been emotionally risky for him to do so. He may well have agreed with Truman Smith who served with the 385th Bomb Group In his memoir *The Wrong Stuff; The Adventures and Misadventures of an 8th Air Force Aviator,* Lt. Smith remembered feeling that " . . . it was best not to get to know anyone too well. Strangers die easier."[lxiv]

***

When in mid-June of 1944 the 45th Evacuation Hospital came ashore in Normandy, it did so in the midst of a horrific war zone. Rev. George W. Zinz, the unit's chaplain, no longer had time for leisurely card games with Mom or even to minister to her spiritual needs-- at least initially. Instead, he found himself in a tented medical ward ministering to maimed and dying young men. In a letter written from her cot at midnight on the evening of July 16, a very tired sounding Mom reported that she . . . *Had a few minutes with Chappie; believe you me he has the cares of the world on his shoulders these days.* More than sixty years later, Rev. Zinz's daughter CherylAnne Williams recalled hearing of her father being with a mortally wounded young soldier.

> . . . the young man grabbed his hand in the med tent and asked him to stay with him, even tho' they were of different faiths. Daddy did; and the boy did not die alone . . . fifty years later he spotted the name and remembered. I was told this at Daddy's funeral by one of his Normandy/Belgium traveling companions.[lxv]

Even though Dad remained in England, he and Rev. Zinz still managed to maintain some contact, mostly via messages relayed in my parents' correspondence. On July 12 Dad closed a letter to Mom with a suggestion. *Tell Chappie that right now would be a good time for a long talk with him.* About this time, Dad sent a parcel of small gifts to Mom, including a box of cigars for Rev. Zinz.

On July 17 this parcel reached Mom in France. That night she reported . . . *Chappie has already smoked one cigar. . . .* And he wanted her to pass along to Dad . . . *how much he enjoyed it-- more important how glad he is to hear that you are OK.* Surprisingly, it was around this same time Mom was becoming concerned about Rev. Zinz. On July 22 she

> *Sensed that you* [Dad] *felt just a little sad in your letter-- wish you could have a long talk with Chappie, too.* [I] *think Chappie is in need of a long talk himself.*

By September 9 she was worrying out loud about the effect that wartime stress seemed to be having on the Rev. Zinz. In her view, the Reverend was depressed. So she now asked Dad to help her cheer the Reverend up.

> *Chappie is really down in the dumps these days-- have a hunch, more than a hunch, that he doesn't have one to share everything with . . . . If you find time, I think Chappie would enjoy a letter from you 'cause he is very fond of you. In addition to all of this, he has probably the most difficult job in the outfit.*

Her next letter elaborates further.

> *Dear Ricky,*
> *Received much at church this morning. Chappie was unusually informal and talked about 'Prayer.' All during the service, bombers flew over head; what an appropriate meditation, 'Prayer.' . . .*
> *Stayed to chat with Chappie the rest of the afternoon, he just isn't his own cheery self these days; and I felt at a loss for something to say; so I listened instead.*

Because of both the delay in receiving Mom's request and his own flying duties, Dad did not get around to drafting his own letter to Rev. Zinz until September 25.

> *I wrote Chappie a letter tonight at your admonition; but it's more of a gesture than a good letter, I guess. I hope his problems aren't too great.*

In the meantime, Rev. Zinz's depression deepened. On October 9 Mom opined . . . *Chappie needs something or someone but bad; he is changing so.* Apparently Mom was not alone in seeing Rev. Zinz as suffering from some sort of emotional decline. On October 2 she reported that the hospital was currently so busy that she rarely had time to talk with him directly. But she was beginning to hear from the others that he was no longer his usual self. *. . . there is not much chance for conversation; so I don't know how he is getting along, but from reports, not too well.* On October 13 Rev. Zinz finally did receive the letter from Dad that Mom requested the previous month. *This morning, Chappie at breakfast, pulled from his pocket your letter. Gee, he was pleased and happy to tell in detail what you had written.*

By the beginning of November, Rev. Zinz seemed to Mom to have bounced back a bit. *Chappie seemed in good spirits this morning; he certainly needed a change of mood.* At some point Rev. Zinz had asked her if Dad back in England could acquire a coat on his behalf.   No luck.   On November 15 Dad requested that she *Say 'Hey' to Chappie and tell him that fleece jackets are as scarce as staff cars.*

Soon, however, the Reverend's emotional deterioration resumed.   Mom's relationship with him seemed to be going through a sort of role reversal.   Now it was Chappie who was confessing his personal problems.   In a letter written on December 5 she revealed all to Dad.   The Reverend was not depressed about the War, but rather about his marriage.

> *Had a chat with Chappie, and he's really in trouble.   I was acting chappie to Chappie; he said he felt relieved having told someone.   It must be dreadful to love and not be loved in return, to discover it so late, too; you see his wife would like a separation.*

According to Ms. Williams, her parents did not actually married until after the War.   Her father told everyone that he was married to reduce the possibility of straying.   Of course Mom did not know this.   Her letter continues.

> *I've broken his confidence in a way telling you; but you're fond of him; and now you'll understand why I wanted you to write to him before.   You're letter cheered him up because he is genuinely fond of you.*

On the morning of December 10 Mom attended the unit's Sunday church service. *Chappie was more solemn than usual.*   Five days later, Mom happened to run into him at breakfast. During the conversation that ensued, the Reverend further expressed unhappiness about the apparent collapse of his relationship.

> *Had breakfast with Chappie, and I was once again Chaplain.   All that he got off his chest he asked me not to tell anyone, not even you.   I winced a little <u>remembering</u> what I had already written to you.   I hadn't the heart to tell him how much I'd told you.   Of course, he wouldn't understand that it'd make no difference in your feelings toward him.   Boy, his pride is taking an awful walloping, as is his heart.   How can anyone else understand the changes in him? He's so different from his old self.*

A week later, with the Battle of the Bulge now raging, Mom wrote to Dad that, despite the surrounding carnage, Rev. Zinz remained preoccupied with his own problems.

> *Chappie is very unhappy, but I guess time is the best cure.   I see him at mealtime, and I've noticed little change in him.   We haven't had any more long, confidential chats for quite some time.*

By January 4 of the new year, Rev. Zinz's situation had declined even further.   At 8:30 that evening, he stopped off at the mailroom, picked up the letters addressed to both him and to Mom, and then brought Mom's letters directly to her.   By doing so, Chappie was creating an excuse to talk with her.   The resulting conversation was not a happy one.

> *Chappie brought it to me; he's really hitting rock bottom tonight because his brother is missing in action; he's just learned of it.   I can see the tears in his eyes,*

so I decided not to stay and chat.

Despite Mom's earlier decision to leave Chappie to his grieving, she wound up spending much of the evening with him anyway. As it happened, a movie was being shown that evening for the benefit of the 45th's off-duty personnel. Chappie suggested that she join him in attending the show. Afterward, she wrote Dad a second letter.

> *Tonight Chappie asked me to go to the movies with him; he's become quite an isolationist, which certainly doesn't become him. He didn't talk about himself at all, but I noticed his wedding band was missing. He's very unhappy; it's strange that he doesn't want me to tell you anything about his troubles. I don't understand why, not unless it's his pride. Nobody [other than she and Dad] even suspects, else it would have been discussed in the inner sanctum, the nurses' quarters.*

Meanwhile, back in England on this same day, Dad wrote a letter acknowledging that he had received Mom's explanation for Rev. Zinz's decline. *Chappie-- my heart is heavy for him. And you wrote of others sensing the same.* At this point, it seems that Rev. Zinz was hospitalized for depression, because on January12 Mom mentioned . . . *Chappie is in bed, but doing fairly well.* On January 21 Dad acknowledged having himself received a another letter from Rev. Zinz. While this letter has not survived, in it Chappie apparently shared his own personal issues directly with Dad, who now reassured Mom . . . *I have written him* [again].

By January 6 the Reverend finally seemed to be recovering. As previously noted, that day he accompanied Mom to the local airstrip where she hoping to locate some AAF officer who was about to depart for England and who would be willing to relay a message to Dad. *Chappie seemed in better spirits this morning, we laughed gaily all the way to the airstrip, I think he enjoyed doing it for you as much as I.* On January 10 Mom advised Dad . . . *Chappie had a piece of your mother's* [Helen Dunn's] *fruit cake and a marshmallow, needless to say he enjoyed both.* In an undated letter that was written around the middle of January, Mom hoped that he was now was fully recovered.

> *Last night I felt sure Chappie was happier; and this morning verified it-- his text was John 3:16; he was more like his old self than I have known him since we've been on the continent.*
>
> *The phrase which was so beautiful in our responsive reading is this: '-- and the path of the just is as a shining light, which shineth more and more unto that perfect day.'*
>
> Proverbs-- (I've forgotten where
and don't have time to look it up now.)

January 14 fell on a Sunday. Mom did not have time to attend a worship service. Nevertheless, she was still thinking about a message from a chaplain, although not her *Chappie.*

> *I felt badly that I wasn't attending services at the morning hour. But just now in the quiet of the hour I've been reading a little folder that a chaplain on the boat,*

coming to France [back in June of 1944], gave me.

'Who maketh the clouds his chariot: who walketh upon the wings of the wind.' Psalm 104:3. . . .

I've thought a good deal about this verse; it seems to apply to you in some special ways; don't you agree?

On January 17 Mom reported that the 45th Evacuation Hospital was about to be relocated yet again. She also noted that she had not seen Rev. Zinz for a couple of days. By the next day she had found out why: he had been held back at their unit's previous location. But by January 20 he had rejoined the outfit . . . *and he seems much happier; I chatted with him a few minutes at supper; and he seemed enthused about studying his text for tomorrow* [Sunday's worship service]. On February 3 Mom noted that Rev. Zinz had returned to the unit following a second brief absence. " . . . *Chappie had been to Holland on business, he seems almost happy . . . again.* She implied that his recent relationship difficulties were resolved. *I think he's relieved now that it is over and settled.*

Soon, Rev. Zinz was again advising Mom on personal matters. This included the growing likelihood of her marriage to Dad. On February 12 she wrote

This is what Chappie stressed and expanded on in Psalm 4 beginning with the end of the third verse (from the Greek).

Set yourselves apart from that which is common place; stand in awe; search yourself in the quiet of the evening; and be still.

This isn't verbatim; but it was touching as I remember it.

Now the 8th verse seems applicable to us, don't you find it so? How much of the best there is for us to learn, more than can be found in a lifetime. Shall we search together?

By mid-January of 1945 the German Army was in disarray. Consequently, the 45th Evacuation Hospital's circumstances were more relaxed. Mom was able to take an off-duty side trip to Paris at the end of January and another in February to Liege, Belgium. For this latter excursion, where she hoped to purchase frames for some of her photographs, Rev. Zinz escorted Mom. Along the way, there was plenty of opportunity for conversation.

16 Feb. 45
9:15 PM

Dearest Pumpkin Sr.,

You'll never guess, but I spent the whole day in Liege; and it was a beautiful sunshiny day. Most of the officers and nurses went [back] to Paris, so Chappie took me to Liege . . . .

Chappie said that it's no wonder you have an ear condition if they 'burn' every time I talk about you. Maybe I'd better give them a rest.

Also Chappie made the remark that, when you and I are shopping together, you'd better be patient state 'cause you'll need heaps of patience. But don't worry, he enjoyed this day in spite of himself . . . .

At the Sunday morning worship service two days later, Mom found Rev. Zinz's sermon to be particularly inspiring.

> *This morning at church Chappie discussed* [St.] *Peter, his character, etc. It seemed more like a Sunday school class. You know Sunday morning seems like a special time to be thinking about you.*

On March 16 Rev. Zinz acted as Mom's escort to a social event.

> *. . . Chappie and I stopped in at the party held on Receiving Ward but didn't stay long. Instead we stopped at the E.M. mess hall and chatted over a cup of coffee about you (mostly) and our trip to England.*

In Dad's mind, at least, Rev. Zinz was also performing an additional role-- that of Mom's protector. On March 23, after complaining that there had been a recent stretch of days in which he had received no mail, Dad admitted that his old worries for Mom's safety had resurfaced. *For the first time since this mailless spell, I've had a creeping worry about how you are. I try to rationalize by thinking that Chappie would have written . . . .*

From her wartime letters, I have learned that Mom occasionally played the organ during military chapel services. In 1945 Easter fell on the first of April. That morning she wrote:

> *Good morning Ricky,*
> *Perchance at breakfast I met Chappie, and he asked to play for services this morning. As usual I protested 'cause I have an awful struggle with that portable organ. After a little coaxing I agreed . . . .*
> [E]*verything went along fine; I wasn't a bit nervous; and then on the last hymn Chappie said we'd sing the first and last stanzas. After the first stanza, I played a grand amen. Oh-- much to everyone's surprise 'cause they already had the next note half out. . . . . Chappie . . . and I had a good laugh about it afterward.*

Rev. Zinz at Nohra near Weimar, April or May, 1945.
Courtesy of Ms. CherylAnne Williams.

At 8 o'clock in the evening of the same Sunday as the organ miscue, Mom added further musings about what she saw as Chappie's influence on her relationship with Dad.

In my excitement this morning, I forgot to tell you the best about the service. Chappie was especially good. He renewed the meaning and hope of Easter; in turn, our last Easter [back in Wotton] *was relived. It dovetailed with our individual hopes and dreams-- remember?*

***

Rev. Zinz had become Mom's spiritual advisor while she was still in Wotton. However, two other men whom she came to admire both professionally and personally are not mentioned in her correspondence until well after D-Day. Both of these were physicians assigned to the 45th Evacuation Hospital: Capt. Ernest Sachs, Jr. and Capt. Edwin B. Egli. Her first mention of Capt. Sachs, a neurosurgeon, was on August 28, 1944, more than two months after the unit had been deployed to France. She related that she had come . . . *into the Red Cross tent to write you. Began talking to Capt. Sachs, admired the pictures of his baby . . . .*

After Dad departed on his first shuttle mission to the Soviet Union in June of 1944, he was out of touch with Mom for nearly a month. However, when Mom did finally hear from him again, she learned that one of the places where his plane had stopped over was Teheran, the capital of Iran. She must have had been sharing this information because . . . *Captain Sachs just asked if you're 'going back to that harem in Persia?'* Near the end of the letter she added

> *. . .it's now 11:35, oh, it's now 12:15, and I am sleepy. . . . Capt. Sachs and I have had a long discussion on everything, and I do mean everything. You included.*

On September 3, roughly the first anniversary of their first meeting at Grenier Field, Mom wrote a very reflective letter to Dad about the blossoming of their relationship. She then compared it with that of Capt. Sachs and his wife.

> *You know Capt. Sachs said he and his wife often thought they were too happy to be true, so I imagine we're not the only ones with such ideas. That statement was made the night we* [Mom and Capt. Sachs] *sat in the Red Cross tent for so long.*

In her letter of October 19 Mom elaborated on this theme of Capt. Sachs' perfect marriage, the sort of union that she assumed that she and Dad would soon be emulating.

> *Dear Ricky,*
> *Was in the mood to write a very long letter tonight, but instead I've talked about you and listened about Mrs. Sachs since 6 P.M. (supper time). Captain Sachs was very lonely tonight; so he asked me to see his son's latest pictures; and then we both dreamed out loud. Boy, is he an idealist! And is he in love with his wife. To tell you the truth, I envied him just a little cause he's married and has a baby-- he 'bragged' from experience, and I 'bragged' for the future. It was a pleasant conversation.*

By October 22 Mom had persuaded Capt. Sachs to read Dad's favorite volume, *The*

131

Prophet, a collection of poetic essays by the Lebanese-American author Kahlil Gibran, She reported . . . *Capt. Sachs really enjoyed 'The Prophet.' He read several parts more than once. For some reason that pleases me, and I thought it would you too. Does it?* On October 25 Mom again ran into Capt. Sachs. Again they talked about his family. Again she felt a bit jealous.

> *We talked naturally about his family and about my prospective family, namely YOU. He was very enthused about 'The Prophet' and had written a six-page letter about 'The Prophet' to his wife. She sent him a song she'd composed about him and new baby, 'Rusty.' The baby is called 'Rusty' 'cause he has red fuzz for hair. I was pleased to listen, very pleased*; but *in spite of my self I felt envious again.*

On October 29 Mom noted that, since it had been a slow day on her shock ward, she had been given the evening off. So, around 7 PM she had sat down to catch up on her correspondence. As it happened, Capt. Sachs was doing likewise in the next chair. He then asked Mom's permission to write Dad a note, which she might include in her own mailing.

Dear Charlie,
    This is just a note to say hello & wish you good luck-- but it's also to say what a swell loyal lovely girl Alva is, and how glad I am you two have each other. As a guy very happily married, I love to see other people in love, and hate people who take marriage lightly and toy with it.
    Best of luck, and may your future be calm . . . .
                                                            Always sincerely,
                                                            Ernie Sachs

Capt. Sachs then quickly placed this note in Mom's envelope and sealed it without giving her the opportunity to read it first. Mom's letter to Dad the next day explains what happened and describes Capt. Sachs as *a tease.*
    The day after that, Mom offered further insight into Capt. Sachs' views on marriage. Another nurse had recently become engaged to some nearby soldier who she had met just one month earlier.

> *They* [the newly engaged couple] *seem radiantly happy. But you should have heard how very disgusted Captain Sachs was; he thinks there should be a law against marrying someone you just met. I don't quite agree with him.*

On November 1 Mom noted that *Captain Sachs has some new baby pictures; they're very nice. Is he one proud father!* On November 24 Mom was provided with yet another Sachs family update. *Capt. Sachs has reported his infant's (2) new teeth, now I'm anxious to see the* [updated] *pictures. He 'tickles' me about his offspring.*
    There is no indication that Capt. Sachs and Dad actually met at any time during the War. Coincidentally enough, however, the two men did have an older connection. Both had once been Harvard undergrads. Ernest Sachs, Jr. had earned an undergraduate degree from Harvard College in 1938. For his part, Dad, while never earning an undergraduate

degree, had been enrolled at Harvard from 1935-37. On November 29 Dad happened to mention in his letter to Mom . . . *I have . . . Capt. Sachs note* [from one month earlier] . . . . *Seems odd to think of he and I in math class together. That was seven years ago.* Perhaps it was with this older connection in mind that Mom suggested that Capt. Sachs might understand Dad more completely than he did himself. On April 11, 1945 Dad learned that Mom . . . *bet that Capt. Sachs knows more about me than I know myself. I'm curious-- it's a bet! But no fair if you told him.*

On December 4, 1944 Mom contrasted the success of Capt. Sach's marriage with the apparent failure of Rev. Zinz's.

> *Thinking of the comparison of effects letters from home bring to our officers. Capt. Sach's letters from his wife just fill him with joy. Wish you could see him reading one.*

Mom's admiration for both Capt. Sachs and his marriage seemed boundless. In her letter on December 8, she continued with this theme.

> *Dearest,*
>   *Have looked at your picture so very often all day long-- and if only I could really see you; but I try to be content and thankful . . . .*
>   *Capt. Sachs has been in a similar mood;* [he] *told how his heart ached to see his wife and* [that] *it wasn't unusual for him to cry himself to sleep.*
>   *We were standing in the chow line, and I showed Capt. Sachs your picture. He asked about your* [squadron] *insignia on your* [flying] *jacket, and could it be a 'Petty Girl'* [illustration of a pinup girl]. *Of course I emphatically said, 'no.' Then he said something about the high opinion I had of you. Then he wanted to know if I thought he'd have a Petty Girl on his jacket.*
>   *Again I answered, 'no.'*
>   *And he said, "You bet I wouldn't.'*
>   *Of course he was pleased.*
>   *The nice behaving kind of officers are few and far between. It's relieving to talk with Capt. Sachs 'cause he's in the same kind of lonliness we are. Besides, I like to hear about their apartment, their adventures, their honeymoon, and their expectations. Oh, they've never had a quarrel either.*

On December 14 she wrote to Dad

> *Dearest,*
>   *Here's a little secret to tell you. Capt. Sachs writes poetry to his wife ' cause he let me read a poem he'd written about Christmastime, his wife and son. It was very nice as was the idea.*

Mom's next brought up Capt. Sachs on January 17, 1945. *Capt. Sachs happened to mention at supper that his wife had written and asked if he liked the name 'Susan Sachs.'* for a future daughter. For right now, of course, Capt. And Mrs. Sachs could not be having another child together. So Mom . . . *also added that he* [Capt. Sachs] *shouldn't be alarmed, it's just a future dream.*

On January 23 Capt. Sachs returned to the 45th Evacuation Hospital from a visit to a Battalion [first] Aid Station. He asked Mom to pass along the message to Dad that the infantrymen he had met were grateful for the support that the Air Force was providing. Mom's letter added that the G.I.s . . . *pray for clear days* . . . to fight the Germans because the AAF's presence on such days gave American soldiers the advantage.

Not until February 18 was there a hint that the Sachs's marriage was anything less than perfection.

> *Capt. Sachs came over to go for a walk. I thought that rather strange and was a little suspicious that he was in trouble, and sure enough he was. His wife and he, for the first time, had a difference about their in-laws; but now it is straightened out, and all is sunshine again. (I had no part in the matter; in fact the details weren't related; but he needed a girl to listen-- just something you can't talk about to other men.)*

By March of 1945 Mom was increasingly preoccupied with making her own wedding plans. As a consequence, her letters make less frequent mention of her friends. However, in an undated fragment, she reported that Capt. Sachs had promised her a Mixmaster [a small kitchen appliance] as a wedding gift. On March 9 she again found time to provide a brief update on Capt. Sachs.

> *. . . dropped by for a chat on his way off duty; he's on the day shift. He had a new picture of his wife in a blouse he had sent from Liege. She looked charming.*

On March 31 Mom reported to Dad that, though she had just had dinner with Chappie, the Reverend had nothing particularly new to say. But, in a conversation with Capt. Sachs immediately afterward, he provided yet another update on his marriage.

> *Had a long talk with Captain Sachs again. He heard more about you, and I heard more about Jeanne [his wife, the former Jean Sullivan]. This is getting to be a habit; but he's the only one I can air my views to so freely 'cause our interests are mutual; and I don't feel silly' discussing how very nice you are to him 'cause he comes right back with Jeanne's good points. But never fear. I can <u>outdo</u> him. Isn't it wonderful to be in love?*

***

Mom introduced Capt. Edwin Egli to her correspondence on September 18, 1944, about three weeks after the her mention of Capt. Sachs. While she admired Capt. Sachs much like the older brother she had never had, she respected Capt. Egli much as she did the real father who she could not be with.

> *Promised to tell you about my new friend; it's Capt. Egli. Remember the elderly Captain who asked you about the possibility of going on a mission?*
> *It happened he's our best surgeon, 'best gentleman,' and yet he is only a Captain. Oh, and he was in the last war too; so he's really the senior officer of the outfit. One evening when everyone had dates and I sat writing to you, along came Capt. Egli (by the way, that is a Swiss name) and stopped to talk. It was a*

134

nice discussion; I felt that here was another of the few who lived for the beauty of living rather than for what material things I can get out of life when the latter is so temporal. It was a nice discovery; oh, his wife is a nurse, by the way; and to hear him, you'd never doubt his love. It is strange that some find so much contentment and others so little.

Feel that I haven't told you this just as I wanted to, but I hear the influx of patients is great so there may be even less time to write tomorrow. I guess the idea that I wanted to put across is that he is another evidence of the joy and satisfaction in striving to maintain ideals, and it can be done.

Love you so,
Gina

The very next day Mom was worried that what she had said about Dr. Egli's modest military rank would offend Dad. She had no reason to be concerned. Of course Dad already viewed the Army as something less than a meritocracy. So, I was bemused to read this particular letter from Mom.

Thought of something I wrote in my letter yesterday that might make you feel a little badly if you misunderstood. When I said Captain Egli was only a 'Captain,' I didn't mean that being a Captain was not an achievement; but, at his age, with his experience, and with the respect of all, he seems more like a Colonel-- and deserving to be one. Understand, Captain Dunn?

Dad's reply to Mom on October 7 professes admiration for Mom's description of the man.

Thanks for writing about Captain Egli. It's swell learning about people like him. You know it's fine to be believe in certain qualities and ideals & strive for them; but the biggest, most powerful boost they'll ever get is to see them personified, actually operating, by someone you know.

Mom's letter of October 9 provides an update on her new friend implying that his age was perhaps making it difficult for him to keep up with his medical duties. *Capt. Egli is sick with sinusitis and is going to be admitted as a patient. I think I'll take him some grapes that were a gift from a patient and 'The Prophet.'* Later in the same letter she added that Capt. Egli was . . . *so very good to me . . . Captain Egli, with his kindness and understanding, smoothes out the bumps.* Four days later, he still was not recovered from his illness. Mom's fellow nurses did not necessarily share her interest in spending time with this older physician.

I visited Capt. Egli . . . , he didn't seem at all well today. I'll bet surgery misses him. The kids can't understand why I enjoy visiting with him instead of following their activities; they just don't know the wealth of knowledge and understanding he has to offer.

On October 24 Mom added that . . . *Last night I attempted to play cards with my boss* [probably Col. Abner Zehm] *and Capt. Egli, but couldn't concentrate; so I came upstairs and reread your letters.*

By the end of 1944 Mom was characterizing Capt. Egli as her best Army friend. She now professed to be generally uninterested in attending social events for which Dad as unavailable-- unless Capt. Egli escorted her. On November 4, for example, she noted that . . . *Tonight is my night off, so after supper I went to the movies with Captain Egli and Capt. Sachs.* On November 9 she and Capt. Egli were . . . *planning on a trip in the mail truck.* [This excursion off their base was later cancelled because he was needed in surgery that afternoon.] On November 21 she . . . *Had a midnight supper with Captain Egli and* [fellow nurse] *Jean Hall, we were full of wishes during the whole meal.* On December 11 she wrote

> . . . *I'm glad you don't like parties either, not that kind I mean. I only go if I 'have to,' but I'm fortunate (or have been) because I have Capt. Egli. The kids rib me about it 'cause his reputation around here is what the Chaplain's should be. He's leaving and being sent to a hospital in England; that* [is] *the only way he can get a promotion. The news made me feel a little sad 'cause he is my best friend here . . . . But Capt. Egli will contact you, and you must try to see him if he is at all close. I'm selfish wishing Capt. Egli to stay, but I'm glad for this opportunity he has. There will be a let down in this whole unit when he leaves 'cause he has the respect and admiration of every one. I wouldn't be surprised if he left the army soon 'cause I think he is old enough to be out.*

However, the Battle of the Bulge delayed Capt. Egli's departure. On December 21 Mom wrote to caution that Capt. Egli was still with the 45th. The next day, not yet having learned that Capt. Egli's travel arrangements had been disrupted, Dad wrote that he was looking forward to contacting him in England. He was now . . . *waiting to hear from Capt. Egli. I hope he gets to a hospital near here. There will be so many questions to ask.* By December 29 Capt. Egli had still not had the opportunity to depart for England. But by then the Allies had largely repulsed the German offensive. As a result, life for the 45th Evacuation Hospital was returning to normal. Mom described evening playing cards with some doctors, including Capt. Egli.

> *Last night we didn't play bridge long but drifted into a rather deep conversation. Capt. Egli accused me of idealism, nicely though; but later the other Captain, Captain* [Phillip A.] *Lief, proved Capt. Egli was just as idealistic, never to be outgrown either. How about that?*

By January 3, 1945, with the Germans in retreat, Mom was able to get away from the hospital more frequently.

> *We're not restricted* [to base] *so Capt. Egli and I went for a walk into town, we stopped in a little shop and had a caramel ice cream sundae, not like American ice cream, but the idea was very nice. We visited a British tank group and naturally I had to climb inside the tank. It was interesting, but as the Limey* [Englishman] *explained* [the workings of the tank], *I did not hear him but you (your B-17-- that Sunday ride).*

Perhaps Capt. Egli's relatively advanced age was again catching up with him. On January 12 he . . . *had an abscess lanced and is feeling under the weather.* On January 17 Capt. Egli finally received some revised orders. Now he was . . . *being transferred to a General Hospital in France, so we won't be seeing him in England.* On January 20 she added that *Tomorrow, Capt. Egli is leaving and there are many sad people about, everyone will miss him.*

By February 3 Dad had heard of Capt. Egli's impending transfer to France rather than England. But he still hoped that the doctor would pass through England eventually.

> *I'm glad Chappie is something like himself again-- and sorry to hear Capt. Egli's leaving. If he beats you back to England and* [comes] *anywhere near here, I can ply him with questions for days.*

On March 9, despite having departed two month earlier, Capt. Egli provided Mom with a written update about his new circumstances. Mom duly relayed the information to Dad that . . . *he's billeted in tents at the present until the hospital gets set up in a building. It reminds him of our Normandy days sans* [without] *the excitement.*

15
RUMORS OF THE CBI

 As their feelings for each other deepened, my parents were increasingly haunted by fears that redeployment to the Far East would disrupt everything. The first written mention of this possibility came from Mom. By mid-January of 1944 she had not seen Dad since her departure from Grenier Field in early November of the previous year. When they had parted, Dad was still rehabbing his surgically repaired leg. Once he recovered to the point where it would be possible to resume his flying duties, there was no guarantee that he would be returning in England. In the meantime Mom herself arrived in the U.K. in late November of 1943. Over the next weeks she received no communication from him. During this time she worried that the absence of letters might be the result of his redeployment elsewhere. On January 20, 1944, comforted by the fact that she had begun receiving letters from him via his 482nd Bomb Group APO, a unit she knew to be stationed in England, she confessed to her fears. *It's been a long interim in your letters; it had me guessing for a while-- I kept imagining you were sent to the Pacific.*

***

 During the first half of 1944, when Mom and Dad were both in England and seeing each other frequently, they seem to have put aside concerns about possible redeployment to the Far East. But after Mom's unit was sent to Normandy in June, it all re-emerged. In September these fears began re-appearing in their correspondence. At this point the Allied advance toward Germany was making steady progress. Consequently, rumors were sweeping the Anglo-American armies to the effect that the Nazi regime would capitulate before the end of the year. It was further rumored that an Allied victory in Europe would be followed by a massive redeployment of forces to the Pacific Theatre of Operations [PTO]. On September 3 Mom wrote Dad a letter in which, due to wartime military censorship, the return address was given only as of *Normandy*. In fact, her specific location was at a place called Senonches. In this letter she worried out loud . . . *the speculations about the Pacific War give me the 'willies.'*

 Coincidentally, not yet having received this letter from Mom, Dad reported four days later . . .

> *The Stars & Stripes started a terrific wave of speculation today with their article about demobilization. Everyone is trying to figure out their priority and when they will go home. I tried it myself; but I honestly don't want to go back to the States 'till you do; and yet I want to stay here rather than go to the Pacific theater.*

By September 9 neither Mom nor Dad had yet received the other's most recent letter on this topic. Nevertheless, on that day Dad wrote

> *There is much talk here about moving to the CBI* [China, Burma, India] *theater when hostilities end here. Of course it is all in the* [illegible] *stage, but I could very well be included. Should it come to pass-- well, you have been forewarned.*

[Because the Japanese had invaded various Asian mainland countries in addition to their Pacific island conquests, both my parents frequently referred to the overall war against Japan with the acronym *CBI*.]

On this same day, September 9, Mom's 45th Evacuation Hospital was at La Capelle in France. Almost telepathically, since she would not receive Dad's letter of the 9th for another week, she now asked

> *Is there any possibility of you going to the Pacific? If you should, I want to go too. I suppose there will be little choice for me. . . . If you have finished your missions, I still hope you will accept what you have earned. But I shant 'lecture' anymore. The above is a favorite topic for the 45th.*

Mom understood that-- because Dad had been in a theater of war since August of 1942, compared with her own arrival in England in November of 1943-- it was likely that he would be demobilized and sent back home than she. In effect, she was very gallantly suggesting that Dad should welcome any such opportunity to return to the States, even if there was little likelihood of her joining him there. By September 24 Mom's hospital unit had crossed the border from France into Belgium, specifically to the town of Baelen. On that day she wrote a letter to Dad explicitly urging that he take advantage of any opportunity to rotate back to the States that his seniority might provide.

> *In regards to the CBI situation, will you please promise me this-- please! If you have a chance to stay here in the ETO or go to the States, take it; and I'll do the same. Because if you should go to the CBI . . . I should be able to get overseas again if I want it . . . . And, if you go home, stay there, because there is much you can do for me in the States if I should be in the CBI. Now, don't think I am being unfair to myself. I'm definitely not. Your work is more risky than mine; and I won't forget it even for a short time; furthermore, in the States you could be singing.*

On September 28 Dad expressed the hope that there was nothing to the rumors his 96th Bomb Group was being transferred to the CBI forthwith.

> *How I wish you were here-- somewhere that I might go to you. It seems that just that would be enough. But I am quite fortunate at being able to stay here in England at least as long as the group does, & the rumors have completely died down about Pacific or any other theater.*

On October 4 he closed another letter with the suggestion that both he and Mom should . . . *forget CBI and just concentrate on your return to the UK & our return to the States-- & home.*

In mid-September Dad returned to England from his second shuttle mission to the Soviet Union. On October 7, now at Eupen in Belgium, Mom received, in a bunch, the first three letters he had written afterward. She now gushed that his continuing survival filled her with a *radiant feeling*. But not yet having read Dad's October 4 admonition to stop worrying about possible future Asian redeployments, she inserted a paragraph in her current letter . . . *Read in the S&S about ETO airman going to the Pacific.* She then went on to ask: *How do you score?*   On the evening of October 11, when Dad's October 4 letter did arrive, Mom, who rarely conceded to having lost her cool, admitted that this particular letter upset her.

> *I wrote a long letter* [in reply] *last night but couldn't mail it this morning, I'll give it to you someday. I didn't mail it 'cause I felt panicky when I thought of you in the CBI theater. Tonight any fearful thoughts are gone, and I'm glad that letter wasn't mailed.*

By December, it was military news from the Far East itself that was again fueling Mom's fears. In her letter to Dad of December 14 Mom asked: *The China news has me concerned about you again-- what thinkith thou now?*

As my parents began to talk about making wedding plans, their mutual anxiety about possible Asian redeployment intensified. On October 25, still writing from Belgium, Mom post scripted her usual letter to Dad with her own wedding proposal. Her explanation for being so forward was . . . *I'm thinking or trying to imagine what you may be thinking about the CBI situation.*

By April 12, 1945, the eve of their marriage, Dad optimistically speculated . . . *Perhaps the Pacific won't be so bad. We seem to be surely going there-- according to the S&S.*

16
TEMPTATION

Even in these modern times, most couples would probably still agree on the importance of faithfulness to one's beloved. But should an exception be made for a couple separated by war? Do geographic distance, lengthy separation, loneliness, stress, and future uncertainty-- in the aggregate-- justify intimate encounters with someone other than one's professed lifetime partner? Perhaps so. However, if my parents' correspondence is to be believed, they remained faithful to each other from the moment Dad returned to England from Grenier Field throughout the remainder of their wartime experience. And this was despite numerous opportunities to stray. Indeed, the letters from both Mom and Dad-- especially Dad's-- repeatedly express disapproval for the promiscuous behavior of others. When my parents both were stationed in England and seeing each other as frequently as their respective leaves from duty allowed, the topic of fidelity was rarely broached in their letters. But, after Mom's unit redeployed to France, it became a preoccupation.

***

As the war progressed, Mom's 45th Evacuation Hospital was repeatedly moved further eastward to maintain close proximity with the shifting front lines. This mobility, especially in the early months, required that the unit's personnel live in tents and sleep on cots. In an attempt to reduce Mom's discomfort, Dad once even mailed her an inflatable air mattress. This air mattress prompted teasing from Mom's fellow nurses. On November 5, 1944 she described such an episode.

> *The kids* [Mom's fellow nurses] *are beginning to 'heckle' me.* [Marian] *Sebring has just said, 'Look at Northy sitting on that air mattress like the Queen of Sheeba* [sic].*'*
> *Johnny* [Sellers is] *saying, 'She's higher than all the rest of us-- those reporters should write about 'army nurse writes letters on air mattress.'*

Perhaps some of these other nurses were jealous that Mom was in a committed relationship. In any event, on November 27 she was teased again, this time for spending so much time writing Dad. On this particular evening, Mom added a postscript to her letter that described fellow nurse Marian Sebring as . . . *G-2ing* [interrogating] *me about my love letter for you 'cause this letter isn't long enough-- hmm, she should know.*

Within a month of coming ashore, the Evacuation Hospital's activities settled into something of a routine. From the point of view of the nurses-- at least among those who were single-- it was better still that they were now living amidst American men who outnumbered them by perhaps 100 to 1. Social opportunities were everywhere. For those seeking male companionship, dates were easy to come by. As early as July 17 Mom reported . . . *All the nurses in my tent are out on dates tonight . . . .* But Mom herself professed to be not interested. *. . . I'm sitting on my cot in my little corner feeling pleased to be alone with you.* On August 20 she described an incident.

> *Last night I saw Chappie for a few minutes. In fact I had walked to the mail tent to mail a single letter, your letter. He walked back with me; and we stumbled*

between the couples [in compromising positions]*; and Chappie said, 'No one could doubt your love for Charles.'*

Soon Mom's letters began mentioning how even the orderlies, who were only enlisted men, were teasing her about her long distance romance with Dad.   On September 21 for example, during a slow night on her medical ward, she happened to be reading one of his letters while still on duty.   As she did so, Mom broke into tears in front of the other medical personnel.   After describing the ribbing that resulted, she asked Dad . . . *Are your ears burning?   They should be.   My face still feels crimson; what brought this on is 'cause I cried on the ward when I read . . .* Dad's letter. *All I hear is 'if only some girl would cry about me,' etc.* Mom's letter of October 13 claims that many within her medical unit now perceived her as

> *. . . sort'a standoffish or seemingly so to most of the kids.   But as long as a few, my ward boys, and ward officer doesn't think so, I'm happy.*
> *Boy, I sure take a beating on 'why I'm so sure of you;' 'what makes you* [Mom] *think you* [Dad] *don't have a blond on the side;' or 'you*['re] *nuts for staying in all the time.'   It amuses me 'cause no one could make me doubt you, nor my feelings toward you.   Furthermore, I don't expect everyone to understand why or why not my behavior is as it is.*

Back when Mom was billeted in the Sims household in Wotton-under-Edge, Reg and Marj Sims had to some extent played the role of surrogate parents.   So it was appropriate that she concluded her letter of October 13 with the observation that Reg would approve of her chaste behavior. *Reg Sims would be pleased with it (recalling his fatherly instruction).*
   On October 9 Dad expressed curiosity about the romantic activities of Mom's fellow nurses.

> *I suppose this will seem odd, but I like to hear of the girls having dates-- not because we aren't, but because it doesn't make life feel <u>quite</u> so bad.*

When Mom received this letter on October 22, her initial reaction was that he was really accusing her of dating other men in his absence.   To this she took exception.

> *This sentence from your letter I misunderstood: 'I s'pose this will sound odd, but I like to hear of the girls having dates-- not because we aren't, but because it doesn't make your life seem <u>quite</u> so bad.'   When I first read it, I thought you thought <u>I</u> was having dates and I had the most sinking feeling.*

Further, she pointed out that, in her current circumstances, social opportunities that abounded.

> *If you think girls are at a premium in England, just think of what they are here. Anyone could have a star* [a brigadier general] *or two to date if they'd chose.   But my confession is this, and I'm very proud of it.*

142

Nonetheless, she reaffirmed her commitment to their relationship.

> *Whenever it has been necessary to have an escort to a 45th function, its been good little 'ole Capt. Egli; and for some strange reason I love being with him and very proud too-- and mostly because he respects you and I so, too. It's wonderful having you with me all the time.*
>
> *Being confronted with so many men constantly, never for even a second have I doubted my love for you, nor could one even compare with you in my eyes (nor in Chappie's eyes).*
>
> *Our future holds no doubts, after all this it could only be happy. I feel so confident in you.*

Elsewhere in this same letter, she reminded Dad that he, too, had come to view Capt. Egli as her chaperone.

> *In your last four letters, you mentioned Capt. Egli in two of them, in regard to the quelling effect he had when you were tempted to be a little envious, as you put it.*
>
> *That pleases me so 'cause that is the effect he has* [on me] *here, and he shall be so pleased when I tell him.*

By November 4 Dad was on the defensive.

> *I am awfully sorry if you really thought I believed you were going out on dates. When I said I like to hear of the nurses dating, I really meant that, if it were possible to have dates at all, then it must be at least a bit less rigorous than if dates were* [im]*possible-- whether anyone* [here Dad had written *you* and then crossed it out in favor of *anyone*] *was really having dates or not-- well, I . . . meant the 'can I' and not the 'shall I;' and that if you all 'could'-- well,* the [illegible] *must be better than if you had no chance. Please push off that sinking feeling. Even if you had had dates, I know where your heart must be.*

On the other hand, on November 22 Mom did admit to a close call.

> *I'm writing this in the* [officers?] *club. Our pictures are out beside me, and one of the visiting officers (a doctor) just asked me if you were my husband. I casually answered 'yes.'* [I] *Don't feel ashamed about fibbing, in fact I feel amused and pleased. It'll save me trouble 'cause I sensed another question about to arise about how I intended to spend the evening.*

Late in the evening on November 29 she observed that it had been

> *A pleasant day working with Major* [William] *Birch and Captain Egli, supper with them, a shower* <u>*without*</u> *them; and now I am sitting atop my air mattress in pajamas feeling supreme and almost regal.*

On January 4. 1945 Mom described a unit party which their new commanding officer expected all the off duty nurses to attend.

Tonight is party night . . . . I'll walk in and walk out. Our Col. is a social beaver, so we make an appearance. Gee, I don't even feel the slightest pang of envy watching the gals get dressed 'cause you're right here with me in this feminine dormitory . . . .

Two days later, responding to a recent letter in which Dad had mentioned his own reluctance to discuss sexual topics even with other men, Mom continued with her own abstinence theme.

Reviewing the discussion you mentioned about sex, I know just how you feel; for some reason I don't go over too well with the majority of the nurses. I never argue with them; yet I never accept dates nor pair off with an officer; and constantly they [her fellow nurses] remind me of the time I am wasting. Prissy, perhaps, but the officers and enlisted men like it; and I value their respect. There are some consciences that ached hereabouts, 'married' ones at that. But in all sincerity I am happiest when I am with you now. Idealistic and sentimental as heck, but deeply content in your love.

On January 24 Mom professed to have no interest in a social event that she was obliged to attend that evening. She would rather be alone just thinking about Dad.

Tonight the chief nurse is entertaining some General; and I'm invited with two other nurses to attend the dinner-- we leave at 6:30 p.m. Instead of feeling pleased as I should, I'm disappointed; with all my heart I would rather stay with you.

Mom was not only protective of her own reputation, she also took a dim view of the promiscuity of others. For example, on February 13, in the middle of the afternoon, she was off duty and sitting at a table drafting a letter to Dad. A couple that she knew entered her area.

. . . so I'd better take the hint and go into the next room, although I shouldn't 'cause he's married to someone else and . . . shouldn't object to my presence. Don't you agree? On second thought, I'd better leave or I might be the embarrassed one.

***

Over the ten months of their geographic separation, Dad continued to reassure Mom that he was harboring no doubts about her faithfulness. However, he was quite aware of a potential competitor. Indeed, during the previous months back in England, there had been a rival-- a young RAF Reserves officer, Flt. Lt. John Peter Vickery. In her postwar stories Mom described *Peter* as a dashing young pilot who flew a Spitfire, the graceful little elliptical-winged fighter plane with a Rolls Royce engine that had become a symbol of British defiance against Hitlerism.

I have only recently come to learn that Peter had received his initial flight training in the United States. He had then stayed on in Canada for a time as in instructor. However, none of his postings in North America place him at any of the same locations as Mom. In all likelihood, Mom first met Peter shortly after her own initial arrival in the U.K. This must have occurred sometime between Mom's arrival in Wotton-under-Edge on November 24, 1943 and Dad's first visit there on about February 10, 1944. Lt. Vickery's first RAF posting in Britain was in Yorkshire-- a considerable distance from Mom in Wotton. A bit later, he was reassigned to Eshott near the Scottish border in Northumberland, a location even more remote from Mom. She would have had no reason to be at either of these locations. Moreover, since Wotton was not a center for RAF activity, Peter would have had little reason for journeying there-- unless it was for personal reasons. On the other hand, Mom would have had every reason to visit London. Knowing Mom, she would have been eager to exchange Wotton's rural tranquility for London's urban glitz. Her service record indicates that she was granted a pair of two-day leaves during the period just prior to her reunion with Dad. The first of these began on December 17, 1943. Mom would later recall for me having once sat in the visitor's gallery of the House of Commons during a Parliamentary debate on the question of whether coal miners would be allowed to volunteer for the army. She described seeing Prime Minister Winston Churchill speaking out against any restrictions on their military service. The historical record indicates that a debate on this issue that dragged on for many days did begin on December 2, 1943. So it seems probable that Mom was in London in mid-December. If so, it is quite possible that it was on this occasion when she first met Peter.

Whatever the actual date of Mom's initial meeting with Peter, it was definitely prior to Dad's first visit to Wotton. This sequence of events is made clear by yet another of Mom's postwar anecdotes. According to her story, Peter had been at the Sims home on Long Street about one week before Dad's first appearance there. Since Dad's had first called on Mom in Wotton on about February 10, 1944, Peter's prior visit must have been around February 3. Mom's second two-day leave had begun on January 31. If Peter had been with her on this latter occasion, perhaps he had escorted her back to Wotton on February 2. This would place him in the Sims home roughly one week before Dad first showed up. In any event, when Dad first stepped into the Sims home a week later, Marj Sims got the two young flying officers confused. She greeted Dad with pleasantries to the effect that she had enjoyed his earlier visit the previous week-- as if Dad were Peter! Mom adored both Marjory and Reg and considered them to be her friends. But she was nonetheless mortified by Marj's gaffe. Whether, up to this point, she had advised Dad of Peter's existence isn't clear. But she most certainly had not mentioned having invited the other guy to visit her in Wotton only a week earlier. When Peter had first entered the U.S. as an aviation cadet back in October of 1941, an immigration document described him as 6 feet 1 ½ inches tall, with a "fresh" complexion and "fair" colored hair. This could just as easily have been a description of Dad. Moreover, both men would have been in uniform complete with aviator wings and lieutenant bars when they first entered the Sims residence. Nevertheless, from Mom's point of view, her landlady still should have been able to tell the men apart. After all, as she reminded me when later sharing this anecdote, RAF uniforms were grayish blue in color; those of USAAF officers combined brown jackets over tan slacks.

Over the next four months, Mom, Dad and Peter all continued to be stationed at various locations in England. During this period, Mom's letters to Dad make no mention of Peter. Of course, if Mom were continuing to maintain some contact with him, she would not have wanted to share that fact with Dad. But her unit's busy training schedule of field maneuvers-- combined with the frequency of her meetings with Dad on those days that she did have off --would have made it logistically difficult for her to continue any significant relationship with the Peter. Indeed, it is an undated letter from Dad, probably written in April of 1944, that first mentions Peter. While Dad may have suspected that Mom was continuing some long distance communication with Peter, the tone of his letter suggests to me that he no longer regarded Peter as a serious rival-- if he ever had. After devoting four pages to various other subjects, he closes simply with: *P.S. Any news from Peter?*

In June of 1944 the logistics of the situation changed completely. On June 9 Peter reported to the RAF's No. 1 Base Personnel Depot at Warrington in Cheshire for overseas deployment. Within a month he was in the Mediterranean Theatre assigned to the RAF's No. 43 Squadron on the Italian front. In the meantime, On June 16 Mom went ashore with her unit at Normandy in France. By early November of 1944 Mom and Dad had not seen each other in five months. Perhaps their prolonged separation was causing Dad to feel insecure about their relationship. In a letter written on November 4, Dad asked a question implying his unease . . . *'member how I used to tease you about Peter?*

***

In later years, while Mom was happy to discuss her past relationships, Dad was completely the opposite. If he ever had been involved with another girl, he made no mention of it to me. In his younger years he was a very good-looking guy. After he left home and enlisted in the AAF, he presumably dated. However, his dating experience may well have been limited. The Dad whom I remember in later years was not exactly shy. In the midst of social situations, however, he could be quite reserved. It is difficult for me to imagine him "hitting on" women in pursuit of casual relationships. Indeed, during the war he could joke with Mom about roguish behavior without fear that she might believe it. For example, after hearing that Mom had run into some of his flying buddies on a train, he wrote her on May 8, 1944 . . . *remember Lt. Grau and, indeed all of Lt. White's crew who rode on the London train with you, telling you what a wolf I am? Well-----. Dammit!*

Even before Mom had departed for the Continent, Dad's letters were already professing a lack of interest in the social opportunities around him. His March 15 letter, for example, previews his intended faithfulness, should Mom's unit be redeployed.

> *Last night I played bridge 'till just before 10 & then just went to bed quietly. The night before was best. I was all alone-- all evening long. I can tell what direction you are from here, and I like the thought of meeting you every night.*

As previously noted, in mid-March of 1944 Dad was transferred from the 482nd Bomb Group at Alconbury to the 96th Group at Snetterton Heath. In and undated letter, written about April 23, he described for her a Saturday night party at his new base.

> *Last night I was the duty officer 'till nine, and then I stole into the party that was well in progress. I didn't give two whoops for it. One of the fellows said, 'If your girl had come she'd be the only nice girl here.' Gee, it was awful drunk in there.*

Dad always insisted that Mom provided him with all the only social life he needed. For instance, on May 8 he described a recent visit to the officers' club at Snetterton.

> *Every now and then during the noon-hour at the club, I look around at the others and wonder how much they lack that I have-- if any of them are longing for what I seldom realize I really have.*

Further, he always insisted that he had no interest in attending his unit's social events. For example, on May 27, a Saturday evening, Dad wrote . . . Party *night tonight. Naturally, It just* happens *that I'm duty officer tonight. Oh well, I didn't want to go anyway . . . .*

After the departure of Mom's medical unit for France in mid-June, Dad could no longer look forward to their next date. Nevertheless, his letters suggest that he now reverted to type, choosing solitude over sociability. On August 16 he mentioned . . . *There is a movie* [on the base] *tonight, but not for me. I want to be with you.*

At a time when a "double standard" was applied to the respective conduct of men and women, a second area of temptation in which only male misbehavior was acceptable regarded alcohol. But Dad professed to have no interest in liquor either. On August 28 Dad described an incident.

> *Almost went into the nearest city for a binge tonight. One of the fellows from my old station* [Alconbury] *was over this afternoon with a friend, and they tempted me. Naturally I would have been slightly AWOL tomorrow morning, but I didn't go for the prospect of a general debauch somehow.*

On October 29 there was another social event at Snetterton, but Dad chose to skip it completely.

> *Last night was 'party' night. You could tell easily by the people missing this morning & the ones with eyes like 'limped pools of mercurochrome.' Well, I cleaned up & dived into bed before eight last night to read & write some letters.*

On December 8 Dad again chose to be alone.

> *Sitting all alone-- sounds lonely saying it that way which is misleading because I am doing it deliberately, and it's nice, the more to be with you . . . .*
> *Oft times, as I think very longingly of you and thankfully for your safety, I'm thankful, too, in a half-understanding that we are now apart. It seems that everything will be ever afterward clearer and more dear. We are not alone. For when I am most thankful, I realize that I have never before been so 'in company' with anyone. Nor ever before so beloved.*

His letter of Saturday, February 3, 1945 is also illustrative.

> *Party night tonight. I left the* [officers'] *club after supper* [meaning before the party] *with a tremendous inner joy that all the immediate hilarity and 'girls' (not*

very respectful-- some not very respectable) didn't stand in the balance to YOU.
It was evening twilight, and there was a single star.

The next Saturday evening provided more of the same. *Parties are raging tonight. Wing party, group party, 200th mission party, GI's party & a stag party. The war room is deserted.* But Dad clearly was not into it. Instead of attending any of the parties, he went over to an operations room where a few men were required to remain on duty.

> *Lt. Olsen, the controller on duty tonight, and the sergeant and I have been talking about the Army & marriage and stuff. 'Ols' was s'prised when he learned I was single-- because he never saw me with any 'gussies'* [women who dressed provocatively]; *he assumed I probably had children.*

On November 12 Dad did concede to having attended a *party night* at his Snetterton base the previous evening.

> *. . . last night was party night. What an orgy! By going, I had my only chance to collar some of the rascals I'm supposed to look after in the group. Well, it wasn't worth it. Remember, they had a party about the first time you were here; but just having you made the party seem as nothing?*

After describing the event's main entertainment-- a female dancer known to fellow partiers as *Short Stride,* but who Dad described as the *local dipsomaniac*-- he insisted that he spent most of his time that evening by the fireplace.

> *I was standing before one of* [the fireplaces] *warming my fanny when somebody (you know how brotherly everyone gets) said 'How come a good-looking guy like you hasn't picked up anything tonight.' I just smiled a bit thoughtfully-- & before I had made up my mind what to tell him according to how crocked he was-- he said, 'You must be particular as h-l.' That seemed about right. I wonder if he'll ever guess how lightly he touched the truth. Would you like to be given a 'little girl' hug?*

On January 22, 1945 Dad described a night spent in Cambridge on his way back to Snetterton from an official visit to his old base at Alconbury. On this trip a fellow AAF officer he named only as *Ernest* accompanied him. While in Cambridge, he and Ernest were invited to a party being hosted by a third AAF friend. Dad admitted

> *There was a curious familiarity to it all that we were quite immune to. I guess it was that curiosity that kept me at the party. I just had to see what all the fuss was, <u>and</u> I <u>had</u> to leave before ten. Believe me, I left an exhilarated person.*

[Regarding this and his many previous visits to Cambridge, Dad may have been less than transparent about his motives. After all, Cambridge was about 50 miles from his AAF base at Snetterton Heath in Norfolkshire while the City of Norwich, the county seat, was less than half that distance in the opposite direction. Both cities possessed roughly equal populations. Yet, Dad and his friends seemed always to opt for the former. While he was not admitting as much to Mom, I suspect that Dad preferred Cambridge because it was a college town with a reputation for offering more nightlife.]

Dad professed to be uncomfortable discussing sexual matters even when no women were around. On December 17 he wrote from a ward at the Snetterton AAF base infirmary, where he had been sent to recover from stress, describing

> *A heated bull session on sex that lasted all evening. Of course it's a very popular subject; and the Lotharios were each trying to outdo the other with stories of their amour-- who, what, where, when, but no why. Some of them were incredibly sordid-- VD is included very blithely. Nonchalant is a better word. Everyone was in the discussion but me. I rather get left out of most things being the only capt. [meaning the others were all lieutenants] . . . .*
>
> *He [an unnamed lieutenant] finally asked for my philosophy, and I told him quite seriously I didn't believe in trifling with it. At any rate I'm afraid I made some of them feel a little ashamed when they saw that I was in earnest. It's odd that, if you stick to your guns, people will always think the better of you for it . . . .*

Like Mom, Dad also took a dim view of the irresponsibility of others. August 19, for example, was a Saturday evening.

> *Dearest Gina:*
>
> *Party night is upon us again, and I am not the duty officer tonight. Just had a spasm of unselfishness, so I went down to the orderly room to call the fellow who is D.O. and offer to take over for him if he is party-minded. Got a big surprise when I found out he wasn't even there. I feel more brassed off than charitable right now.*

On December 23 Dad participated as a singing "wise man" in a costumed Christmas nativity pageant at his Snetterton base. His letter afterward condemned the behavior of some of the other participants as irresponsible.

> *One of the kings and two of the shepherds were 'fortified' for the ordeal and decided to present themselves at the club [afterward] (where a terrific 'party' is in progress) in costume. It nearly caused a riot. Some of the lads, who were really blotto, had varying stages of mental collapse at the sight of Eastern figures: make up, beards, and caboodle.*
>
> *I felt antagonistic . . . to everyone there. It was because I simply couldn't laugh and horse around and get tight. Oh, I suppose it is a Xmas party-- but some of the fellows there are due to be called for the mission tomorrow, if there is one; and with the things at sake, they can't afford to give less than their best.*

As previously noted, by the end of 1944 Dad had been relieved from any further operational flying. His new duties as a desk officer-- first at 96th Bomb Group Headquarters and later with the 45th Combat Wing-- were not only less stressful, but, judging from the tone of his letters, less time consuming. On January 13, 1945 he reported that

Wing is throwing one [major party] *tonight. Do you know that one of the boys had me dated up with some dish' from London-- that's what he thought. The idea didn't* [illegible] *very well. Incidentally this fellow was home this past summer and got married. Tonight he describes himself as being a 'stupid sob' for doing it.*

On Sunday, February 11, Dad described the hangover symptoms exhibited by partiers following yet another AAF social event the previous evening.

The afternoon was comic. Party panthers emerging and looking beaten-- wailing about those double scotches and telling tales out of school about their 'commandos.' It's fine to listen. Eventually they always ask why I'm so happy, but I can't seem to make them understand.

On May 5, 1945 Dad reported

There is a party in the wing club-room tonight . . . . Gorgeous creatures have been imported from all around and the bar is heavy-laden. [Illegible].
I put in an appearance there not long ago. Things were well under way, and I felt quite sorrowful as I left. Some of the fellows I have talked with quite intimately who have shown me snaps of their homes, wives, and children and told me how wonderful such things are-- they were there and strictly in their cups [drunk]. *Their affections were being lavishly strewn on their companions. I felt a little sick.*

Ever the loner, he retreated from the boisterousness of the party to the solitude just beyond the door. *In the mist and drizzle of this night I feel warm and glowing, it is impossible to keep the visions of our week from my mind.* He rather poetically concluded this letter with

Outside there was only the dark soft velvet sadness of the rain. All acts seemed to fade in bowed shadows. A thousand days or nites, it does not matter. Look for me-- I shall be standing in the sun.

***

As I remember him in later years, Dad-- unlike Mom-- was neither overtly religious nor denominationally oriented. So I once asked if he really believed in God. His response was that, given his own survival of the war when so many others who shared his job description never made it home, there must be a god who watched over him. If there were no God in his life, then why had he survived when s so many others had not?

Other WWII veterans came back home sharing similar convictions. For example, Sidney Scheinberg described a mission to bomb a tank factory in which he asked himself

Why did the plane next to you go down in flames and not you? Why did the German fighter plane shoot down the plane two planes over from you in the formation?[lxvi]

Elsewhere in his memoir, Lt. Scheinberg attributed his survival to good luck. But he also asserted . . . "Everyone prayed in his own way to get through this and go home."[lxvii]

Charles Alling flew with a different Bomb Group, the 34th. Like Dad, he faced the additional risk of being in a pathfinder plane leading the formation. In his postwar memoir *A Mighty Fortress; Lead Bomber Over Europe,* Capt. Alling later wrote that he could not

> . . . understand why or how we [his plane's aircrew] made it through, except to think we were watched over and protected. We could have never done it by ourselves.[lxviii]

If Nassim Nicholas Taleb, the author of *Fooled by Randomness*, had been party to my postwar conversation with Dad about religion, he might have suggested that Dad's opinions-- and those of Lt. Scheinberg and Capt. Alling, as well-- are really the result of "survivorship bias." In other words, the post-war views of the survivors are a non-random sample of the total population that was obliged to participate in it.

***

While Dad needed a god to watch over him, Mom needed a partner who shared her faith. Indeed, the correspondence reveals that her religious commitments played a significant role in their mutual effort to be led " . . . not into temptation." While neither of Mom's parents was religious, she, along with many other young children in her family's Chicago neighborhood, was recruited to join a Sunday school program. This Sunday school, which originally met in a garage, gradually evolved to become the Grace Gospel Mission, a denominationally unaffiliated "evangelical free church." Mom grew up with this church. Throughout her life, she considered herself to be a "born again" Christian.

Because Dad, on the other hand, had not been particularly interested in religion until after he met Mom, the discrepancy explains why her letters are filled with biblical passages, prayers, and anecdotes about her personal religious experience. She was subtly converting Dad [who apparently had been raised as an Episcopalian] to her persuasion. And while her letters never say so directly, the overall impression one gets from reading them is that willingness to adopt her religious views was a prerequisite for any future husband. Dad understood this. His correspondence never explicitly acknowledges this reality. But he knew that converting to Mom's more evangelical brand of Protestantism was necessary in order to win her hand in marriage. For example, as early as February 25, 1944 he assured Mom . . . *I want to be all you want me to be.* Subsequently, a significant portion of his correspondence was intended to demonstrate to Mom that he had been converted. Toward that goal, Dad suggested that Mom's chaplain-- Rev Zinz, a man he knew she relied on for spiritual advice-- could also play a role in his own religious education. On May 18, for example, he made a request of Mom. *I've been wondering if you could get Chappie to give me a list of advised reading. I don't quite know how to get started on the Old Testament.* Further, in an undated fragment, Mom passed along a promise from Rev. Zinz. *Chappie thought there were more verses on predestination than what I gave you, so he will look them up for you.*

Dad's correspondence soon begins to claim that his conversion was not only making it easier for him to resist temptation, but that was also positively affecting those around him. The first letter to this effect was written on May 16.

After I placed the call [to Mom in Wotton], I returned to the Club and pulled out your pocket Bible and started in on Luke again . . . .

. . . one of the fellows, almost a complete stranger, detached himself from the bar and asked if he might speak with me. He seemed very earnest.

What he wanted was to tell me that he had seen me reading Luke & instantly was filled with admiration that I should sit reading it as naturally as you please. He was a bit incoherent about much that he said, but it was plain to see that he respected me for it no end and was moved. I suppose it was a contrast to all the soaks [drunks].

It made me feel good all the way thru, and to think that I should have unwittingly stirred him. Who knows how many others who were silent.

Further, on September 5, he described an incident that occurred while traveling by train from Wotton back to Snetterton at the end of a leave.

Had quite an incident on the way here-- let me tell you.

I was reading the pocket Bible . . . which I had with me; and, after a while, I turned to the inscriptions you had put in the front for me; and when I had read that, I just sort of dreamed, I guess. Well, in the compartment & sitting next to me was this elderly lady (slightly deaf as it turned out); and she was curious to read it, too. She just beamed 'cause it was the same verses that she wrote in her son's Bible before he went overseas in the last war. He was a flier, too.

Then she looked up the sources that I had looked for and never found-- it's Proverbs III, 5-6. Of course she was downright amazed to see me reading a Bible (of all things) and finally got off at her station with the best wishes in the world.

On the other hand, Dad's newly found religiosity also occasionally led to conflict. On January 12, 1945 Dad found himself in a debate with a fellow officer.

Last night I got into a religious discussion that lasted two hours. Lt. Cole, the group's engineering officer (and one of the group characters-- a big beary guy), caught me reading the Bible and asked me if I believed in it; and I was on the defensive all the way; he argued for a long time that the Ten Commandments is [all there really is to] religion.

The best he could do was hold his ground.

You just can't say that ethics or moral law or laws are religion. I could have made a better cutting edge for my argument. I was in the position almost like the man with the tiger by the tail who didn't dare let go. I couldn't disprove the things he said very quickly, and some of them not at all; but neither could he sell me anything. It was a grand argument, though. 'Member the time you & Chappie & I had a discussion in his office-- remember how he said we were just right for each other?

152

On March 5, 1945 Dad described a conversation in which a fellow officer expressed curiosity about the origins of his religious demeanor.

> *Last night Mac [?] really started something. He asked me if I came from a very religious family because religion seemed to be a big thing in my life. He wanted to know why & what my personal philosophy was. We talked about it ' till two in the morning. Mac is an exploring agnostic.*

Exactly one month later, his Bible again prompted the curiosity of others.

> *Went to the show tonight and was reading Acts while waiting for it to begin. One of the newcomers at wing who was sitting two seats away finally worked up enough curiosity to ask me what it was I was reading. When I told him, his first question was 'Are you Catholic?' When I told him I wasn't, he looked so dumbfounded . . . .*

17
ENGAGED

Despite the Hollywood-style circumstances of my parents' initial meeting, and despite the intensity of the feelings that they soon shared, the correspondence is surprisingly unspecific as to how they reached the decision to marry. None of their surviving letters make explicit who was the first to propose. Nor do any of the letters indicate when they considered themselves to be officially engaged. Nonetheless, my overall impression is that Mom and Dad, from nearly the beginning, perceived themselves as being destined for each other-- provided they both survived the war. However, both also recognized that they were in the grip of historical forces beyond their control. When they first met at Grenier Field, neither could be assured of redeployment to the European Theatre. And even when both arrived in England, neither-- especially Dad-- could feel confident about surviving from one day to the next. What good would it do to plan for the future if there was not going to be a future?

***

Superstition may have played a role. Mom's letters in particular suggest that she was more superstitious back during the War than I remember of her in later life. In April of 1944, for example, Mom was still in Wotton-under-Edge. On April 11 she informed Dad that she was knitting him a scarf.

> *You'll never guess how I spent the afternoon and evening. Working on a scarf for you. I'm not sure you'll get one or not. That piece of material is in six pieces, and not one section is big enough for a scarf. If I can put one together without having it look too much like a patchwork quilt, you shall have it.*
> *It is a marvelous feeling spending time sewing for you. Just think how centralized my thoughts were, and around whom.*

The next day, Mom thought the project was completed.

> *Dear Ricky,*
> *Just finished your scarf. I shall send it tomorrow. It isn't so nice as I would have liked it to be. I hope it isn't too short. If you don't like it, use it as a dresser scarf. I had to use the thread out of the piece you gave me; and sort of the cord unraveled; so it is 'home spun.' [I] couldn't get new thread.*

By the day after that, however, Mom was having so many troubles with the scarf that she decided to delay sending it. Informing Dad of the delay, she made a rather superstitious request.

> *Dearest Ricky,*
> *Have had my troubles with your scarf. I finally discovered you can't iron that material, but just let it dry. Will send it with Capt. M. [?] Would you grant me this request? Don't ever wear this scarf or take it with you on a mission. Ever since I started on it, it's been a jinx; and there is another reason I don't want you*

to wear it flying-- the important reason because of the material it is made from. Can't be more specific now. __But__ I'm starting to knit a [second] scarf that you can wear flying or anyplace you like to compensate for this one. Sounds crazy, the request, my reasoning or lack of reasoning. When I see you, I shall try to explain.

Apparently it had been Dad who started this whole knitting project, albeit unintentionally. In an undated letter probably written in mid-April of 1944, he implied that he had given her some yarn as gift, but with no intention that she knit anything for him.

I'm really looking forward to the scarf. I really didn't mean for you to make anything of the stuff-- I regretted the suggestion 'cause I gave it to you so you would have it for yourself.

His letter further implies that she had inaccurately accused him, perhaps over the phone, of giving her a bit of British money for any related expenses. *. . . honestly, I didn't put the pounds in your purse.*

On April 19 Mom tried to reassure him that she was knitting only because she wanted to.

About the scarf-- don't you dare feel badly about the material I used. There is ample left for anything I wish to make for myself when we get home. About the three pounds [which had appeared in her purse]-- *it's still a mystery. Can't understand it.*

On the very next day, Mom began work on this second scarf. *The wool for your scarf-- guess where I got it? I'm unraveling an old sweater of mine. How about that?*

Mom knitting. To her left are Fred Breadman and his daughter Jeannie.
To Jeannie's left is her childhood friend Marie Williams.[lxix]
Courtesy of Ms. Karen Anstice.

By April 25 Dad was wondering if this second scarf would be an improvement over the previous one. *So I'm going to have a 'good' scarf. Are you going to make it a nice one?* On May 2 she reported *. . . your* [second] *scarf is 14 inches done. Worked on it all* *evening.* The next day she added . . . *Your scarf is 16 1/2 inches long; may work on it again tonight.* Two days later she reported . . . *Your scarf is now 23" long, and after this letter I'll' get busy on it again.*

Three days later Dad acknowledged receipt of the first scarf.

> *Aha! Your scarf came today and it is very, <u>very</u> nice-- to the admiration of all. I show it off & most of them say 'I didn't think a LIMEY could do something as nice as that.' Naturally I say 'She's not a limey.'*

Given Mom's previous concerns about the bad luck a scarf might have the power to invoke, Dad now inquired about the extent of the restrictions being imposed on the first one's use. *Shall I wear your scarf as a ground scarf or not at all? I won't wear it in the air if you don't want me to.* He then closed the letter . . . *Sometimes I wonder if you <u>can</u> love me-- sometimes (more often) I wonder at the wonder of your love. Mine seems pitifully small beside it.*

In an undated letter written around May 16, Mom responded to the news from Dad that he had received the first scarf. *Glad you didn't think the scarf was too bad. Wear it whenever you want, but not flying.*

Regarding the second scarf, by May 8 Mom was receiving unsolicited advice on how to proceed further. That afternoon she was making her way back home to the Sims when she decided to stop off at the Breadmans to phone a message from Dad. *While I visited with him* [Fred Breadman], *I worked on my knitting. He suggested I sew it up the middle and add sleeves-- How about that?* Perhaps it was this suggestion that led to a third project. Without telling Dad, Mom began working on a sweater as well. Eventually she let him in on her revised plan.

> *23 May 44*
> *10:15 P.M.*
> *downstairs* [at the Sims]
>
> *Dear Ricky,*
>   *Am as pleased as punch tonight 'cause today I was able to get some 'extra' fine English wool to knit you a sweater. The wool is beige, and I've done about an inch in the back this evening.*

By May 24 the second scarf had arrived with Dad who intimated that he was now wearing it on combat missions.

> *Guess where I went today! Aha-- right. The very first time. My eyelids are really sagging. Had a bad moment this morning-- no, yesterday evening when I . . . couldn't remember where I put your scarf. I was almost panicky. But when I remembered & had it on, I felt almost safe as pie. Proud? -- why everyone knows all about it, and you.*
>   *Fox ('our girl')* [probably a Red Cross volunteer] *was serving coffee on return. I'm afraid that it (the scarf) will show the signs of combat, but it'll mean all the more.*

Here Dad was implying that he had been unnerved by the mission and was, as a consequence, shaking so badly that he had spilled some coffee on the scarf, or possibly even vomited on it. In any event, on June 2 he again wore this second scarf on a bombing mission.

> *Just back from a 'trip.' Tried to call but the operator couldn't put me through for quite a while. Here I am in the barracks & thoroughly pooped out. Happy-- your scarf is wonderful-- so are you.*

On June 15 Dad indicated that it was now his intention to wear Mom's second scarf only when flying.

> *Today I got all dressed up for a mission that I didn't have to go on, but I'd rather have gone than wait around sweltering in two sets of underwear. At least I had a chance to wear your (MY) scarf, which is only worn on op's* [operations].

On June 1 Dad received the sweater that Mom had made him. *A sweater! I shall have love for armor.* On the evening of on July 18, returning from a bombing mission to Kiel, Dad wrote to Mom, whose unit was now positioned at La Cambe, near the Normandy beachhead.

> *. . . it would be nice to see your picture. When I came back today I got my own taken all with your sweater and scarf showing most conspicuously. If they ever get into Yank or S&S, it'll be a huge surprise.*

Dad wearing his sweater from Mom at the end of a mission, July 18, 1944.

Six days later he received copies of the photographs. He promptly forwarded them to Mom and asked her to . . . *Notice how conspicuous your sweater and scarf are!* On August 6, after a particularly long mission over Germany, he wanted Mom to . . . *Think of all the places yours sweater and scarf will have been.* On August 14 he again mentioned Mom's good luck charms, this time noting their frequent use. *Your sweater & scarf especially will be soaked* [with perspiration] *when I finish (magic thought), but are they precious-- wow!*

***

At Grenier Field there had been no need for correspondence because Mom and Dad were seeing each other nearly every day-- if not socially, at least on the basis of their nurse-patient relationship. Later, when both were stationed in England, there were frequent opportunities to meet whenever the other could obtain either a full leave or day pass from duty. Moreover, there were also frequent telephone communications on those days when they were not free to meet. For the most part, I can only speculate about the subject matter being discussed during my parents' English meetings and telephone conversations. Nonetheless, even this pre-invasion period, much can be inferred from the letters that they did exchange.   In them it was Dad who was the first to broach the subject of marriage. In a letter written on February 27, 1944, following a weekend visit from Mom at his AAF base near Alconbury, he reported that he . . . *was asked twice today if I was about to marry you. Now you know how possessive you looked when you were holding hands at the Grand* [local cinema?].

On March 2 Mom responded with one of the few expressions of displeasure to be found in any of her wartime letters.

> *Strange-- I have a bone to pick with you. Maybe I <u>appeared</u> to act possessive; but I hardly think you looked like you were trying to run away-- so don't blame me <u>entirely</u> for questions in regard to any new marital status of yours.*

At this early stage in their relationship, it may have been Dad who was the first to mention the marriage issue, but it was also he who hesitated to commit. While in England, both he and Mom occasionally communicated via telegram.   The problem for Dad was that the contents of a telegram had to be shared with a third party, namely the telegraph clerk. Initially, he was reluctant to express his affection for Mom in the presence of this clerk. And this was despite knowing full well that the contents of all his letters to Mom were also being shared with a military censor. Nonetheless, on March 8 Dad complained that the signals officer [telegraph clerk] was trying to figure out who the *Gina* to whom Dad was addressing his telegrams actually was. He then went on to admit . . . *I still haven't screwed up enough courage to sign it with 'love.' He* [the telegraph clerk] *might think that a bit too odd.*

While Dad was the first to mention the possibility of marriage, it was Mom who was the first to weigh the pros and cons of getting hitched while in England.   On March 13 she wrote

> *Remembering that you asked me if I'd like to be married in England (Before you read any further, DON'T PANIC), I guess I'd had Pumpkins on my mind a great part of the day when I answered you. I seem to forget that it would have to be a long time, perhaps, before there could be any Pumpkins because there are so many things you have ahead of you.*

Pumpkin was, of course, my parents' nickname for Bernice Breadman, the younger niece of Mom's landlady Marjory Sims. Here, Mom's letter rather wistfully uses this nickname in the plural to refer not to the original *Pumpkin* but to the daughters that Mom herself would someday like to have. Still, at this stage of the war Mom's desire to marry Dad was tempered by uncertainty about their future, especially Dad's.

> *<u>Just</u> being <u>Mrs. Gallagher would</u> <u>be</u> <u>a</u> <u>crowning glory;</u> and <u>don't</u> <u>think</u> <u>I</u> <u>wouldn't</u>*

want to be it anytime regardless of any situation: economic, war, postwar, etc. In fact, it would be rather wonderful to be married in England in view of what has happened-- your being here. BUT I am not sure it would be fair to you. This is no proposal.

A month later, Mom still did not consider herself formally engaged. In her letter to Dad on April 12 she noted that her unit's chaplain, Rev. Zinz, had asked her-- perhaps teasingly-- if she and Dad were getting engaged.

Chappie asked me today if he was going to have to write a letter of recommendation for us yet. Of course I said 'no.' And the conversation became a bit embarrassing-- you know 'Chappie'-- WOW!

As previously noted, on May 2 Mom attended the wedding of fellow nurse Elizabeth Dean.

Went to Deanie's very lovely wedding at 3P.M. [and] was very much embarrassed. Mrs. Elliott [Rev. Zinz's landlady] sat up in the balcony and, when I was seated, called me to look up, and then in a loud whisper said: 'This should be Charles' and your wedding." Oh!!!! etc.

During this period, Dad, too, was receiving inquiries about the status of the courtship. By May 27 he had been stationed at Snetterton Heath for about two months. Mom had already visited him there on at least one occasion. Moreover, his friends knew that he was spending every leave with her somewhere. Among his fellow airmen, his relationship with Mom had become an "item." In his letter that evening

Lt. [illegible] keeps asking me outright when we are going to be married. So I confess that he seems to be a bit of ahead of things. Today, his retort to such a naïve assumption was: 'Ha! With that gleam for you in her eyes! She'd marry you quicker than she'd pick flowers in the spring!' How about that! Pat (Lt. Mackey) just stood by and grinned. The rascals!

On June 14 the 45th Evacuation Hospital found itself at a place called Hursley Hants, which was being used by the Allies as a marshaling area in southern England. That evening Mom again wrote about the possibility of marriage.

Dear Ricky,
Just had a long chat with Chappie; we talked about everything, but mostly you. He has as much confidence in you as I have, and you know how much that is.
Hope this won't be too much of a surprise-- but I said we talked about everything. Chappie said he'd like to perform the ceremony someday-- and he'd make the trip to wherever we'd like in the States. And he was serious 'cause that's the kind of mood he was in. It was nice to have you [be] the object of conversation. Capt. Welden [?] asked about you today, too.
The events of the day will have to be saved for one of our fireside chats.
Remembering our hour--

Love,
Gina

Dad had telephoned Mom in Wotton on June 12, just prior to her departure for Hursley Hants. Had he proposed marriage in this phone call? Subsequent letters are ambiguous. Five days later-- probably too soon for Dad to have already received Mom's letter of June 14-- he wrote

> *Dearest Gina,*
> *Hello Mrs. Gallagher!*
> *Pardon the double salutation, but there is a big grin on my face; and if you could see it, you'd say it was worth it. It's a wonderful thought.*

Regarding this letter, was marriage the antecedent of the pronoun "it" in . . . *It's a wonderful thought*? In her own letter of June 29, written amidst a battlefield, Mom complained of not having spoken with Dad since that last phone call just prior to her unit's transition to Normandy. She also returned to the theme of marriage for the first time since her arrival in France.

> *The honorable Chaplain Zinz paid a visit professionally to my ward at 4 a.m. last night. The first I've seen of him since we've been here* [in France].
> *Guess what he said (verbatim)? 'Most of all, I want to be the one who marries you kids.' The statement was entirely out of the order under the circumstances last night. I was surprised and* <u>deeply</u> <u>touched</u> *'cause you see he was called to see one very ill.*

For the next several weeks the correspondence made no further mention of marriage. By September of 1944, however, it seemed that German military resistance was crumbling. Gen. George S. Patton, commander of U.S. 3rd Army, was beginning to speak publicly about the possibility that German would surrender before the end of the year. Moreover, both Mom and Dad were now growing increasingly fearful that one or the other might now be transferred to the war against Japan. While not explicitly saying as much, they both seemed to have concluded that having seemingly survived one maelstrom, they should take advantage of any opportunity to marry before being swallowed up by another.

On September 30 Mom wrote that she had received no letters from Dad in several days. Then-- enigmatically-- she added that *'no news is good news;' and* [it is] *time to take out* <u>THE</u> *letter of all letters, and renew 'Our Faith.'* . . . Was this the letter in which Dad wrote to formally ask for Mom's hand? If so, perhaps Mom kept it with her for strength on the battlefield rather than placing it in her footlocker for safekeeping. In any event, if such a letter existed, it has not been preserved. Mom again revisited the subject of marriage on October 25.

> *My Darling Mr. Gallagher,*
> *This is the third letter I've written to you in the last two days, and haven't mailed the 1ˢᵗ two because I couldn't say just the way I felt, the way I wanted you to understand. Then, last night, two letters came from you postmarked the 7ᵗʰ and*

the 12th. They made me happy, tearfully so, because I felt so alone until I read them at ten p.m. I felt comforted; you seemed so very near-- by eleven I was sound asleep . . . .

In your letter of the 12th you were wishing for what I want more than anything else, to be just Mrs. Gallagher. And it's what I want more each day.

In my possession are letters from Dad written on both October 7 and October 12. However, neither of these letters mention anything about transforming Mom into *Mrs. Gallagher*. Still, both Mom and Dad often drafted more than one letter on a given day. Perhaps there was a second-- unpreserved-- letter written on October 12. If so, it probably was in this second letter that Dad further pursued the subject of marriage. Indeed, since Dad had just learned that he was being relieved from any further combat flying, it would be understandable if he were now to begin thinking more about the future. In her own letter of October 25, Mom reflected both on how providential it had been for both of them to be assigned to the European Theatre and how forbidding the possibility of a Pacific redeployment now seemed.

To think we found each other before this invasion, your coming to England made so much difference.

Perhaps to better see 'His' [God's] stature-- yes to be sure.
So humbly, thankfully

In love with you,
Mrs. Gallagher.

This letter then adds a postscript that might be interpreted as Mom's wish that they seal the engagement by agreeing on a date for the wedding ceremony.

P.S. Would you like to hear this again? <u>Whenever</u> you want me to be Mrs. C.W.D. I shall be more than willing . . . .
P.S.S. Time cannot be measured-- when we see each other again, every minute apart will have been worth the joy of that meeting.

Dad himself returned to the topic of marriage in letter drafted on November 9. In it he shared with Mom a conversation that he had that day with a photoreconnaissance officer named *Bill Barnes*. During the conversation, this Bill Barnes asked Dad to listen to a personalized phonograph recording that his wife in the States had sent him.

. . . it was an ecstatic moment listening to his wife play [Brahms on the piano] and hearing her voice; and he said that being married was wonderful and that I just better had get married, or else I wouldn't really be living. I told him I was doing my very best under the circumstances.

In a second letter written about this same time, Dad daydreamed . . . *just think, we <u>can</u> get married when we get home & make goo-goo eyes for fun over maple walnut sundaes.* However, contrary to all the evidence that my parents already considered themselves to be engaged prior to November 14, on that evening Dad wrote a letter the postscript of which reads like a rather clumsy initial marriage proposal.

161

Started this at ten o'clock. And I want you to be Mrs. CWD NOW! You see I went to division today and read your letters, especially your letter of the 25th as we rode there in the command car. I wasn't anywhere in that car at all. Instead, I was remembering how you had told me that you would be Mrs. Gallagher any time, & in my heart I was a bit afraid of being secure. I think my mind really crystallized on that side. Do you have any anxieties about it now? I have none. Why was I such a dolt?

In February of 1945 Mom sent Dad a Hallmark-type card that begins . . . "To My Husband on Valentine's Day." She signed the inside page *Mrs. Gallagher.*

***

On December 1, 1944 Dad accepted a Christmas invitation from the Breadmans back in Wotton. Armed with a weekend pass, he made another of his solo visits there. His letter the next afternoon was composed while still with them.

Dearest Gina:
   Fred wants me to begin by giving you his love. Of course the children chorused in theirs too; when I said good-bye to Marge a few minutes ago it was the same.
   I'll be leaving in about half an hour. It's been my shortest stay.
   Last night I came on the bus. It was dark and everything seemed just like the first time. And for complete surprise Jeannie & Pumpkin jumped out of the darkness & tugged me to [illegible] with squeals & much excitement. I had called from London the night before.
   What an evening. I had presents for them and for Fred, Phil, Reg & Marge, too. I popped down to see them just after nine, and just like always it was very late before we stopped talking. Rather? Before I left,-- you see we had just begun to talk, and about everything.

At this point, his letter becomes somewhat enigmatic.

During the evening a very wonderful idea came up that you will hear more of later. Marge helped me carry it out this morning. It is for more than Christmas. Yes, far more.

The December 1 letter was posted forthwith. Two days later, Dad explained what he had been up to.

Marge, Reg & I had a big pow-wow about Xmas gifts-- that was the thing that kept us up so late. And since the pictures won't be finished for a long time, there seemed to be a real Xmas problem still with us.
   It seemed that there weren't enough 'practical' things we could think of, & we were stumped by [ration] coupons on lots of other things. That started us off on jewelry. Marge thought that a ring was a far better idea than a bracelet, and somehow the idea of an engagement ring by mail didn't quite ring the bell. Then

we stumbled onto just a ring. I'd never really thought of it before, but it grew like wildfire.

Marge, Jean & I bought this the next morning. It was quite a ceremony. Marge said you should decide what finger to wear it on. Does it fit?

This is not meant just for Christmas, but for all days and all hours; and that each of those hours may be richer in love and joy and the wisdom of these things.

<u>Ricky</u>

Dad included the December 3 letter with the actual package containing the ring. He then posted the combined parcel on December 5.

A week and a half later, Dad's December 1 enigmatic letter was delivered to Mom, but not yet the parcel containing the actual ring and its December 3 cover letter. When Mom read the original letter, the *wonderful idea* that it mentions caught her attention. She responded like an exited schoolgirl. *Wonder what you and Marge are cooking! A hint please, just a little one, hmm?*

However, the delivery of Dad's package did not arrive for a further six weeks. This delay was probably due, in part, to it having been shipped as a parcel rather than in an ordinary envelope. But the prime cause for this delay was an unforeseen event, the massive German counterattack known as the Battle of the Bulge, which began in a snowstorm on December 16 and raged on until January before the Germans conceded failure by pulling back.

On January 6, 1945, just two days after learning that Mom had survived The Bulge, Dad attempted to redefine his still yet-to-be-delivered parcel as a birthday gift inasmuch as the Christmas season had passed and Mom's 25th birthday was now only weeks away. *I think you're going to have a very nice birthday gift this year. Something that says '1 love you.' And oh-- how I do!* But by February 3, still having received no confirmation that the ring was safely in Mom hands, Dad worried out loud that perhaps the APO had misplaced it in the commotion of the battle.

> *On the radio today I heard of the many thousands of packages & letters lost to Runstedt* [German Army Field Marshal Gerd von Runstedt] *and wondered if they might include your Xmas package that Marge & I 'cahooted' on . . . . I won't be able to duplicate the present.*

In other words, Dad was admitting that-- should the parcel's contents be lost-- he could not immediately afford its replacement.

Unbeknownst to Dad, on January 26 the ring had reached Mom at Spa, about two hours by car from Brussels in Belgium, along with Dad's original cover letter defining his gift as . . . *just a ring* . . . . Nonetheless, judging from her reaction to its arrival, Mom most certainly regarded this particular ring as of the engagement variety. She could not contain her happiness.

Dearest--

Tonight your Christmas present [a sapphire ring] *arrived, and it couldn't possibly have been nicer surprise. It's beautiful.*

Guess which finger it fits perfectly? Right the first time; and it's been on my left

163

hand ever since I opened the box. And that is where it shall remain until it is
replaced [when a real diamond ring can be afforded].

> *After I opened the package and put the ring on, I* flew *down the hall to show it*
> *to Chappie and then to Capt. Sachs. Bless Marjory and Jeannie too, I can*
> *visualize the three of you shopping.*

She then concluded this giddy letter with . . .

> *Oh, but I'm bubbling over with joy, happiness, and*
> > *Love, for you alone,*
> > *Gina*
>
> *P.S. Good night, my Darling--*
> *P.S.S. Just 'right' finger & left hand-- hmmm-- I can't stop looking at it, how will*
> *I ever fall asleep tonight? 'Wide awake dreams.'*

On February 5, 1945 she added . . . *Your ring is twinkling merrily; and, if I were trying to*
tell you this, I can see you twinkling with pleasure, as [is] *the ring, in return, at my*
attempts.

By February 6 Dad had learned that Mom had received the ring. He was thrice
relieved: it had arrived safely; Mom welcomed it; and it fit. He wrote

> *Had a letter from you postmarked the 28th. Now if that isn't special delivery, I*
> *ask you! Special news too-- you have my Xmas present. I must call Marge and*
> *tell her how right she was. That was some morning we went shopping.*
>
> *Best of all, I'm glad you like it. I could picture your surprise-- the wrapping*
> *wasn't very gift-like, but it seemed protective-- and to think that it fits and you like*
> *it. I feel practically smug. Only yesterday or day before I had serious doubts*
> *about your ever getting it.*

On February 9 Mom was complaining, tongue in cheek, . . . *Your ring interferes with*
your letters; every time I pause and see your ring, I become lost in dream; it's the
loveliness of the blue lights. On February 16 she added . . . *It's good to know you know I*
have my ring . . . .

***

As my parents took these steps toward their formal engagement, Dad's made an attempt
to write Mom a love poem. But, on December 29, 1944 this first effort ended in failure.

> *You force me to a confession . . . . I tried writing a poem . . . and could not*
> *satisfy myself. It was even impossible to write each letter as poetry. Oh, there*
> *would be a moment of clarity-- of those once-in-a-whiles perhaps a letter might*
> *have a fig of beauty . . . .*
>
> *At our hour I was reading a collection of letters (poems)-- 'This is My Beloved'*
> *by William Benton. It is terrific. They are very emotional utterances, and, were it*
> *not for their beauty, their eroticism would be even more extreme.*
>
> *How many opposites there are! We are apart-- yet you are with me and as one.*
> *Many things are chaotic, yet for the future, a rock is standing. So shall I stand for*

you.

On the evening of January 22, 1945, Dad sat down for a second time to write Mom a poem, a composition he titled *Ten O'Clock.* Throughout the two years of their wartime correspondence, both he and Mom referred to 10 P.M. as *our hour.* What the original significance of that particular time of evening was is never made clear. It could not refer to their engagement because references to *our hour* began well before any serious discussion of marriage. Perhaps it refers to their first evening stroll back at Grenier Field. Nonetheless, regardless of how the notion of "our hour" got started, both Mom and Dad intended that this particular time of the evening was to be a moment when-- if at all possible-- each would pause from whatever else they were doing to reflect on the significance of their relationship. In the letter accompanies the poem Dad said

> *I felt so bumptious . . . . I just had to write this-- oh what a job picking the right way of saying it. Does it help fill in those missing* [delayed or lost] *letters? . . . P.S. I even finished it at ten.*

> ### *Ten O'clock*
> *When there is only gray weariness and pain*
> *Of searing pain; knowing too much*
> *Loneliness that tars each step*
> *Aimless; leaden:----------------pause*
>
> *Alert every sense. . . . . soul open . . .*
>
> *As in a dream*
> *Cool water will be toying at your feet.*
> *Every ripple a tiny sibilance insistent*
> *Saying 'Walk on me, refreshed in surety.'*

In a note at the bottom of the page, Dad added . . . *St. John VI 19-21 was the thought that led to all of this. It took two nights writing to evoke it.* By the next day, Dad was having second thoughts about the quality of the poem he had just mailed.

> *Dearest Gina:*
>
> *If my letter jumped all over itself last night, it was because I had finished the poem and was very pleased with myself, thinking it was just right from title to punctuation and even to a* [illegible] *beginning and a crisp-fresh ending. Well, tonight, after re-reading a few dozen times, it doesn't seem anywhere near that good. Naturally, the real reason I was tickled was because I thought you would think it was just right, too. Tonight it doesn't seem to have that certain point or punch. Don't tell me you like it if you don't-- I'll try again.*

In an undated letter, probably written on February 4, Mom acknowledged receipt of the poem. Her reply gave no hint of disappointment.

> *. . . I received two letters from you, and one poem, 'Ten O'Clock.' Truthfully, I more than liked the poem. I liked its origin, its theme, and 'your' expressions.*

And for one other reason too, perhaps nobody else would or could understand it
completely; so that makes it 'ours' alone. I love its depth of meaning. it is lovely.
You keep me so happy; may I, you.

> *Always,*
> *Gina*

On February 15 Dad wrote back.

> *I kept a copy of Ten O'clock, and it doesn't seem to have the fire I hoped it had.*
> *I'm glad you liked it tho'. It was one of my surprises'-- and lots of fun writing it*
> > *I love you*
> > *Ricky*

***

My parents had always owned a charcoal portrait, about 9 by 16 inches, of a smiling Dad wearing his officer's uniform set against a gray background. Mom once explained to Jane, Bob and me that a sidewalk artist in Paris had sketched it. I had originally assumed that Dad posed for this picture during a visit to the City of Lights that he and Mom made together as newlyweds near the end of the War. However, judging from the totality of the correspondence, Dad himself was never in Paris. In fact, he was never on the ground in France at all except for that one unsuccessful attempt to rendezvous with Mom in Normandy back on September 1, 1944.

Mom, on the other hand, did spend a few days as a tourist in that city. This happened just a days after her unit had been pulled back to Spa in Belgium following its harrowing battle experience at Eupen during The Bulge. On the evening of Monday, January 29, 1945 she wrote

> *Last night lots were drawn; and three nurses were allowed three day passes to*
> *Paris; lucky me! We left at nine this morning in an open weapons carrier and this*
> *[the Hotel de la Paix in St. Quentin, France] is as far as we got; (by the way, we*
> *just arrived). The snow was deep, no map, no male officer, no chains on the tires,*
> *lost several times, followed ski tracks instead of roads & had to push the truck out*
> *of ditches (made by snow drifts) no less than five times. Consequently we're cold,*
> *exhausted . . . travelers tonight.*
>
> *Now I'm glancing at my fourth finger, left hand-- hmmm but I have your ring;*
> *but oh how completely I love the giver. It is the most wonderful Christmas gift*
> *I've ever, ever had.*

The next morning, January 30, she and the other two nurses arrived at the Hotel Normandy in Paris. *Our surroundings are beautiful, 'gorgeous' wouldn't be too extravagant a word to use. Only there is no coal in all of Paris, so there is no heat anywhere.*

Mom's letters during this excursion make no specific mention of a charcoal sketch. But they do provide some hints about how it came to be created. On the evening of January 31, in an effort to escape the cold in her room, Mom wrote a letter from the Hotel's snack bar. Most of the other patrons that evening were USAAF officers on leave rather than local Frenchmen. While drafting her letter, she happened to strike up a

166

conversation with an officer who had been stationed at Alconbury, where Dad also had once been posted. *. . . of course I told him about you . . . but he didn't recognize you from your pictures.* So Mom was traveling with photographs of Dad. There would have been little reason for her to do so, especially on a brief trip to a place where she had nobody in particular to share the pictures with-- unless she had some specific purpose in mind. Further, not only did Mom travel to Paris with several of Dad's pictures in her possession, she spent much of her time there shopping. In her letter from the previous morning, January 30, she had already expressed her intention to do so. In separate note written that evening, she described having *. . . walked all day by myself looking at the shops . . . .* During this jaunt she found a sidewalk artist whose sample work caught her eye. She then hired him to draw Dad's likeness from one of the photographs. Her January 31 letter closes with another hint.

> *Today I went sight seeing, it was much as expected, and did some shopping. Paris does seem gay, adventurous, and romantic even despite the cold.*
> *The disappointment of the day, I didn't find a suitable watercolor, but I did buy something for 'our home.'*

Charcoal sketch of Dad, January 31, 1945.

[Today this picture hangs on my home office wall.]

***

Dad had not made an overt attempt to rendezvous with Mom on the Continent since his failed attempt in the Normandy area back on September 1, 1944. But he continued scheming for a way to do so. By the beginning of the new year, they had not actually been together since the previous May. On January 17, however, Dad expressed his intention to *. . . soon . . . be meeting you again.* On this same day, Mom's 45th Evacuation Hospital was being redeployed from Jodoigne in Belgium to the previously mentioned resort area of Spa, further back from the front lines. Here the unit set up operations on the grounds of the "Caserne du Premiere Lancier," a former Belgian Army horse cavalry base.[lxx] Surgeries were performed in a stable, which had been sanitized for this purpose.[lxxi] On that day Mom reported

. . . we're set up on a horse stable-- how about that? Not quite as crude as I imagined it would be, the E.M. [?] are still cleaning up before we can set up the hospital. Tomorrow morning we begin to set-up; I hope we do. We live on the second floor; at least the aroma isn't too bad up here-- there are ten girls to a room, a coal stove so it's not so bad, and not too cold.

In late January of 1945, Mom was one of four nurses from the 45th Evacuation Hospital who were invited by the Signal Corps to pose as off-duty skiers for some publicity photos. [See Appendix A.] The Signal Corps photographer who took them made notations about when and where they were taken on the back side of each print. An Army censor then covered up this information up with black crayon marks before allowing them to be mailed. Around February 17 Dad received several of these images from Mom. He cleverly used them to uncover where she was-- or at least where she recently had been.

The other . . . pictures came today-- well censored by not quite well enough. The first one we tried to undo . . . with a solvent, but it didn't help a bit. [Then] I worked on these-- slicing the black crayon off with a razor to see what was underneath. It's wonderful to know where you are again . . . .

Skiing in Belgium, January 24, 1945. Mom is second from the right.

Dad now knew that-- as of January 24, 1945, at least-- Mom had been in Spa. Two days later, her correct position in hand, he asked . . . *Did you know that you're only 215 miles away? Less than two hours flying time. It plagues me.* By February 23, Dad had further come to learn that the in the nurses' accommodations had now been upgraded from the stables to a chateau about two miles from the Caserne. *In a chateau now! Pretty ritzy. It sounds ever so much better than a stable.* How Dad came to learn all this is unclear. Perhaps information about her new quarters had been passed along by word-of-mouth via one of Mom's suggested couriers.

On February 24, with the Germans in retreat, Dad wrote very candidly that he would soon be departing for Belgium. He had good reason to believe that Mom was still there. Moreover, in contrast to his rendezvous attempt in Normandy the previous September, there was no need for him to pose as the co-pilot on a medical plane. Instead, he would accompany a party of Air Force brass on an official visit to the Continent.

I am at division tonight feeling very wriggly. You see I am flying over to the continent . . . to you. That's tomorrow morning. As yet, I cannot find out much about it except that we are leaving in the morning and supposed to be going to Brussels. There is a colonel at the head of all this, and what the purpose of the trip is I don't know yet. Let's hope that you can read this letter fondly with a . . . smile.

In other words, if this second rendezvous plan succeeded, this message could not possibly reach Mom before he did. If it did succeed, the letter would serve merely as a reminder of their meeting.

On this occasion Dad's scheme did work. It is not clear exactly where in Belgium Dad's plane landed on February 26. But that evening he was somehow able to excuse himself from the tour group and make his way to Mom in Spa. In her first letter afterward-- written at 2 PM on her 25th birthday, February 27-- she raised the censor's eyebrows for reasons other than any possible breech of Allied military secrets.

If my ribs weren't so <u>pleasantly</u> sore from being held close to you, I'd think it all a glorious dream.

You must be dreadfully tired by now, perhaps you've been able to catch a little sleep. I do hope so.

After you left I went straight to bed, but I couldn't fall fast asleep. But rather I relived every precious minute of your visit. . . . I'm still smiling about you preparing breakfast this morning the way you took charge [in] very masculine fashion. I don't think I'll be the boss, and it was a 'just right' thought as you left.

[Also, it was presumably here that Mom first shared the charcoal sketch that she had just a few weeks earlier commissioned in Paris.]

By the afternoon of the next day, Dad was back in England. It is not clear whether the colonel who sponsored this Belgian visit was aware of Dad's hidden agenda. Indeed, to locate Mom, Dad may have slipped from his official party without permission. A letter he wrote the next day seems to imply as much. . . . *Red* [another officer] *and I reached the airport at 1040* [the previous morning], *which was early enough to beat the colonel* [Engersall, leader of the tour group].

Mom was relieved to hear that Dad had been . . . *delivered safely to the airfield.* Because Dad had not missed his return flight, he could not be accused of having gone AWOL. Both Mom and Dad now savored their brief time together. In her own letter written the day after, Mom said

Today I'm almost back on earth, and I've been thinking of all the things I should have asked you in person. Nothing really important; but, in 'our' excitement and eagerness to fill each minute, I wasn't quite sane. Oh for the time that we will be able to talk at our leisure.

Back in England, Dad expressed similar sentiments, but added a comment implying the colonel may been aware of Dad's personal agenda all along.

169

Meeting you with joyous surprise, dancing, together at ten o'clock, talking, looking, magic hours. Do you know I was in Belgium less than 24 hours altogether and with you for twelve? If I ever see Col. Engersall again, I'll wash his feet.

Since Mom and Dad had rendezvoused in the same chateau where she and her fellow nurses were quartered, his presence had been observed. As a result, my parents' relationship now became even more of an "item" among the personnel of the 45th Evacuation Hospital than before. Still, Mom was not the least bit embarrassed. Indeed, her February 28 letter suggests she was basking in all the attention.

This time I've felt that our romance has been one that the 45th has been reading, and they're anxious for the last installment of the serial. Everyone probed me with questions yesterday; and all said how pleased they were to see you, even the chief nurse. And when were you coming back? Oh, if I only knew that, too.

In a postscript to her next letter, Mom returned to the subject of her sore ribs, this time to tease the censor who would be reading about them.

P.S. My ribs are o.k., but yesterday every breath reminded me of a very happy night; it was wonderful.
P.S.S.-- If that should get censored-- oooo! (Sorry to disappoint you, censor, but what you're thinking isn't correct.)

Of course neither Mom's nor Dad's letters written immediately afterward could state exactly where the rendezvous had taken place. However, in a letter written after V-E Day, Dad did mention in passing that their tryst had occurred in Spa.

***

Dad's next poetic effort is actually typed. Though undated—and untitled-- it must have been written sometime during the weeks leading up to the wedding. While conceding that he and Mom are apart, it looks forward to their being together.

Now is a time for greatness.
f ever two have loved, then we.
If ever two have dreamed, then we.
Such as happiness is, we have known
And lived exultant yet humble;
Aware of time and timeless together--
Together! And while so awake
To all that is of earth of air, we made
Of dreams reality-- saw future loom with hope.
Apart! For awhile we shall be
Guided by what is born.
Nor is it an elfin thing. Perhaps apart
We can better see his stature.
Look! Ahead our goal

Yet a little while and we shall be there.
Fear not the journey.

At the bottom of the paper on which this was typed, Mom asked, in her own handwriting: *Who complained about the difficulties of writing poetry? I've never read anything more beautiful nor anything that meant more.*

***

Being engaged, both Dad and Mom now sought a wedding ceremony in an Anglican Church. Their correspondence does not explain why an Anglican ceremony was so important. After all, Mom's Christianity was of the more evangelical variety, a faith which, culturally at least, is quite different from that practiced by the more traditional Anglicans. Perhaps all of this was to please Dad's adoptive mother, Helen Dunn, whom Mom had met back at Grenier Field and who apparently was an Episcopalian, the American equivalent of Anglican. More likely, though, it was to oblige the Sims and Breadmans who had treated Mom like a daughter and who most certainly were Anglicans. Moreover, a wedding at the local Anglican Church in Wotton-under-Edge would make it convenient for the entire Sims-Breadman extended family to attend. This was a hope that both the Sims and Breadmans shared. On February 21, 1945 Dad made his final solo visit to Wotton-under-Edge.

> *. . . I've talked the legs off the chairs since I came yesterday noon. Oh, what talk! We talked about everything in the past and the future too. Of course they won't have us married anywhere else in England but Wotton.*

However, he soon doubted that a Wotton wedding could be arranged. On March 14 he wrote:

> *Let's see, tomorrow I have to call Wotton and day after a trip to head of the Diocese. I'm having quakes for fear we won't be able to get married in Wotton.*

These fears proved justified. In spite of having sung in the choir at the small Anglican Church in Wotton, Dad was now obliged to inform Mom-- still mired in war-torn Germany-- that their application for a Wotton wedding had been rejected. The very next evening, Dad reported

> *Dear Gina:*
> *I've been nosing about most of the day-- into the affairs of church and state. Of course there was a visit to the Red Cross, Chappie* [Dad's AAF chaplain]*, a long telephone call with the division chaplain-- oh, and one to Wotton. I talked to everyone but Pumpkin. Jeanie sounded full of fun.*
> *Perhaps the best talk was one this evening with the Rev. Mitchell. He's the rector of the local church* [near Snetterton Heath]*, very kindly, ear-whiskers-- you'll like him. It seems quite definite that we can't be married in Wotton. You see, it appears that you (one of us) must have been residing in the parish where the wedding is to be held, at least fifteen days prior to the wedding. So here is the only possibility. The division chaplain is going thru all possible exceptions, but*

171

didn't seem to offer much hope. At next best, perhaps Reg can come here [to Snetterton Heath]. *It will work out over the phone when you come to England. Don't fret about trying to rush a letter back in answer.*

My papers are still at division, and I can't get them thru until five days before they become valid. Boy, is this exciting! I never had dreams better than this.

I am in love with you,
Mr. Gallagher

By the day after that, Dad was anticipating a visit to the cathedral in Norwich to formally request permission to marry at the Anglican Church nearest his Snetterton Heath AAF base. Meanwhile, back in Wotton, Fred Breadman had not yet given up the fight. On March 19 Dad reported to Mom

> *Fred wrote saying that he thought it will be possible to be married in Wotton-- something I had given up on as impossible-- so now I've got to tear into it and its possibilities.*

The next day Dad was still hoping. *Won't it be something if we can be married in Wotton after all?* Nonetheless, he thought it wise to proceed with plans for a wedding at the Anglican church nearest him. On March 26 he wrote

> *It's really crept up on me tonight. . . . I went after supper to have another chat with Rev. Mitchell. We* [Dad and fellow navigator Bob Harnish] *have things pretty well worked out by this time and feel quite smug inside about our accomplishments. I came away with a Book of Common Prayer and have been reading the service and other things.*

By April 1 it was reconfirmed that an Anglican wedding back in Wotton would not be allowed. Consequently, Dad was obliged to revert back to his "Plan B," a wedding at the Anglican Church nearest to his AAF base at Snetterton Heath. This was St. Andrew's, a modest medieval structure in the nearby hamlet of Quidenham.

> *It is going to be necessary to be married here. I wrote to the vicar at Wotton with Fred behind me, and it is well nigh impossible to be married there. In addition there is not a single thing that either the Breadmans or Reg & Marge can do about it. So-- he advised me to be married here. The general is waiting to give you away.*

By April 6 Dad was sounding confident that all church arrangements were in place.

> *The big thing of the day was the trip to the cathedral* [in Norwich, about 24 miles to the northeast] *for your (our) license. It reads like an excerpt from St. Paul and is quite impressive to look upon. In there at the time was a young English girl for the same purpose. She was about eighteen and very excited. We struck up a conversation. It seems her fiancé is so young that he, too, must have his parents' consent. He is in the Forces and very much expecting to embark soon for-- India perhaps. They plan to marry during his embarkation leave. It made her seem*

very young before such long hopes. I felt completely burdenless. Oh-- the license was without any difficulty at all. You are described as a 'spinster.' It looks quite out of place here.

***

The Battle of the Bulge had temporarily disrupted all personal communication between Dad and Mom. By early February of 1945, however, Dad was feeling confident enough about Mom's safety to encourage her to complete the Army's marriage permission paperwork. In the meantime, in an undated fragment, Mom teasingly cautioned Dad to *BEWARE 'FEMALE' WILES!!!*

Now, in a letter dated February 3, 1945, Dad responded

> *. . . I* [previously] *sent a formal typewritten letter asking your CO's permission. Perhaps you'll have it by now; but if you don't, tell me so I can send another. I sent it to you. That was a beaming afternoon when I typed it out-- I just couldn't keep a straight face-- excited? 'Wow! Beware female wiles!' My foot! It's your confidence in me that's frightening* <u>sometimes.</u>

On February 6 Mom received a letter from Dad instructing her on how to fill out the Army's paperwork for requesting permission to marry.

> *Why Darling,*
> *Your letter of December 27th arrived and I am blushing. And trembling too. Of course I shall fulfill the 'you're willing' part immediately. Why, I can hardly believe it. When I wrote 'trembling' it was with joy and amazement. Oh, I do love you so . . . .*
> *Now I must run down and tell Chappie and Capt. Sachs the good news, I wish Capt. Egli were here to share it.*
> *Just think, really being your wife; may I be all you desire.*
> *All my love,*
Gina

However, several questions in Mom's mind remained unanswered. For instance, should she delay taking a week's leave of absence until after the Army approved all of the paperwork? Or should take the leave at the first opportunity on the assumption that everything would be approved in the meantime? As of March 3, Mom was leaning toward the latter alternative.

> *Dearest,*
> *A week from tomorrow another nurse and I will be leaving for England for one week. I'll come straight to your place.*
> *I hesitated accepting the leave now, but so much can happen between now and June that I thought it best to accept it now. Perhaps you can come here in June.*

By late afternoon on that same day, however, in a second letter, she had changed her thinking on this.

You'll think I'm nuts for sure, but the Col. suggested I postpone my leave until our [marriage] papers come through. He felt quite sure leaves for the U.K. would be coming through right along-- so now we can definitely plan (as much as one can in the army) getting married in England.

She ended this latter note with the postscript . . . *Chappie is planning to come too, even if he can't perform the ceremony.* Even this did not quite resolve everything. A second question lingering in Mom's mind was whether the wedding should really be held in England at all. This was because her fellow nurses were now pressuring Mom to hold the ceremony wherever the 45th Evacuation Hospital was on the Continent where they all could attend. At 8 P.M. on that same day, March 3, Mom wrote a third letter to Dad.

. . . the girls cornered me today and so much want us to have a very formal wedding. (Maybe it's because they think perhaps they can be bridesmaids and wear formals). It would be nice, but I explained that I didn't know if we'd be married here or not. Julia [Ramacciotti] even suggested they send home for material to have dresses made here. I thought this was very sweet, and I was very touched. If you should come here to get married, you'd like bridesmaids, wouldn't you?

Within four days however, Mom had dropped that idea, too.

. . . the chief nurse came in to awaken me to tell me that my approval is back and [I] may be married after April 7th. She seemed very pleased and eager for my reaction. Just think, that is a month from today.
    My permission came through in record time, and I can hardly believe it. Now you'll have much planning to do in not as much time as I expected you'd have. Will I be surprised? Hmm-- a whole week in England and us.

Shortly after midnight on the morning of April 5, Dad was still fretting about all the things that could go wrong.

So many things keep popping to the top of my mind-- things I can't do anything about. For instance, my papers aren't back yet; when will you be here; where are you now, and the little wordless jigs that like to pop up with those. Odd-- when you write these down, they don't seem so big, do they?

***

Although it is not mentioned in Mom's correspondence with Dad, somewhere along the line she had written to her mother Sarah North back in Chicago requesting that a wedding gown be ordered as quickly as possible from her favorite dress shop in Chicago and shipped to her APO address. At the time, Mom's sister Louise was not quite 14, but already was about the same size as her. Aunt Louise later remembered their mother now taking her to this Chicago dress shop where she herself was measured for Mom's gown.

***

On March 9 Mom was taken aback when another nurse from the 45th asked about legally changing her name.

Tonight Jeanie [Hall] asked me if I was going to change my name officially before the war was over. Her question amazed me 'cause I never considered it before, but I think I will even if it involves much red tape. You'd like that, wouldn't you? It will be thrilling to be writing Dunn three times on the envelope. Ever since she mentioned it, I've been swept to the clouds and am not completely back to earth yet.

By March 13 Dad was beginning to sound a bit frazzled.

And you're going to be here sometime after April 7th. This is staggering! Everything rushes me at once-- Reg, Marge, Louise, Chaplain, papers, cake, reception & heaven only knows the things that haven't dawned on me.

But he persevered. On March 17 he was able to announce that a best man had been lined up for the ceremony, Bob Harnish, a fellow navigator. In the same letter, Dad also reported that he had acquired a wedding ring for Mom, although he wasn't certain that it was the right size. Overall, he was now feeling more confident that everything would work out.

We even know pretty well what time we'll be married . . . where to go for the honeymoon and how to get there. And the framework for a lot of odds and ends are set up.

On March 27 he was still attending to details.

Bob and I started for town to arrange some things, and take care of practical things like shoe repair & stuff. On the way he said 'Wouldn't it be funny if Alva was there when we get back?' The fiend!

On April 7 yet another necessity was brought to Dad's attention. *The rector* [Rev. Mitchell] *was in tonight. In all our plans it turns out we still need someone to pump the organ.*

***

In Wotton-under-Edge, my parent's friends were closely following developments. On April 17 Mom reported having just received new letters from both the Sims and Breadmans, letters that had been hand-delivered to her in Germany by other personnel from the 45th who were just now returning from 30-day leaves in England. Mom took satisfaction in observing . . . *All Wotton seems excited about our wedding, as am I.*

***

Maddeningly slow mail deliveries continued to make things difficult. On March 27 Dad received letters from Mom written several weeks earlier. One caused him some momentary panic.

The earliest one today was written on the 3ʳᵈ and said you were leaving for here in exactly a week, and you were taking a furlough now because so much could happen between now and June. Of course, that was sent from Belgium, but it had me breathless. I'll bet it was a very long moment before I realized that you hadn't left for UK and were still 'over there.'

Indeed, right up until near the actual day of Mom's departure for England, it remained unclear exactly when her leave would go into effect.

Remember, let me know, as soon as you find out, when you will be over; and, if you can't send a letter quick enough, I think your local Red Cross can send a cable to Red Cross Director-- 96ᵗʰ Bomb Group. That's the big thing that has us stumped-- where to get reservations [for Mom prior to the wedding]. If that fails, give a buzz as soon as you can; the extension is 89. If that's busy, I'm sure the lads here will dig me up for you.

Look at the traveling you're going to have to do. It's better than any story I ever dreamed of. Oh-- if it's possible, I want to come down to London to meet you. . . . I'm practically laughing with excitement-- it really shakes me-- Wow!!

Honestly-- I can't write any more now. I need to take a deep breath.

So happy-- <u>so</u> in love,
<u>*Ricky*</u>

Mom, too, worried about last minute glitches. On March 30 she wrote from Bad Honnef in western Germany.

Your letter came tonight telling about your anticipation of the visit to the Cathedral the next day. And all of a sudden it occurred to me how very disappointed <u>we</u> both would be if I can't get to England. You know the war is progressing very rapidly; and we are now a good way in, making England further away. Just be prepared to accept it, if I can't get a leave; and I'll try to do the same. It would be a bitter pill to digest though.

Four days later, it seemed as if Mom's fears were about to be realized.

3 April 1945
Germany

Darling,

This note I dread writing. We'll be on the move again, this time <u>so far</u> that I'm very much afraid [that] leaves to England will be cancelled. <u>There is nothing official yet</u>, but it nearly breaks my heart to have the plans we made spoiled. Yet it means that the war here is that much closer to the end; so I would have it no other way; and I'm sure you feel the same.

Mom was right. The 45ᵗʰ Evacuation Hospital did move again, this time to Bad Wildungen. She continued to worry that all leaves would be cancelled. And she continued to look for ways to improve communications with Dad. On April 6 she thought that perhaps such a way had been found.

Among the slightly wounded patients was a . . . flyer, who had been shot down over Germany . . . and now evacuated to our hospital. I gave him a message to give to you; it will probably get to you before this letter will.

Dad also continued to fret. In his April 7 letter he returned to the problem of how to coordinate everything. *Don't you <u>dare</u> come before the seventeenth now. I don't see how your papers can be valid before the first of May, but I'm worrying until then.* On the other hand, at least he now had a better idea of where she was. Given the Allies' growing military ascendancy and the commensurately reduced need for censorship, it now was possible for Dad to ascertain the 45th Evacuation Hospital's current location from publicly available sources.

1950 Sunday evening
8 April 1945
Dearest Gina:
Everything seems to be in a roseate glow tonight because again I know where you are; and along with all the places you have been, this little Rhine town [Bad Wildungen] *will have its very own meaning with me.*
The Stars and Stripes came, too, with the handy little map on the back page. I have a special pin put in the big war [room] *map on the wall.*

On April 11 Dad received Mom's April 3 letter cautioning that all leaves might be cancelled. His response was stoic.

On of these [recently received] *letters brought* [illegible] *warning that you might not be able to return to England. I have been preparing for just that. Oh, not that I can come to Germany for a week, but somehow not to make the disappointment seem so harsh to you. I haven't said anything about that possibility before, but I had been thinking of it exactly as you had.*

By now Dad was grasping the irony that good news about the military situation was potentially bad news for their wedding plans.

15 April 1945
Dearest Gina:
The sergeant just brought in your letter of April 3 telling that you are about to move again. Of course, it was no surprise, really-- watching the Ruhr collapse and the [Allied] *armies moving incredibly forward from the Rhine; I had been rather waiting for such news. But, in spite of it's being expected, it <u>is</u> a blow; and it gives a very numb feeling all over.*
I am thinking of how <u>you</u> must feel, and I know that your real anxiety is not for yourself. Honestly-- if we can't be married in England-- wouldn't you say that much wisdom is at work? It seems that, wherever and whenever we become Mr. & Mrs. . . . it will be right in every way.

In the meantime I shall try to live toward that 'right,' and being yours and having you; I count myself with gods and not with men.

I love you
<u>*Ricky*</u>

He need not have worried. Wheels were turning. On this same day, the 45th Evacuation Hospital issued a memorandum again granting Mom a leave. This memo was stamped as "received" on April 17 and approved by Gen. Courtney Hodges' at U.S. 1st Army Headquarters on April 18. Yet Mom had already gotten wind of all this by April 14. Needless to say, she was exceedingly relieved. She could feel confident that the English wedding and honeymoon arrangements that Dad had made would now go forward.

Oh, I'm just bursting with happiness tonight. Today, I was informed that I am to leave for England on the 24th of this month.

When I came to my senses, the first thing I did was to send a cablegram through the Red Cross as you directed; now that I actually have a leave, I simply can't come down to earth-- dreaming an planning. Just think, in ten days--

As yet I don't know who to thank for the leave, because I did try several possibilities; and one must have worked, 'cause I'm the only one in the unit to receive one.

A day later she added

Received some wonderful news; it's possible that I may be able to leave for England on the 19th; that's only four days from now. Wouldn't it be wonderful if by next week we'd be together? I won't believe I have a leave until I'm on the way.

On April 19 Mom's commanding officer issued a memorandum authorizing her military flight arrangements from Germany back to England. The first word at the top of this memo is "restricted." Why the Army would want to restrict information associated with my parents' wedding plans is hard to imagine. It is true that Hitler and his Propaganda Minister Joseph Goebbels were still holding out in a bunker below the Chancellery building in Berlin. It is also true that what little remained of the Nazi regime would continue to resist for another couple of weeks. However, even if the Germans knew that my parents were taking some time off from their military duties, I doubt that this would have given them much additional hope.

On April 20 Dad wrote his last letter prior to the wedding. In it he reported having just seen the movie *When Irish Eyes Are Smiling*. It was an appropriate title-- both Dad and Mom claimed Irish heritage on their respective mothers' sides.

18
WEDDING & HONEYMOON

On April 21, 1945 Mom's military air transport flight landed at Biggin Hill, an RAF base in the London area. Here Dad had arranged for a smaller military transport to fly them both on her final leg to Snetterton Heath. Not mentioned in the letters is an anecdote Mom would share in later years. Gen. Archie Old was commanding officer of the 45th Combat Wing, the unit to which Dad was now attached. It seems that Gen. Old had made arrangements for an engagement party at the base's officers club. According to Mom, when she arrived for this event she was taken aback to discover that she was the only female present. And, to make things even more awkward, Dad had so much to drink that he promptly fell asleep. Consequently he was in no condition to discourage other officers from flirting with his fiancé. Mom later professed to have been mortified by this turn of events, suggesting that the other officers in attendance had intentionally encouraged Dad to drink too much. However, while she never admitted as much to me, she was secretly flattered to be the center of all this male attention.

***

St. Andrew's Anglican Church is located near Snetterton Heath in the hamlet of Quidenham. Dad would later characterize St. Andrew's as already being old 600 years earlier. This is where the ceremony would be held. Back on March 25 Dad had described for Mom the Airman's Chapel inside St. Andrew's that had been dedicated in November of the previous year.

Palm Sunday today. Chapel was jammed. Easter Sunday is going to be a sunrise service in the chapel [that] the base has built in the local church. There is a special stained glass window commemorating the airmen.

The Airman's Chapel in St. Andrew's church, Quidenham,
Courtesy of Mr. Dan Shields.

***

On a Tuesday, April 24 the wedding did go forward. This arrangement was made in such haste that none of Mom's compatriots with the 45th Evacuation Hospital in Germany were able to attend. Nor did the wedding dress Mom had ordered from a dress shop in Chicago arrive in time. Consequently, Mom was obliged to walk down the aisle wearing her 1st lieutenant's uniform. About 100 flying officers from the 96th Bomb Group were in attendance. But other than Mom herself, the only other woman present was an employee of the base's Red Cross Office. The same Rev. Mitchell who had helped Dad make the arrangements also conducted the ceremony. Gen. Old assumed the role of father-of-the-bride. Dad's fellow navigator Bob Harnish stood as best man. Immediately afterward, Mom and Dad posed for a professional photographer outside the Airmen's Chapel entrance.

Outside St. Andrew' church immediately after the ceremony.

The wedding party and guests then retreated back to the air base where a modest reception was held.

***

As it turned out, no one from either the Sims or Breadman households attended the wedding, no doubt due in part to the lingering uncertainty about the ceremony's actual date. Indeed, because the wedding was held on a Thursday, Jeannie, at least, would have had to be taken out in school. Perhaps, too, the travel and lodging expenses were a further deterrent. In any event, subsequent correspondence sheds no light on why no one from Wotton came. Nevertheless, they did send congratulatory telegrams from Wotton-under-Edge that morning. All were addressed to

CAPT AND MRS. CHARLES DUNN 0=789764 96 BOMB GROUP 413

BOMBER SQD 45 COMBAT WING APO 559 USARMY.

The first was wired at 8:56 AM by Fred Breadman's parents, who were the proprietors of a local public house in Wotton called "The Rising Sun," a public house being a sort of small tavern operating in the living room of an otherwise ordinary home.

ALL BEST WISHES FROM THE RISING SUN

The second was sent a minute later by the Sims. [On this message it was the telegraph operator who misspelled Marjory's name.]

CONGRATULATIONS AND BEST WISHES FOR THE FUTURE
REG MARGERY[sic]

Immediately after the Sims' message, a third telegram came from Fred and Phyllis Breadman.

MAY ALL OF YOUR TROUBLES BE LITTLE ONES FRED PHYL AND FAMILY

***

By May 11 Mom had been back in Germany for more than a week. On that day she finally received her first post-wedding letter from Dad. She replied immediately.

> *Mr. Gallagher, 'darling'--*
> *Your first letter since we've been Mr. & Mrs. .Gallagher! and I'm oh so happy to have received it 'cause I've been longing to hear from you.*
> *I am very fond of our 'cutting the cake picture' . . . .*

Cutting the wedding cake.

Following the reception, Dad and Mom had proceeded to London by car. According to my brother Bob, Mom once told him that Gen. Old had made his London apartment available to them as their honeymoon suite. Needless to say, during the honeymoon itself there was no need for correspondence. No letters at all were exchanged between April 21 and May 1. However, Dad's first letter afterward does provide some details. On May 2 he asked: *Say-- did you know we started on our way to London with some cans tied to the car? I don't remember hearing them at all-- or anything else.*

What is certain about the honeymoon, however, is that at some point Mom and Dad traveled from London back to Wotton-under-Edge to say hello to the Sims and the Breadmans. There is no reference to this side trip in any of their later correspondence. But many years later, sometime during my own teenage years, I once happened to tell Mom that I did not particularly care for the boiled asparagus she had prepared for the evening meal. Mom glared at me as the ungrateful son that I doubtless was. But she verbally responded only with another of her wartime anecdotes. It began with her account of how she and Dad, during their honeymoon, had traveled back to Wotton because she herself had not been there since June of the previous year. Upon their arrival, the Sims served them a special honeymoon dinner that included lamb chops and asparagus. Mom said that she and Dad were particularly appreciative because so many consumer items were then being rationed. Fresh meat and produce were particularly hard to come by. They understood that Marjory Sims had been able to prepare such a meal only by hoarding her ration coupons in anticipation of their wedding.

My only other insight into the honeymoon comes from some tiny photographs. These first came to my attention when I began sifting through the contents of Mom's footlocker. Several images, taken at a photography studio in London, were in the same envelope as the first letter Dad sent to Mom following her return to Germany. About these photos Dad commented . . . *Well, here they are-- ain't they fine, and aren't we the lovingest pair!* On May 21 he added . . . *I like the laughing one as well as any of them. . . . In the smiling one I look like a goof.*

Mom and Dad, April 28, 1945.

Upon receiving the photos, Mom was undecided as to whether larger copies of these portraits should be ordered. On May 30 she wrote

> . . . I'd best be practical and answer your questions about the proofs. I liked the smiling one best, too. But they hardly seem 10 [pounds] worth. If we could get one or two prints it would be fine; but as I recall, it seems you have to buy the whole works. I suppose the finished pictures would be better than the proofs, and

182

they would be nice to have. Oh shucks, I don't know what to advise you to do. If we were both sure of being in the States before long, it would be better to wait.

When Mom' leave expired, she was required to return to her nursing duties in Germany. For the return flight her military transport plane departed from Croydon south of London. Of course Dad accompanied her to the airport. Afterward, his letter dated May 2 describes her departure-- and his feelings.

We [?] left Croydon shortly after you entered the plane. They had all the baggage in, and I still couldn't catch a glimpse of you-- the others were waiting for me. It wasn't till I got back to our little 'home' that it really hit me that you were gone. I'm glad you were spared the sight of the empty room and wardrobes and the tousled things-- all mine. It was truly poignant.

***

By the summer of 1945, censorship restrictions had been relaxed. Dad was now reasonably free to describe routine military activities. His letter of June 19, for example, indicates his admiration for Gen. Old.

The general returned from the continent today. He's visiting other headquarters and doing a fair measure of sight seeing using Weimar as a base. Buchenwald, Nordhausen, Halle, . . . a 400-mile trip in a borrowed staff car. Then an aerial tour & return in his personal P-51 [escort fighter]. He's a gutsy character.

By July 10 Mom had been back in Germany for more than two months. On that day she responded to information from Dad that *the General* would soon be departing from Snetterton Heath. She wrote: *Let me know when the General leaves and his new outfit so I can drop him a 'thank you' note. He has been very kind to us.*
On July 27, Dad agreed that she should write to Gen. Old and thank him for all of his kindnesses on their behalf.

No one knows Gen. Old's new assignment, & he may remain unassigned for some time. His home address is simply Brig. Gen. ARCHIE J. OLD, ATLANTA, TEXAS. I'm sure he'd be pleased as punch with a note.

19

A TUMULTUOUS WEEK

When Mom flew to England to marry Dad, her unit, the 45th Evacuation Hospital, was just then redeploying from Bad Wildungen in Germany to Nohra in the same country. By the time Mom returned to the 45th on May 2, 1945, it had been reassigned again, this time to the recently liberated concentration camp at nearby Buchenwald where tens of thousands of innocent people has perished during the Holocaust. The unit's male personnel-- physicians, medical technicians and orderlies-- worked at Buchenwald from at least May 1 to May 8. Indeed, according to Hyman Lebson's narrative, the 45th began accepting Buchenwald survivors as patients as early as April 28,[lxxii] midway through Mom's English honeymoon.

However, the 45th's female personnel were not allowed to share in this work. According to Robert Roberts "This was the first time our nurses did not accompany us, so the task we were undertaking put a very heavy load on the doctors and enlisted personnel, who remained."[lxxiii] Lt. Lebson's account agrees.

> The nurses did not see duty during this operation. When the Unit left Nohra [for Buchenwald], the nurses moved into the city of Weimar. A large home, reported to have been the residence of one of the Nazi party chiefs in Weimar, was requisitioned for their use.[lxxiv]

***

By May 4 Mom had been back with her fellow nurses in Weimar for a couple of days. In her second letter since her return, she observed . . . *in order to have my name changed, I must have a copy of our marriage certificate, and then the changing procedure is comparatively simple.*

***

As Buchenwald and other concentration camps were being liberated, Gen. Dwight Eisenhower, commander of all Allied forces in the ETO, issued an order that the local townspeople nearest each of these camps be required to view what had occurred nearby. At Buchenwald Robert Roberts was assigned the task of leading such guided tours.

> The people from the city of Weimar were led through the camp. I was designated as a guide to lead groups through. Almost to the last person they declared that they were not aware of what was going on here. [This claim] . . . was unbelievable to me as trains and vehicles had to pass through the town on the way to the camp. This had been going on for years. 60,000 persons lost their lives here in Buchenwald.[lxxv]

Despite not being assigned any duties in the camp, Mom would later claim that she had nonetheless chosen to join one of the tours, thus witnessing its horrors for herself. This is confirmed in one of her letters, albeit circumspectly. Perhaps-- as with her previous excursions in January to Jodoigne and in March to Bad Honnef-- Mom did not want to alarm Dad by acknowledging the additional danger of venturing beyond the 45th

Evacuation Hospital's security area. After all, as of May 6 Mom could not have known that the Germans would capitulate within 48 hours. From her vantage point, leaving the relative safety of the nurses' quarters to tour such a camp raised the possibility of enemy intervention. Given this risk, perhaps her letter afterward deliberately downplayed the horror of what she had witnessed. Perhaps, too, having just returned from her honeymoon, Mom was so enamored of her new status that even a concentration camp tour could not dampen the marital bliss. If so, then the enormity of what she was witnessing did not fully register until later. Because of ongoing wartime censorship, the letter in question does not actually use the word *Buchenwald*. Still, it is dated May 6, well within the time frame of the 45th Evacuation Hospital's presence there. Moreover, it does specifically acknowledge that she had just toured a concentration camp.

> *Today I went to Hqs. to get a typhus shot, hand in my marriage papers, and get a few items at the post office. So I looked around the concentration camp somewhat. It is grim indeed. I felt relieved that I hadn't seen it at its ghastly stage, when it was first taken over by the Americans.*

Aunt Louise later spoke to me of Mom of what once shared with her. In particular, Mom described to Louise how some men in her unit, men who had considered themselves inured to the horrors of war, were so nauseated during the . . . *ghastly stage* . . . of preliminary cleanup that they now became physically ill. Lt. Lebson's description of the camp renders this credible.

> Within camp Buchenwald could be found all of the sights and horrors so often described. The Crematorium, the camp 'hospital,' the whipping posts, the living quarters of the inmates, the laboratory with a 'museum' displaying results of cruel, senseless experiments on human beings were all there to be seen.[lxxvi]

Sgt. Roberts reported on a particularly gruesome aspect of the camp.

> One building in the compound housed lampshades made from the skin of tattooed inmates, made by Ilsa Koch, the German Commandant's wife who was referred to as 'The Witch of Buchenwald.'[lxxvii]

***

V-E [Victory in Europe] Day was first announced on May 7th 1945. In a letter written that morning, Dad described some initial reactions to the news.

> *V-E day is upon us. I bet the crowing here is a mere twaddle compared to what goes on over there* [in Germany]. *You should hear the GIs. The most despondent are those who have just come back from pass, and are now too broke to raise the riot they have been planning so eagerly.*

That same evening he wrote a second letter. With what now seems to me to be remarkable foresight, this latter message predicted that the British would adapt to whatever the future might hold with more equanimity than would the Americans.

We're loafing tonight-- a bit rebellious against the blackout and the sobriety of everything. The war against Germany is over; and there is exaltation, the sigh of pausing in mid-furrow. It is so far a mere statement of fact. The beginning of the war seems so long ago. Yet the dead are by our sides. They will be young always. It is so easy for them to fade in hearts at home that have not scarred. I envy England. She will be sober and mindful-- we will jump into the lap of peace like a waggish puppy.

The next day the celebrations began. Perhaps because he was now all the more worried about the possibility of being transferred to the Pacific Theatre-- or perhaps because he was something of a stuffed shirt-- Dad did not entirely approve.

A day of pageantry, speeches and music of victory-- Churchill, the King, Monty [British Field Marshall Bernard Montgomery], Eisenhower, the great, and a few of the little people of the war. Tomorrow the base lets go with speeches and parades. Tonight we have fireworks; last night-- ah, there was a time. Everything went [up in flames] including all of the haystacks in the area. You could call it vandalism without stretching it a bit.

***

Throughout the war Dad remained a keen observer of world events. Three days before the actual surrender, he had already seen it coming and began weighing its personal significance.

The news floods in. Its very certainty can hardly dim its welcome. The total end must be very near. It makes this news all the more interesting. A broad policy covering the disposition of the European Air Forces has been set forth from Washington. It is to be realized as soon as possible after hostilities are over here. We are to be divided broadly into three groups. Those with the least service will be returned to the States for leave and Pacific assignments. Personnel with neither the most nor the least overseas service will make up the occupational air force. Those with the most service including service in Africa [which included Dad] will be returned to the States, with minor exceptions, as soon as possible. Long months of waiting, regardless of category, are to be expected.

It seems that the Pacific is very remote for me and chances of returning to the States the very best. Remember the last time we parted before D-Day? Even then you were confident it would not be for too long. We have infinitely more to cherish now.

In his morning letter on V-E Day, he was also looking ahead for Mom.

I've been reading the S&S and pondering how the demobbing [demobilizing] plan will deal with you. At best it seems you might be flown to the States. It's easy to forget that all the stuff they print hardly applies to the officers who are disposed according to military necessity.

186

That evening he returned to his own future.

> *Already 'the wheels' are busy exploring the angles. Whether to obtain . . . transfer to this unit or that and the best moves to shoot for. The opportunism of the Air Force is boundless.*

For now at least, Dad could emphasize the positive. Pending any future redeployed to the fight against Japan, both he and Mom had survived. In the conclusion to his morning letter, he was philosophical.

> *At least we have our stretch of sunny days again. The fields are white with blossoms; the whole earth stretches sweetly in the sun. Imagine the land to be home with people in the pursuit of normalcy, peace, and happiness. It is odd to think that the trees will give the same shade, and the fields will be no more fertile than before.*

Still, the possibility of eventual redeployment to the Pacific War remained a shadow hovering over their future. Even Dad's adoptive mother Helen Dunn back in Massachusetts could sense the potential danger. The very next day she drafted a V-Mail to her new daughter-in-law. In it she suggested that the relief she felt because they were no longer in a war zone was tempered by uncertainty about their respective military futures. "Dear Alva, Now that Germany has surrendered, my very first thought is where will Willard [Dad] and Alva be going next: home, I hope."

That same day Dad admonished Mom to accept any opportunity to go home.

> *If we [his AAF unit] are held for occupational duties, it will probably mean being sent to the continent. So far there is no sign of how we'll be employed, but scoot for the States if you can.*

***

On the evening of May 7, the same day in which the impending German capitulation was preliminarily announced, Mom received news that Peter Vickery had been killed in a flying accident. Since June of the previous year Peter had been attached to the RAF's No. 43 Squadron then conducting operations in the Mediterranean area, mostly in Italy. However, in mid-January of 1945 Peter himself returned to the United Kingdom. On February 26 he was re-assigned to the RAF's No. 595 Squadron located at Aberporth, Wales. However, on April 5, 1945, less than three weeks before my parents' wedding, he was killed in a flying accident. A few days later he was buried in the All Saints Churchyard Extension of the Anglican Church in his home community of Sanderstead, just south of Central London. At his funeral

> . . . the C.O. of 595 Squadron was present. Floral tributes were sent by the Officers' Mess and Sergeants' Mess of 595 Squadron. Flight-Lieut. Vicary [sic] was highly thought of his fellow officers and very popular in all circles."[lxxviii]

The inscription on his gravestone reads:

PROUD MEMORY OF
OUR DEAR AND ONLY SON
FL. LT. J. P. VICKERY
R.A.F.V.R.
43rd SQUADRON
APRIL 5th 1945
AGED 24
TODAY AND ALWAYS IN OUR THOUGHTS

Twelve days after the crash, a Ms. Doreen Paddock wrote a brief letter to Mom informing her of Peter's death.

> The Croft
> Limpsfield Rd
> Sanderstead
> Surrey, Eng.
> 17 April 1945

Dear Alva,
  You will be sorry to hear that Peter has been killed in a flying accident. Mrs. Vickery herself is too ill to write at the present, so she has asked me to do so for her. I have enclosed the article [obituary] from the Croyden Advertiser. Mrs. Vickery hopes that you & all your people are keeping well.

> Yours very sincerely,
> Doreen Paddock

Judging from the letter's perspective and familiar tone-- Mom is addressed as "Alva" rather than Lt. North-- this was a neighbor of the Vickery family. Indeed, if Peter had once brought Mom to meet his parents, this might explain why his mother now felt obligated to inform Mom of her son's passing.

  In later years, when Mom and Dad were experiencing marital difficulties, I once asked her-- given Dad's alleged shortcomings-- why she had married him in the first place. She had replied rather cruelly-- or so I thought at the time-- that she had married Dad only because her other suitor was no longer available. While Mom had intended this remark as a bit of dark humor, circumstances mitigate against the possibility that it was true. For one thing, Mom and Dad had been making their own wedding plans since February, two month before Peter's fatal crash or Ms. Paddock's letter. For another, Mom did not learn that of Peter's death until after the wedding. Not until May 7, five days after returning from her English honeymoon, did Mom report . . . *in the mail tonight was the news that Peter Vickery has been killed. It happened last month. The news came from his home.* This was her only direct mention of Peter anywhere in her entire wartime correspondence. Could she have feigned ignorance of Peter's death until after the wedding? This is not likely. Given the date on the return address, Ms. Paddock's letter to Mom was posted no earlier than April 17. Meanwhile, beginning on April 21 Mom was in England for her wedding and honeymoon rather than with her unit back in Germany. So there was only a four-day window for Ms. Paddock's letter to be delivered to Mom in Germany before her own departure for the wedding. Even with hostilities winding down, it generally took a week or more for mail posted in England to reach

188

Mom on the Continent.   Moreover, while in England, Mom's incoming mail back in Germany was not forwarded.   So Ms. Paddock's letter was almost certainly either waiting for Mom in Weimar when she returned from the honeymoon on May 2 or belatedly delivered on May 7 as Mom claimed.

On May 15, as soon as he heard the sad news from Mom, Dad responded.

My Beloved:
The first letter [to be delivered to Dad] *since you left England & I came this noon and with it the news of Peter's death. I'm quite sure I felt about it quite the same as you did-- it has been a saddened day.*

***

On May 10 the wedding gown that Mom ordered from a dress shop in Chicago belatedly reached her in Germany.

You will never guess what the mailman brought tonight, a wedding gown-- oh, and is it beautiful! White satin and net with a <u>long</u> *train. I felt a little like crying 'cause my mother must have wanted me to have a gown to be married in. As soon as the opportunity arises, I'll have pictures taken in it before sending it home.*
I tried the whole works on and sailed around the house with Jeanne [Hall] *carrying the train, it fit perfectly. You would have liked me to have worn it, too.*

The next evening she added

Tonight I have had more offers to have people take pictures of me in that wedding gown, without soliciting, by the way; so when I can get up the courage, it will be done.

The day after that, several of Mom's friends in the 45th Evacuation Hospital took several snapshots, two of which are reproduced here.

Dear Ricky
Today I had 'beaucoup' [many] *pictures taken by many, so at least one should turn out well. It took about two hours to press the dress and veil.*

Mom certainly does look beautiful in these informal photos. They show that she was wearing a gown with high shoulders. No doubt she had chosen this style to hide the scars on her back, scarring which had inadvertently resulted from her application back in January of a skin ointment to protect from a possible German chemical attack.

However, to the best of my knowledge, Dad never had the opportunity to actually see his bride wearing the gown. Still, he did soon receive several of the photographs. Of course he was pleased.

Dearest Gina:
Oh boy! It is worthwhile to come back to the base. You see your 'wedding' pictures are here . . ., and they enslaved me completely. You've the most adoring

Mom posing for pictures in the back yard of a local Nazi chief's house, Weimar, May 12, 1945.

Mom in her wedding gown, May 12, 1945.

smile and then the happiest face-- and the gown-- it's beautiful. How I should have like to have seen you wearing it. When we get back to the States, let's get married all over again.

To be truthful, I've been more than a little absorbed in the fantasy of imagining that you are smiling thinking of the happiness these would give me when they came. It makes it seem more than ever that you are very proud, and I am standing there watching them being taken (feeling very proud & happy too).

20
ARMY OF OCCUPATION

Upon returning from her honeymoon, Mom continued her nursing duties with the 45th Evacuation hospital. After V-E day, however, her letters make less reference to her colleagues within the 45th Evacuation Hospital than before. About the other nurses they say nothing at all. Regarding Rev. Zinz, Mom's last reference to him was in a letter written from Germany on May 6. By that time he had stopped over in Wotton-under-Edge, apparently on his way back to the United States. While there, he had called on Mrs. Elliott, the Englishwoman in whose house he had once been billeted. But Dad was unaware that the Reverend was back in England. Shortly afterward, Dad learned from Reg Sims of the Reverend's recent presence in Wotton. His letter to Mom of July 8 laments a missed opportunity. *Chappie had been in Wotton & stayed with the Elliott's. I wish he had called.*

Now that she was married, Mom felt more secure about her relationship with Dad. Perhaps for that reason she felt less need to maintain other close human connections. After V-E day the only Army figure to receive extensive attention in her letters was Capt. Sachs. On May 16 the 45th Evacuation Hospital was still at Nohra near both the Buchenwald concentration camp and the historic city of Weimar. Her letter that day describes how

> *Capt. Sachs and I walked at least eight miles. We set our goal as Bismark's* [sic] [former German chancellor Otto von Bismarck] *monument. The nicest part of the walk was a remark Capt. Sachs made. It was this-- I hope my wife talks about me as much as you do about Charlie.*
>
> *I pondered on this statement and discovered that, if I talk about you as much (to some people), its because you are in my mind . . . so very much.*

While Mom may now have felt less need for her Army friends, Dad now felt less willing to tolerate them-- or at least those who he may have viewed as potential rivals. For instance, on June 8 Mom mentioned . . . *Captain Sachs said he'd written to you the other day; he was going to enclose a picture of Rusty* [his young son]; *but I forgot to ask if he did.*

On that same day, Dad did in fact receive Capt. Sachs' letter. And it did indeed include the picture of Rusty. According to Dad, Captain Sachs' letter described how Mom was doing at the Hospital following her return from her honeymoon. Dad's response was ungracious. He claimed that Capt. Sachs' letter . . . *shook me unaccountably.* His then claimed . . . *I don't feel jealous a bit . . . .* But he was.

Sensing a new undercurrent of hostility toward Capt. Sachs, Mom tried on June 20 to calm Dad.

> *Your 'with Captain Sachs' letter arrived, and I feel very ashamed that my letter to you brought so little joy. But may I add this, that I have no <u>real joy</u> or <u>real fun</u> with anyone else, <u>only</u> you.*

***

On May 23 Dad sent Mom, who was at Nohra in Germany, a brief and otherwise inconsequential letter. However, attached was another poem. Entitled *Perseverance*, it is three stanzas in length and, unlike his previous efforts, written in a traditional A-B rhyme scheme.

Perseverance
Flower in your plot so vast
Fiery shadow thou hast cast.
Spear of grass-- trefoil clover
Hem thee tight and bear thee over;
Giving only room to such
Whose stature threatens lessers much.

Not afar the lofty oak
Serenely gathers shady cloak;
Sweeps it round ' fore burning sun;
Cool caress for everyone.
Mind not stir of ' scordant ranks;
Spread thy tiny arm-- give thanks.

Wanderer with 'scerning eye
Shall thy lowly spot descry;
Stand mid baser tangle dense,
'Tranced by thy white radiance.
Mightily his heart is awed
Thou are eloquent of God.

From Germany, Mom immediately acknowledged receipt of the new poem.

29 May 1945
A bright sunny afternoon

Mon Cheri . . . .

The second verse was especially touching. Did you have the oak in the field [that] *you showed me in mind when you wrote that verse? I liked the way the lofty oak serenely gathered his shady cloak and so obviously offered all a cool caress, yet your little flower needn't mind cause it was cloaked in eloquence, radiant in giving thanks and indirectly to mightily awe the wanderer.*

The more I read it, the various impressions I have change and grow deeper. Poetry was intended by the poet to impart a definite meaning as an artist intends to impart a definite beauty in a picture; yet the longer one looks at a picture, different ideas are created and so with your poem. Were you conscious of all its possible interpretations as you wrote it?

'Mightily his heart is awed
Thou art eloquent of god.'

So am I awed-- I love it and you.

Toujours [Always],
Gina

P.S. Five weeks today.

***

Because redeployment to the Pacific Theatre remained a real possibility, Dad was obliged to keep his military skills sharp by periodically completing a certain number of flying hours. On June 2 he described having flown

> *. . . all afternoon to get in my flying time for the month. None of the others [crew members on the B-17] had any place in particular to go, so we toured most of southern England with special emphasis on Wotton, which we circled several times. I don't think we attracted any attention there because buzzing or just ordinary low flying is strictly to be avoided these days. A major I know got socked $2400 for one case of the latter, among others.*

***

On June 6, 1945 Mom was remembering what had occurred exactly one year earlier.

> *Today should be celebrated, as they say 'D-day +365.' It's been a long year, and If only you don't ever have to fly combat anymore. I never look back to last summer that I don't thing first of the bombing of St. Lo and watching the German ack-ack.*

In mid-July, Mom's unit was at Schwabisch Hall in Germany. At this location she and the other nurses found themselves living in a tent, just like the early days back in Normandy.

> *16 July, 1945*
> *Schwabishe [sic] Hall*
> *8:10 P.M.*
>
> *Darling,*
> *If only you could see the dilemma we're in tonight. Our tent is so old, and it is raining. Can you picture what happened? Not only did the tent leak, but it fell in on me.*
> *We've everything crowed in the center of the tent and covered with innumerable blankets to keep dry.*

This experience reminded her of battles in northern France a year earlier.

> *Strange that . . . a year ago any inconvenience of a tent wasn't thought of because we were so completely absorbed in a task. And, too, it was St. Lo, and about the 17th of July was a certain bombing raid.*
> *I'm so grateful for you and for your safely.*

***

On May 27, a quiet Sunday evening, Dad described a post-V-E Day conversation at his base.

A terrific argument is going on-- and on & on-- about what we should have done in the war and about making a career out of the army [AAF]. Everyone from major on up seems to be sold on it. I feel very much apart from them & very much with you.

By mid-summer of 1945 European hostilities had long since ended. Dad's Bomb Group had little to do except await new orders. On July 19 he wrote

The hour's drill this morning. . . was the first drill I've had since being a cadet. I used to fancy myself a bit as a soldier then (typical cadet cockiness), but the accumulated divergence from the mask of the military sprang out all at once. The army-- ughh!

The next day he again commented on the possibility of making the Army Air Force a lifetime career choice.

Dearest:

Today was evaluation day for the officers, and we were asked if we desired a commission in the regular army. One adjutant may have been a recruiting sergeant early in his career because he thinks that a young fellow is a damn fool not to stay in the Army, particularly so if he is on flying status. As he puts it-- 'Where in h--l are you going to step into a job at $100 per?' Yet, when I look into the faces and minds of most whose life has been the Army . . . that scares me more.

21
A NEW BROTHER-IN-LAW

The only member of Dad's birth family described in his wartime letters is his oldest brother Benjy, who was then Capt. Benjamin Moeller, an Army surgeon. Dad's first mention of *Benjy* in his correspondence on February 18, 1944. *Had a* [belatedly delivered] *Xmas card from my brother today. Here it is. Alberta is his wife. He really calls her Bertie. A swell brother. Older & soberer. Loving.* By the time Mom's unit landed in France in June of 1944, it had been well over a year since Dad and Uncle Benjy had met up back in Africa. The North African campaign had long since been completed. Many Army units that had been stationed on that continent had now been redeployed to Italy. In an undated letter to Mom that must have been written in mid 1944, Dad reported that he . . . *Learned today that my brother is in Italy. Gave me a real start. Somehow I'd pictured him safely tucked away in Africa.* On August 19 Dad received a letter from Benjy. It included . . . *this picture taken at* [illegible] *where he was sent for a rest. He's much more serious looking than I. I'm always Mickey to him* ["Mickey" being Dad's Moeller family nickname].

With the Mediterranean Sea now largely under Allied control, on August 15, 1944 an amphibious invasion of Southern France called Operation Dragoon was launched. Uncle Benjy was soon part of that campaign. Moreover, Uncle Benjy was now providing Dad with updates on his situation. On November 22 Dad noted . . . *I have heard my brother was in France. So, you see I'm anxious about the north and south of the Western front. That's no picnic either.*

All this meant that Benjy and Mom, who had been serving all along as members of the same Army Medical Corps, were now both in the same country as well, albeit hundreds of miles apart. There was a real possibility that their paths might soon cross.

By early 1945 Mom had survived the Battle of the Bulge. It would be another two months before the Allied Armies would cross the Rhine River and enter central Germany, but the end of European hostilities was in sight. Was it now possible to travel about for personal reasons on the American side of the battle lines? On February 12, 1945 Mom suggested to Dad . . . *if your brother should ever be in this vicinity, invite him to visit the 45th; it would be very nice meeting him-- or would you rather introduce us?*

***

A message directly from Benjy finally reached Mom at Nohra near Weimar on May 18. It indicated that he knew of my parents' engagement but not their actual wedding, which had occurred about three weeks earlier. Still, Mom was impressed by its tone.

> *Benjy's letter was so warm and friendly. It was dated the 6th of May. He wanted us to let him know the approximate date of the wedding so he could be present, that is, if I didn't mind having a brother show up. It is the first time I'd really thought about acquiring a brother since we were married.*

Most of the letters from third parties to which Mom and Dad refer in their own correspondence have not been preserved. However a letter from Benjy to Dad on May 25 did make it into Mom's footlocker.

Well brother, supreme happiness for you two!

Got a letter from Gina today in answer to that 'show her what kind of a brother you are' letter. Mickey, [I] can tell by [the] tone of her letter you all have the real thing. Regardless how very much you are in love now, its just beginning. You two will be more so each day.

On May 27, when Dad heard that a message from Benjy had reached Mom on May 18, his response to Mom was . . . *I hope you will like him as much as I.*

***

On June 2 Mom's unit was still located at Nohra near Weimar, but about to move again. Her letter that day expressed the hope that this newest relocation might bring her closer to Benjy's position to the south. Five days later she wrote to Dad.

> *Today the application to change my name* [from North to Dunn] *bounced 'cause a new form is out; and one has to know where their husband is born; and I'm afraid I don't know the town you were born in. So I wrote and asked Benjy to tell me, thinking his mail* [from elsewhere in Germany] *would reach me more quickly than yours* [from back in England] . . . .

On June 10, more than 18 months since she had first met Dad, but too soon to have received a written response from Benjy to her recent query, it finally happened: Mom met someone from Dad's birth family. At 10:12 that evening she was sitting in her new living quarters at St. Wendel, Germany writing her usual letter to Dad. After drafting a page and a half, there was an interruption. When she resumed writing the next morning, an explanation was included.

> *Where I'd stop writing last night @ 10:30 pm, there was a rap on the door and a male voice asked for Lt. Alva North Dunn; guess who? Right, Benjy.*
>
> *Say, he's swell! He stayed until about 4:30 a.m. We talked and talked and talked. He came down as soon as he'd learned I was in St. Wendel; he's about 140 miles from here. I wished he could have stayed longer 'cause it would have been so nice, but he had to be on duty at 8 a.m. this morning.*
>
> *Oh, he told me you'd promised to paint the town* [New York] *red after the war with Alberta. Let's.*
>
> *Don't be surprised if he visits you in England soon, he expects to leave about the 19ᵗʰ of June.*
>
> *He saw all of your pictures; it was easy to see he thought you were pretty swell. He told me about being with you in Africa, about his honeymoon, about your sisters, about your parents, and his postwar plans, and asked questions about you and us. It was no less than wonderful.*

Two days later, she reflected on the significance of Benjy's visit, professing surprise that he and Dad seemed so much alike despite having been raised apart.

12 June 1945

Dearest,

    Last night I crawled into bed right after supper and slept until this morning; so you didn't get a letter last night; but considering that i[t] *was 'Benjy' who kept me up, I'm sure you wouldn't mind.*

    For a change I had another man on my mind today and yesterday in relation to you. He is like you more than I thought he'd be. He said he'd try to come down before I left for England, and I am hoping he can.

Three days after that, Mom added still more impressions.

    Now let's talk more about our apartment some more, which reminds me. Benjy went into detail about his 'honeymoon' and later how they fixed up their little place. It sounded like fun; evidently Alberta really made it easy. Benjy and Alberta think they are the happiest couple, but I argued that we are.

Back in England, Dad finally learned on June 20 of this family introduction. Because he was never comfortable discussing the circumstances of his childhood adoption, he now expressed the hoped that his older brother had provided Mom with information that he could not bring himself to share. Of her recent meeting with Benjy, Dad said . . . *I am glad beyond words. I know he told you many things that I could never tell. I think you have perhaps seen a bit of myself, too.*

***

On June 16 Mom learned that it was feasible for the three of them to gather in England.

    The best news today. It's possible that I may get a leave to England on the 20th of this month. Boy, are my fingers crossed-- Benjy hopes to leave for England on the 19th; so <u>perhaps</u> we three will be in England together. Won't that be exciting.

By the next day she was trying to coordinate travel plans with Benjy, writing that she was . . . *curious to know if he'll be starting for England on the 19th as a he planned.* After failing to reach Benjy by phone, she went to a movie being shown on the base that evening. Upon her return, she learned . . . *Benjy phoned while I was at the movies. The message he left was for me to go ahead, and he'll be in London on Thursday.*

    Mom herself actually made it back to England on June 22. Her time with Dad and Benjy included stops at his AAF base in Snetterton Heath, the medieval church in Quidenham where Mom and Dad had been married two months earlier, and, of course, London.

    Her leave ended on June 28, after which she was obliged to return to Germany. But Benjy was able to hang around for a couple more days. On June 30 Dad reported: *Benjy came up* [to London] *from Bournmouth to find me sound asleep in a real nap. We've been buzzing ever since.* Later in the same letter he added . . . *This time when you left, it was really something to watch you off.* He closed the letter by adding . . . *Benjy and I are going back to Snetterton tomorrow. You are always in my heart.*

    The next day Benjy and Dad also said their goodbyes.

*Benjy left on the first train this morning on his way back to London &
eventually Worms* [in Germany]. *We spent most of Saturday in London and came
back to the field yesterday evening. Actually, we didn't do very much besides
talk; but last night was full of long silences with each of us thinking his own
thoughts; and mine were curving toward you.*

By the day after, Dad was wondering if he had previously mentioned . . . *Benjy & I
stopped at 47 Grosvenor to check on your flight, but there had been no word, and they
hoped you had gone straight through to Wiesbaden.*
The first of Dad's two letters to Mom on July 4 implies that he wanted to make his
older brother's marriage a template for his own. *Think-- married ten weeks! Benjy has
an anniversary system that sounds very nice. Remind me to tell you of it-- with a kiss.*
On July 10 Dad sent Mom some photographs that had been taken during her most recent
leave in England. Again thinking of his brother, Dad now requested that Mom forward a
portion of the pictures to him . . . *the ones you think he'd be most interested in.*

Mom and Uncle Benjy at Snetterton Heath.

Dad and Uncle Benjy together.

On that same day Mom was also remembering her new brother-in-law.

Benjy should be back by now [here in Germany], *I hope that I can see him again
soon. Before I can make any plans to visit him, I'll have to wait until we've
moved. The hospital is closed and will probably move to another area to bivouac.*

By July 15 Mom was writing to Dad from yet another German location, Schwabisch Hall. For first time since her arrival in England back in 1943, the 45th Evacuation Hospital was . . . *now in a 7th Army area, so we should be getting a new APO.* She grumbled that at this new location . . . *We're quite far away from Benjy, darn it!* However, in the Army there is never a shortage of rumors. Within two days, she reported hearing a new one that the 45th would soon be moving again to either Mannheim or Heidelberg. She added . . . *If this is true, I'll be near Benjy.* On July 18 Mom recalled . . . *our second visit to Quidenham Church, and the things that Benjy said about Religion; they were few but pertinent. Remember?*

22
PREGNANCY, HOME

Paradoxically, the end of European hostilities was increasing Dad's unease about the future. His letter to Mom on May 10, 1945 offered the following advice:

Had a chance to talk with Col. Mallory for a while. There weren't any secrets tossed around, but he was interested in what was going to happen to <u>us</u> *from now on. At least one very definite thing needs to be said as a result-- if you* <u>volunteer</u> *to go anywhere, volunteer for the States. We don't know yet how we'll be moved here, but it may be very sudden.*

The next day he added:

If the army intends to move all but 400,000 from the ETO, it seems that you could hardly miss being returned to the States. It is reassuring-- just the probabilities of the numbers involved.

Mentions of the Far East were sometimes quite casual. On May 12 Dad described local efforts to deal with the post-V-E Day boredom.

It's been positively hot in England. Baseball is in full swing, and those who can loaf are lying in the sun getting brown. We count it as part of the training program-- getting ready for the Pacific.

On that same day Mom reacted approvingly to a recent letter from Dad suggesting that he would soon be sent back to the America. The . . . *letter held a surprise, the likelihood of your return to the States. Wouldn't that be wonderful . . . ?* However, she did not feel as confident about her own fate. *Rumors here about what is to happen to us* [are] *not as optimistic.* She then described her thoughts about being in the United States together.

Our being stationed in the States-- another dream which I haven't really dared to dream, that is not until the war with Japan is over. But it would be grand; why even if we were States apart, there'd be leave with <u>no</u> *English Channel separating us. We could really begin on our plans. Happy thoughts!*

On May 22 Dad reported on yet more rumors. Among the day's events,

The two lows are <u>really</u> *low. Of course they may not materialize, and we worry too much about what* <u>might</u> *happen-- but. It seems increasingly definite that I'm going to stay right here in the ETO. That's rumors only. Number two, you probably know about; but I just found out about this evening-- your army* [1st Army] *is tagged 'Pacific.' Of course the 45th may not go; and, if it does, the nurses may not; & even if that should come to pass--* <u>you</u> *may not.*

He then rather poignantly added

I have elaborate hopes that you will stay here and go home; but the thought of my being here and your being out there somewhere gives me a numb, unbelieving feeling. Even now, how close you are. I can whisper with my being 'I love you,' and you can hear me yet. I can shout if need be. The wonderful part is awaiting the echo . . . .

Two days later, certainly not enough time for Mom in Germany to have received the letter that Dad had just posted, her thoughts returned to this same subject.

You won't have a letter for a few days 'cause I'll be a patient at the 180th General Hospital. Some of us are going there for physical exams tomorrow, to see if we're fit for the CBI. It seems that our unit is going to the CBI. This is nothing to be alarmed about. If I pass the physical & go, it will be via the States. This is all supposition, and it's possible that our unit won't get to the CBI. So don't you volunteer for it 'cause I certainly am not going to.

A week later Dad passed along information that was more than mere rumor.

I expect that this will really make your heart catch at least once, but here is the big event of the day around here. Division finally put out orders sending lots & lots of us to the Z of I [Zone of the Interior, i.e., the United States] *as a permanent change of station. Well, my name is just about at the top of the list.*

But Dad was not sure that he would be treated the same as the others. After all, he had arrived in England in August of 1942-- far earlier than virtually anyone else still with the 8th AAF. The letter continues

I expect that the majority of the others will remain in the States for a fairly short time [before being sent on to the war in the Pacific]. *If I could stay there* [in the U.S.] *by virtue of experience with pathfinder stuff & length of overseas service, then I would be scratching my palms.*

On the other hand, the length of his combat tour had been stretched out by a combination of factors: his own pathfinder training, his temporary redeployment to the States, his medical injury, and his recent duties as an instructor. Consequently, he assumed-- indeed feared-- that some unspecified, perhaps uniquely dangerous assignment had been chosen for him. In his letter to Mom the previous day, May 28, he had described one general [perhaps Archie Old] implying that his fate would be different from other navigators.

Dearest Gina:
Orders are beginning to come out for pathfinder navigators to return to the States. I wonder if I will be among them. I don't feel excited over the prospect. The general asked me a few curious questions this morning that makes it seem as if I'll stay with the wing, if he has anything to say about it.

With this uncertainty in mind, his letter of May 29 continues

All the boys here think I'm getting a raw deal; but, if the general has me taken off of the order [returning Dad's unit back to the States], *and I expect he will, it will only be because of a very powerful alternative that he has to offer.*

Two days later he was still in limbo.

Dearest Gina:
What a whirl! I had too much to do last night to have put much into a letter that would be very coherent, and I am about to fail again now.
The gist of things is this. My orders didn't *get rescinded, and that means I'm supposed to start for the States today. I packed and cleared the post ready to leave this afternoon, & now the General says not to leave because he is trying to swing a deal to hold me. So, here I sit tense as a mousetrap.*
Last night I felt out & out blue. *I had everyone wondering if I was off my nut-- being on orders to home and then not wanting to go.*

Nonetheless, he still wanted Mom to go home.

Now the mail is here with the news of your physicals & prospect of moving to the CBI, then *the States. I hope you just move to the States. If I should be removed from the present order, it wouldn't be too bad. I have a pretty strong feeling that I'll get to the States before fall, & then I'm going to see about what comes next.*

Going into June, Dad's perceived redeployment status took yet another turn. On the first day of the month he reported

I am not going to the Z of I immediately myself. The general had me removed from the orders, and I'll stay with the wing now. It's full of good points-- I'll be assigned and not a casual; I'll probably be in the States longer when I get there (remember you aren't there yet); the necessity of returning to combat is far less. Wouldn't it be wonderful to be on leave together at home . . . .

By June 1, Mom had not yet learned that Dad was arranging for his own departure from England to be delayed. From Nohra in Germany, she grumbled . . . *that I am eager to know, too; gee, if only you don't have to go the CBI, and, if you should, that you* won't *have to fly combat.*
Until the beginning of June, Mom's unit, the 45th, was classified as an evacuation hospital. This meant that it was mobile, always staying within close proximity to the front lines. Being close to the fighting made it possible for the 45th to provide the equivalent of emergency room services to wounded soldiers before transferring them to more complete medical facilities further back. However, after V-E Day, the 45th's ability to relocate was less important. Given this change in circumstance, it is not surprising that by June 3 Mom was hearing rumors . . . *we are going to function as a station hospital; nothing really definite, but in a few days we will know.* But, in the same letter, she opined that any change in her unit's job description would not reduce the likelihood of

redeployment to the Pacific Theatre. *Even if we do* [become a station hospital], *it doesn't mean anything definite about the C.B.I.* By June 5 the 45th had moved yet again, this time to St. Wendel in Germany where the station hospital rumor became a fact. Still, Mom remained uncertain as to whether or not this change either increased or decreased her unit's chances of redeployed to the CBI.

> *Darling,*
>   *Today we took over* [as] *a station hospital. The setup seems rather temporary, not many patients, mostly displaced p.o.w.s. So, from the looks of the situation, it would be hard to tell whether or not we'd be army of occupation; and that is most doubtful. If I just knew you would be army of occupation, I* [would] *get out of the unit fast 'cause it could easily be CBI bound. With you, I'd like to be A. of O.* [Army of Occupation].

For his part, Dad had reason to feel optimistic about his chances to be sent home. According to my brother Bob, Dad later told him

> . . . that people were sent back to the States based on a point system. The more time overseas and more missions flown, the more points you earned. He said that he had more points than anyone in the 8th Air Force and would have been the first person sent home had he not made an effort to stay overseas.[lxxix]

Based on this point system, on June 10 Dad concluded

> *I'm going back to the States for <u>sure</u>. I expect to be back not later than my birthday* [August 14]. *I don't have any chance of being occupational at all. When I get back there, I expect to be there a decent period for training and stuff and eventually go to the Pacific-- but not on combat status (I hope). It <u>may</u> be that, once in the States, I <u>may</u> never have to leave again (136 points)! Don't you toy for a moment with Army of Occupation.*

On June 13, still writing from St. Wendel, Mom continued to fret.

> *Dearest Ricky,*
>   *Tonight your letter of June 1st arrived, and it contained some very startling news, that you now belong to wing and that the General had you taken off orders for the Z of I. Now you'll be here longer . . . .*

On June 15 Dad was still trying to decipher the Army's plan for his unit. On that day he expressed discouragement that no one at Snetterton Heath AAF base had received any mail for quite some time. On the other hand, he was somewhat buoyed by the resulting rumor . . . *that all units scheduled to leave for the States within 30 day have their mail diverted to their port of eventual arrival.* By July 4 another rumor had become more specific, if not more probable.

> *The latest rumor is <u>really</u> good. This one has the wing moving into headquarters*

at Miami and staying there most of the winter. It doesn't have the ring of fact to it, but we are trying to believe.

Assuming that Dad really was about to be sent directly home, he tried to "pull strings" so that he and Mom, as a married couple, would be assigned the same destination. On July 11 he advised her that . . . *the A-1[?] section has written an official letter for you to use to pry yourself out of the 45ᵗʰ & to the Z of I. I hope it has enough information.* By July 30 Dad knew for certain that he, at least, would be shipped home pending any later redeployment to the CBI. But he remained unable to divine the Army's plans for Mom. Still, he took comfort in the document just provided to her.

> *The redeployment plan for nurses was in the S & S today. I'm glad you have the certificate of my transfer to the Z of I, just in case. I hope you don't have to fall back on it though -- don't you?*

***

Amidst these rumors, on July 12 Dad composed another untitled poem. Despite its brevity, the first stanza shifts uncomfortably between first, second and third-person perspectives.

> *Pale blossoms we*
> *Our leaves a chorded scent*
> *Read not of roads so bent*
> *He dreaming turned along*
>
> *Yet chorus we*
> *Once stood bright & fair*
> *Yet this be our despair*
> *His love for thee-- alone*

He then closed the letter with: *You see what you bring out in me-- the nicest thoughts. I give these to you.* As far as I know, this was Dad's last attempt at verse.

***

As it turned out, Dad needn't have worried about any redeployment to the Far East-- at least for Mom. On July 15, from Schwabisch Hall, she offered an intriguing explanation for not having sent letters in several days.

> *Darling,*
> *This is the first letter I've written to you in four days. By the time this reaches you, you'll have every right to be furious with me. But I knew you'd be counting the days since the tenth of last month, and each day I couldn't be sure.*
> *So, up to [the present] date, it seems that we might be parents. Now, don't take this as meaning it's a positive fact, 'cause it won't be definite until I've seen a doctor; and I won't be able to do that for a week or two because it's now too early for any positive signs.*

I hope you can understand why I was unable to write. The probability of being parents has me a little bewildered, and it seems a little unbelievable.

Two days later she reiterated . . . *Our parenthood is still possible, and I'm getting anxious for two weeks to pass so that I'll know for sure. I can visualize your anticipation, too.* A day after that . . . *like a good girl I'm taking vitamin capsules and calcium capsules just in case.* On July 23, now at Bretten in Germany, Mom reported

> *At the end of this week I'll have an examination, and then we'll know about Pumpkin, Jr. Gee whiz, but I'm eager to know if we are going to have one. And I know you must be too.*

Following an unusually long delay in routine mail deliveries, on July 25 Dad received several letters from Mom, including the one first raising the possibility of pregnancy. After returning from a training flight to Liverpool, he responded, explaining

> *It used up the afternoon and gave me a badly needed outlet for my excitement, which wants me to run in four directions at once and jump up in the air at the same time.*
> *You see, I've been snowed under by four letters from you-- two with airmail stamps and posted the 17th. If it turns out to be true, I think the booby hatch will claim me after a Section 8 [unfit for duty]. I don't have a chance to be 'furious' with you for not writing because the letters you wrote . . . came at the same time; & besides, I didn't expect you to write them.*
> *But what news!*

On July 26 Mom wrote confirming that she was indeed pregnant.

> *Darling,*
> *Tonight I'm writing you first 'cause I want you to be the first to know that we are going to be parents-- the report of my examinations today. I leave at 8 a.m. in the morning, flying to Paris. Just think, we'll be in the States together. And, that isn't the end of the good news. The first of your letters arrived, very recent ones [from the] 15th and 16th of July. I don't know how long I'll be in Paris before I leave for the States, but maybe I'll know in a few days. Now, to write the news to my Mom and Dad, also to Benjy in case he plans a trip to the 45th and finds I'm on my way home. Are you excited and pleased? We'll be together soon! And in the States.*
> > *Oh, but I love you so,*
> > *Gina*
> *P.S. How does it feel Pumpkin Sr.' to realize that you are going to be a 'Daddy'-- to a 'Pumpkin Jr.'?*

On that same day-- not yet having learned the happy news-- Dad wrote that he soon would be embarking from Scotland for home on the RMS *Queen Elizabeth*. Moreover, not knowing Mom's situation, he and former best man Bob Harnish even speculated about . . . *the possibility-- incredible odds-- of your being on board with us.*

Mom, unaware of Dad's embarkation orders, wrote on July 30 from Paris that she was still waiting for results of some additional medical tests. *I am just waiting for Col. [Isadore] Feder's diagnosis to be verified and then for transportation home.* Later in the same letter . . . *For myself it is still very difficult to believe that* <u>we</u> *are going to have a baby-- gee, but I wish I were with you right now.*

***

While censorship was easing up, the problem of slow mail deliveries remained. Mom might now mention a specific location inside her letter. But Dad would know for certain only where she had been a week or so earlier-- never where she was on the day the letter actually reached him. Consequently, he and Mom both kept looking for opportunities to speed up their communications. On June 2, for example, Mom heard of

> *. . . a B-17 landed at the airstrip* [near Nohra] *so I rushed down to see if the crew would take a message to you. The crew wasn't around, so I'll go down first thing in the morning.*

The next day she reported that

> *This morning was spent at the airstrip trying to get a message to you. I missed Church, but felt very close to you watching the planes and especially the B-17 on the field.*
> *A Colonel said he'd phone you, and a Sgt. Mich?ovich said he'd mail you a letter. So at least one letter should reach you.*

***

During the air war over Europe, the 8th AAF employed its huge fleet of B-17 Flying Fortresses and B-24 Liberators almost exclusively as bombing planes. Once hostilities ended, however, these same aircraft were often re-tasked for more humanitarian purposes. Back on May 3, for example, just a few days before the official end of hostilities in Europe, Dad had reported

> *Operations have been confined to the dropping of supplies to the Dutch. The crews took it as quite a lark flying over Holland at a few hundred feet and waving back at everyone.*

On May 8 Dad had indicated that he would be participating in one of these operations. To his way of thinking, this created an opportunity.

> *Tomorrow I'll be flying a regular tour of France, Belgium, and Germany. It promises to be an all day jaunt. I wish we might get lost or wander off to Weimar, but it looks as if that must come another time.*

The next day Dad did indeed find himself on a bombing plane transporting American soldiers from one German city to another.

> *Dear Gina:*

Just back from the Ruhr and other places. It was a long ride, but the GI's we were toting liked it immensely, that is, for the first three or four hours. After that, one gutted town was just the same as any other; and they all began to get tired and a little sick.

From there on the only things which brought them round were a buzz job of Paris, a look at a blasted flying-bomb [V-1] launching site-- oh, and England again. We were in that damned plane nearly 10 hours; I'm sore all over the back of my lap. And the nearest we got to the 45th was Kassel-- woe!

On May 17-- just over a week after V-E day-- he noted that

Today has been a bit busier than expected. More stuff to fool around with. The big business at hand is the evacuation of prisoners from the depths of the Reich.

On June 14 Dad learned of an opportunity to travel to Germany but judged the specific location not close enough to St Wendel, Mom's most recent address.

Tomorrow there is a flight scheduled to land on the continent, but it doesn't bring St. Wendel within reasonable range. I wonder if you have moved again.

As it happened, Mom's 45th unit departed St. Wendel for Schwabisch Hall on that same day, July 14. Eight days later her unit moved again, this time to Bretten. Significantly, however, Dad would not learn of this latest relocation until early August. In the meantime, on July 25, the same day that he first heard Mom might be pregnant, he proposed yet another new rendezvous scheme. Still, any such rendezvous would have to be squeezed in before Dad's scheduled return trip back to the United States.

Remember my telling you that the 96th is assigned to OAF [Occupational Air Force]. Well, this field (to be) is about forty mile north of Schwabisch Hall. And so-o-o-o-----maybe------! It'll have to be before the 2nd of August. We are supposed to be leaving for our embarkation area then.

Thinking that he would be departing for the United States by August 2, on July 27 he calculated that he had . . . *five days more before the 2nd to catch a possible ride to you.* The day after that, he outlined his new plan.

Tomorrow a plane goes on a tour of the Ruhr and a few other places; but the crew is coming from the 96th; & the passengers are all ground-pounders. No planes are going to Wurzburg. I still have my fingers crossed hoping to promote something. The crew of tomorrow's tour was originally coming out of the wing; & I, as navigator, was to select a desirable route, at my discretion. Now right below is Schwabisch Hall, famous for----------!

The next morning, July 29, Dad was on the move again. His letter the following afternoon describes what happened.

> *Yesterday was my big day-- and a long one. We took off for a flight to Wurzburg . . . . [Schwabisch] Hall, & its airfield was the place we worked over. There were at least two hospitals there and two in tents. We buzzed them both, but we couldn't land and turned north [for] Wurzburg. The problem was how to get back to Schwabish-Hall the quickest. A colonel-- bless him-- gave us a magnificent answer. He had a Piper Cub, which we could use but we would have to go over to Kitzengen to get it.*

In World War II helicopters were experimental technology. In Europe no American helicopters were yet available. Consequently, the Army used the equivalent of single-engine private planes that could land in small, unpaved areas. The Piper Cub was such an aircraft, providing seats for two occupants inside a fabric-covered airframe. As Dad quickly discovered, its 65 horsepower engine gave the Cub a top speed no higher than that of a compact car.

> *Well-- we [Dad and Bob Harnish?] got it and started off at full throttle & half-cocked for Hall without a map. We thought we could simply follow the highway, but we got lost and returned to Wurzburg for a map & gas.*

In later years, when retelling this story of this rendezvous attempt. Mom expressed more than a little amusement that an experienced navigator had gotten lost on such a short flight. At the time Dad

> *. . . was mentally kicking myself for wasting 40 minutes; so we gassed up (7 gallons) in no time and started off again-- 75 mph for Hall. That time we made it. There wasn't anything on the field but two sergeants and a field phone, which they let us, use; and-------- the 45th had moved two days before. None of the other hospitals could give us any information about where or how we could find out.*
> *On the way back to Wurzburg, the Cub was pretty low on gas; so we stopped off at another field we came across & gassed up [again]. We really needed it. The cars were making better progress than we were. When Wurzburg showed up, our 17 [B-17] was gone. They had given us up.*

At this point-- if Dad was unable to return to his base in England with his tour group and as a result missed his connections for his return to the States-- he was in danger of being declared AWOL. Luckily, the other crewmen who were on that B-17 return flight from Wurzburg back to Snetterton Heath managed to prevent disaster.

> *Actually they thought we either [were] lost or still at Hall; so they flew to Hall and, seeing we weren't there, took a long shot on our being back at Wurzburg. Sure enough, there sat our Cub when they came back; and we all got back [to England] at eleven last night.*

He concluded his description of the failed rendezvous attempt with a rationalization.

> *I don't feel bitterly disappointed at missing you yesterday because I should have had to leave by tomorrow morning at the very latest. But it would have been*

grand-- remember our 12 hours at Spa! I had an unearthed bottle of vitamin capsules for you too.

At the end of a letter written the next day, he asked: *Where are you now? I reach for you.*

On the evening of August 3, Dad belatedly received three letters from Mom. To his chagrin, he now realized that he hadn't gotten as close to her at all. *The first one was written on the 23rd, and you were already at Bretten. I must have missed you by a week instead of just two days as I thought.*

On the actual day of this rendezvous attempt, Mom had been in neither Schwabisch Hall nor Bretten, but rather in that Paris hospital.

> *31 July 1945*
> *Paris*
>
> *Dearest Ricky,*
> *Wonder what you're doing at this moment, even where you are.*
> *Now to report the event of the day. I had the examination and the diagnosis was confirmed as much as can be this early (for pumpkins). Somehow I still can't believe it, and probably won't until I can see some signs for myself. Haven't yet learned when I'll be leaving for home.*

Her prediction in the next paragraph proved to be all too accurate. *I shouldn't be surprised if I'm home before this letter reaches you, 'cause it will go to England; and I hope you're on your way home.*

***

Meanwhile, back in England from his failed rendezvous attempt, Dad observed two good omens. First, at 7:30 A.M. on July 30 his heavy luggage was collected for shipment back to the States. Second, the next day he was paid in American money, which seemed to him to look . . . *very strange.* The day after that, the 8th USAAF held an open house at its Snetterton Heath base to which local English civilians were invited. *Can't you just see dozens of English kids & their equally interested parents scrambling all around-- a regular carnival.* The following day he flew in a military plane over England for a final time.

> *In the morning Col. Henry had borrowed a Fort [B-17], and anyone interested in piling in his 4 hours flying time for the month climbed aboard. We didn't have any place to go, but the weather swept us away from Wotton. We stayed right in Eastern England, mostly close to the coast. For the first time I flew over Broadstairs. I'd been over that section before, but never over the town. Say! It's a wonderful looking town . . . .*

Dad's troopship, the converted luxury liner RMS *Queen Elizabeth* was now scheduled to depart from Glasgow on August 6. In preparation, he and many others were ordered to depart by train from Snetterton Heath for Scotland on the morning August 3. The evening before, he wrote

Dearest Gina:

The thought on everyone's mind tonight-- just one more night here; and then we leave for Scotland and the States. In way of celebration, practically everyone went down to the pond this afternoon for an outing. We had sandwiches, juice, a barrel of beer, tow rubber dinghies, and clear skies. We had a rare old time. Some of the boys stayed there; but when we came back at five, there was that 'Sunday afternoon after a long day at the beach' feeling. I guess it is always the way after being out in the sun just soaking it up.

I wish I felt as peaceful inside, but I just don't. Perhaps it is the product of doing so little, this unrest; but I do so long to be with you-- to let my love sing out again. It seems as if every act, every bit of understanding begins with you.

Precious one,
<u>*Ricky*</u>

On what he thought would be his final morning in Snetterton, Dad continued.

3 August 1945

Good morning darling:

Everything was swathed in mist this morning when I left my roommates sleeping; but after breakfast it was clearing fast; and things stood young in the sun. Is it any wonder the birds are singing or that I am writing to you?

I wonder if I should tell you of the prayer of you that begins every day or of living by rote, said blind, waiting for your light.

<u>*Beloved*</u>
<u>*Ricky*</u>

In the meantime-- on that same day-- Mom was ordered on to a military transport plane for return flight from Paris to the United States. Out over the Atlantic, she miscarried.

By that same day, and contrary to his previous understanding of the travel itinerary, Dad still had not yet actually departed from Snetterton. That evening, three earlier letters from Mom were belatedly delivered. He now blamed himself, at least in part, for the missed communications.

. . . I don't like the mail situation for you. Why on earth haven't I been writing air mail! You said you'd know on the weekend of your letter-- that was the Sunday that I was at Schwabisch Hall-- about Pumpkin Jr. Oh, that you have my letters now. <u>You</u> need them so.

I love you-- so much
<u>*Ricky*</u>

The next evening, August 4, he finally received Mom's July 26 message confirming her pregnancy. He immediately wrote back to say how delighted he was.

Dearest Gina:

I'm far too wound up inside to be coherent. Your letter is already here from Paris with the results of your exam-- wow! WOW!

And you said you might be home <u>before</u> I got this letter. I'm not supposed to be here to get it, but I 'm really thankful knowing that you will be home very soon. We're all packed and retraining for Scotland tonight. Everyone is strictly sober-- and with a party on-- at the orders of the CO. I can't get my mind off <u>our</u> being in the States and beginning to <u>believe</u> all this-- together.

> *I love you*
> *Always*
> <u>*Ricky*</u>

On the evening of Sunday, August 5, Dad boarded a troop train for Glasgow without knowing either that his bride was already back in the States or that their first child had been lost.

Darling Gina:

On board! We left Snetterton just one hour after posting your letter last night. Everyone was in the highest spirit . . . .

The train left Attleboro sometime after midnight and brought us here just after three this afternoon. It was a long ride. We stopped twice for coffee & a general stretch, but the highlight of the trip was the part which took us along the coast just as we started into Scotland. Most of the view might have a characteristic of solitude. but it was also of serenity and beauty. It seemed as if, in such places, you would have to become as simple & pure as they [the Scots]; and it would be impossible to mold-- only to be molded . . . .

<u>We sail tomorrow night.</u>

***

The next evening, Monday, August 6, RMS *Queen Elizabeth* cast off from her moorings and began its journey toward Virginia. Soon after departure, the ship's captain made an announcement about an event that would change the world.

The nine o'clock news is coming over the address system, and the announcer is talking about an atomic bomb being used against the Japanese. All I can make out is that it's terrific.

At this point Dad still had no idea of either Mom's current whereabouts or her miscarriage. He concluded his shipboard letter that first night with the hope . . . *Perhaps at some port you are preparing to sail. Godspeed!* The next day he was describing the ship's lounge as . . . *a den of iniquity.* By the fourth day he had reason to resist temptation.

. . . it was too wet to be on deck, and I was sitting in the lounge by myself content with myriad thoughts of you. Up popped a nurse and asked me if I would mind joining in with cards at her table. I didn't have a good excuse to stand on, so I agreed. On the way over to her table, she said that she hoped I didn't think she was too forward, etc.; but that's about what she was. It turned out that she had her eye on me for quite a while before she got around to it and wanted to know

*why I had been sitting by myself. I told her I was thinking about my wife. Boy!
She was so surprised. I was grinning right out loud.*

Meanwhile, throughout the voyage Dad continued to receive updates on world events.
On the morning of Thursday, August 9 he was playing bridge in the ship's passenger
lounge. *Everything was a* [illegible] *'till the announcement was made of Russia's
declaration of war* [against Japan]. *After that things just weren't the same.* The next day
he added

> *The immediate item is that we dock tomorrow and move to Camp Kilmer.
> Morale and appetites have jumped enormously. To boost everything, there is
> quite a persistent rumor that the Japs have stated some terms of surrender which
> are acceptable to us. Wow! What a time to be coming home for both of us.*

Dad disembarked in Norfolk, Virginia on August 10 still not knowing that Mom was also
back in the States-- or that she had miscarried.

***

Immediately after Mom's plane touched down on American soil on August 3, 1945, the
Army ordered her to *Station Hospital, bldg. C., Mitchel Field . . .* in Hempstead on Long
Island where she was admitted to recuperate from her miscarriage. When Dad
disembarked, Mom was somehow able to reach him with information about both the
miscarriage and her current whereabouts. In his turn, Dad was somehow able to obtain a
leave of absence, travel from Norfolk in Virginia via Camp Kilmer in New Jersey to
Long Island in New York, and attend to Mom at her hospital bedside-- all within 24
hours. Mom's letter on August 12, drafted at seven that morning, was her first to Dad
since July. Neither on this occasion nor in her subsequent letters did she mention the
miscarriage itself. But she did thank Dad for visiting her in the hospital.

> *There was and is still the warmth of your visit, your flowers, and the things you
> said and your happiness-- I'm really cheered, warm and happy. Hmmm-- I love
> you.*
> *The roses at my bedside table are at their best this morning, and oh, so
> fragrant. You must have been very, very tired yesterday. I hope you weren't . . .
> too busy when you got back to* [Camp] *Kilmer.*
> *It's fun thinking about the phone calls you made today. It's fun thinking about
> us' in the good ole U.S.A.*

By that date a second atomic bomb had been dropped on Nagasaki. Rumors were now
flying. Nonetheless, hostilities continued-- at least officially. If the war in the Far East
dragged on, the possibility remained that Dad would be redeployed to that theatre. If on
the other hand, the Japanese did surrender, a turning point in my parents' relationship
would have been reached. Mom's letter the next morning casually mentioned this latter
possibility.

> *Darling,*
> *Good morning!*

Are you 'all slept out' this morning? I do hope you're well rested, enough to be really well rested, enough to really enjoy this possible V-J [victory over Japan] *day.*

Golly, but I'm excited with all that V-J means, and for all it means for you and me, together.

The two majors [attending physicians] *were just in, and it seems that at 3 p.m. I'll learn all I should about getting out of this bed, etc. Jiminey* [sic] *Crickets* [a Walt Disney cartoon character]*, but I am eager for a leave.*

Your telephone call last night was a wonderful nightcap, an incentive for the sweetest dreams.

A kiss with

> *All my love,*
> *Gina*

The day after that did indeed turn out to be V-J Day. It was also Dad's 27th birthday.

> *14 August 1945*
> *7:30 P.M.*

Happy Birthday-- Happy V.J. day
Darling--

Happy? Hmmm-- I'll bet you are.

It's so hard to believe that the war is over, that we are home, that we'll be beginning so many new experiences together, and [that] *they'll be built on our past experiences. Thrilled? I am.*

Here's a bit of news you'll want to hear. After my examination today, I learned that I'll be discharged for reassignment in a day or two [with] *a possibility of a four-day pass if my disposition papers take any time at all.   Then a 21 or 30 day leave.*

P.S. *I'm relieved that no surgery is necessary and that I'm exceedingly alright. You are a 'sure-cure.'*

The kids in the 45th Evac must be exceedingly joyous tonight . . . . I'll wager there'll be more celebrating in the ETO and CBI than in the States, although there seem to be plenty of excitement here on this post.

From now on, it's not unlikely that we'll be celebrating future birthdays together.

> *Good night-- a kiss*
> *I love you,*
> *Gina*

***

On August 16 Mom was indeed granted a 21-day leave, during which her address would be 99 Centre St., Danvers, Mass. This was the home of Dad's adoptive mother Helen Dunn. Coincidentally, a number of Mom's father's relatives also happened to reside in that state. One of these was her great uncle Knut North, who lived in Worcester, Massachusetts. On November 29, *Uncle Knut* wrote a holiday letter to other relatives back in Sweden. One purpose of his letter was to inform the Swedish side of Mom's family about what the Americans had been up to of late. Among these North family news items was the following.

Now Brother August's grandson (daughter's son) [Mom's second cousin John Russell] and Alva, daughter of your brother Albert, are back on this side of the Atlantic, safe and sound from the disastrous war. We have seen and talked to both of them. Alva had her husband with her; we were happy to see him, a nice young man. He doesn't drink or smoke or has any other bad habits, and she is happy with him. Alva is a devout person, so they will probably live a good life together. [lxxx]

By mid-September of 1945 Mom was living with her parents back in Chicago. While she was still waiting for her discharge from the Army to made official, she had already been granted an extended leave of absence from duty, no doubt out of deference to her recent miscarriage. Dad, on the other hand, was now posted to an AAF base in Grand Forks, South Dakota along with thousands of other military personnel who, like him, were impatiently waiting for permission to go home. *Most people sleep late in the morning after the usual round in town, which is said to boast 65 bars.* Frequent phone calls to Mom were now possible, but Dad continued to write letters as well. The one on September 26 is fairly typical.

Today they continued to fill us full of separation poop but very little was of real value to me. I have to report to my draft board so I won't get drafted again, and I can't start studying under the GI bill [providing college tuition for returning veterans] *until my terminal leave is over. I have to change my will, fix up my insurance, pay my income tax, get a driver's license, and settle down to housekeeping and studying.*

Finally, on October 3, immediately after receiving his discharge papers, Dad boarded a train for Chicago. While in transit, he composed a prayer of gratitude that he personally delivered to Mom upon his arrival.

> *Written on the train*
> *at night, 3 Oct. '45*
>
> *Father:*
> *For bringing us to this*
> *hour in love and safety, we offer*
> *our humble and hearty thanks. Give*
> *us grace in thought, word & deed*
> *that in forgiveness our need will*
> *be slight. Fill our love's garden*
> *with the fruits of thy worship,*
> *and in thy wisdom make us*
> *strong together thru Jesus Christ*
> *our Lord. Amen*

Father:

For bringing us to their home in love and safety, we offer our humble and hearty thanks. Give us grace in thought word & deed that in forgiveness our need will be right. Fill our love's garden with the fruits of thy worship and in thy wisdom make us strong together thru Jesus Christ our Lord. Amen.

Dad's letter to Mom, October 3, 1945.

When the war ended, more than twelve million men and women put their uniforms aside and returned to civilian life. They went back to work at their old jobs or started small businesses; they became big-city cops and firemen; they finished their degrees or enrolled in college for the first time; they became schoolteachers, insurance salesmen, craftsmen, and local politicians. They weren't widely known outside their families or their communities. For many, the war years were enough adventure to last a lifetime. They were proud of what they had accomplished but they rarely discussed their experiences, even with each other. They became once again ordinary people . . . .[lxxxi]

Tom Brokaw
The Greatest Generation

23
REMINDERS

After the War, my parents chose to settle in Chicago near Mom's parents. By the spring of 1949 Dad was in his second year of medical school at the Loyola University Stritch School of Medicine. Because of financial troubles he also was working full time as a night watchman at the Zenith television factory. For that same reason Mom was temporarily living on Dad's birth family's Wisconsin farm 240 miles drive to the north. Here Dad's Grandmother, Hannah Moeller and his two unmarried aunts could babysit for my newborn sister Jane and me so that Mom herself could take a nursing job at a nearby hospital. [Our little brother Bob would be born two years later.]

Being again apart, my parents temporarily resumed their correspondence. For example, with their fourth anniversary approaching, Dad reminisced by opening Mom's Army footlocker. He was soon reminded of the wedding dress that he had never actually seen Mom wear. He then wrote

While I was in the footlocker I pulled out one of your letters at random. It was written the day your wedding dress came and filled me with poignancy for the trials and joys of those days. Does it seem possible we have been married almost four years? . . . it brings up in a rush the deepest happiness and the highest points I have ever know. Can I ever tell or show how much I love you!

***

Back on January 23, 1945 Mom had written from Belgium to Dad in England promising . . . *I'll more than love you even with a double chin redoubled; that's a very truthfully stated.* By the spring of 1949 Dad was only 31; Mom was only 29. But both were already encountering medical problems. Metaphorically, at least, the *double chins* were beginning to appear. On April 5, for example, writing from Chicago, Dad updated his old wartime leg injury. Because of an abscess at the site of his wartime ankle scar, he had gone to the office of a Dr. Doherty, an orthopedic surgeon.

He had office hours till five, and I just squeaked under the line. His X-ray equipment was nearly as elaborate as the hospital job. The outlook is favorable, but, in nonprofessional talk, I'm fine. I have a bony union between my tibia and fibula at the site of operation but no signs of any infection of any sort. You see, your womanly intuition was perfectly correct. He didn't look for any similar recurrences. We chatted about things for a while. He was with the 15th Air Force in Africa and Italy. What surprised him a little bit was that I wasn't getting a disability.

The next day he added

. . . the bone man the school sent me to [Dr. Doherty] *said I ought to be getting disability. We'll talk about it when I come* [to Wisconsin]. *I don't know whether to follow through to find out such possibilities.*

On April 14 he did go to a Veterans' Administration [VA] office in Chicago to make a claim. Mom later told me that the Army did offer him a 10% disability. However, I do not remember our household ever any receiving envelopes from the VA. Indeed, according to what Aunt Louise recently added, when Dad learned how little the VA was willing to pay, he declined the benefits.

Beyond this, Mom had reported back on March 21 about the recurrence of a wartime physical problem of her own. As previously mentioned, sometime late in the war she had acquired a large number of keloid scars on her back. Her later explanation was that they were an unfortunate reaction to an ointment that the Army provided as protection against enemy gas attacks. None of her wartime letters specifically mentioned the existence of these scars. Now, however, she wrote to Dad *. . . my scars are becoming increasingly painful all the time . . . . It seems that, after a period of four years, they shouldn't hurt like this.* At the farm, she was receiving a *. . . slippery elm . . .* treatment from Dad's Aunt Emma, a firm believer in homeopathic remedies. But, by April 6 he was urging Mom to *. . . get some competent opinion.* In her later post-war conversations with me, Mom rarely complained about these small disfigurements. And when she did, it was usually something to the effect that, since she considered herself to have a good figure, it was a shame that she could not wear lower-cut dresses. In saying this, Mom's tone always seemed cheerful. But she was no doubt troubled by her declining physical appearance.

***

In 1953 the family moved from Chicago to Michigan where Dad began a five-year medical residency program with that State's Department of Mental Health, initially at the large psychiatric hospital in Traverse City. It had been only eight years since Mom and Dad had been on active military duty in a war zone. But so much had happened since then that the war must have seemed to them a distant memory. Nevertheless, there were occasional reminders. One afternoon in the early Fall of that year, just as we were beginning our life on the state hospital grounds, I happened to be playing touch football on the lawn of our apartment building with some other boys. Dad arrived home from work and parked his car in front of us on 11th Street. As was normal for that time of year, he was wearing a long coat over a jacket and tie. So I was pleasantly surprised when he accepted my challenge to race him across the yard. At first it appeared that he was going to beat me easily. But, after a few more yards he pulled up limping, his face grimacing in pain.

During these Traverse City years, I became aware that Mom was carrying around an ordinary looking one-dollar note that she referred to as her *short snorter bill*. Back during the War, the term "short snorter" referred to anyone who had accomplished one of several air travel feats, such as crossing the Equator or traversing the Atlantic. Prior to the War, commercial air travel between Europe and America had hardly begun. Crossing the Ocean by air was considered something of an adventure. During the War, the captain of a transport plane on a trans-Atlantic flight would autograph a dollar bill for each of his passengers. This bill then became the short snorter's certificate of membership in a sort of unofficial travel fraternity. Unfortunately, Mom's short snorter bill has long since been misplaced. At some point she had inadvertently spent it.

Also, Dad had been keeping various wartime medals-- including his Distinguished Flying Cross, his Bronze Star, and his aviator's wings-- in small, hinged boxes similar to the hard-shell cases used for carrying eyeglasses. When I was seven or eight, I asked for and received permission to show then to my elementary school classmates. When I failed to bring them home that evening, neither Mom nor Dad said anything about it. Indeed, they did not seem to care. Looking back now, however, as a son seeking reconnection with my lost parents, I deeply regret this childhood miscue.

In the summer of 1956 our family took an extensive motoring trip that included a stopover in Tennessee to visit Dad's older brother Benjy, his wife Alberta and their daughter Marilyn. Uncle Benjy was now working at a VA hospital in Memphis where he specialized in the treatment of spinal injuries. While we were in Memphis, Mom insisted that Dad drive us all to see the *Memphis Belle,* a B-17 about which a wartime documentary film had been made, now on outdoor static display in that city. [See Appendix A.]

Throughout this period my parents subscribed to *Life* magazine, a large weekly publication featuring excellent photographs of current world events. In January of 1957 a *Life* cover story was about three of the Air Force's new Cold War-era bombers that had just completed the first non-stop jet flight around the globe. This circumnavigation was achieved through the use of in-flight refueling, a technology not available back in WWII. This flight's leader was Dad's former commanding officer, Gen. Archie Old. I remember Dad looking at the magazine's cover and saying that Gen. Old had been his wartime friend. He added that he now intended to contact the General to offer his congratulations. However, I was never told whether he followed through on this.

***

In the summer of 1959 our family returned from Michigan to Chicago where Dad opened up a private psychiatric practice. An event the next year caused Mom to expand the subject matter of her wartime anecdotes: Israeli intelligence, the *Mossad,* kidnapped former Nazi war criminal Adolph Eichmann from his place of hiding in Argentina and brought him back to Israel to stand trial. Eichmann's trial for war crimes and crimes against humanity began in 1961 in Jerusalem. Soon the image of Eichmann-- sitting inside a bulletproof booth in a Jerusalem courtroom while listening through earphones to a German translation of the Israeli prosecutor's accusations-- was gripping the world's attention.

For her part, Mom had already begun sharing anecdotes about her other wartime experiences when I was quite young. But it was only during Eichmann's trial that she first opened up at what she had seen for herself at Buchenwald. At the time I was only a high school freshman. But I was fascinated by all the media coverage nonetheless. Indeed, this was when I first became aware of genocide as a concept. Moreover, unlike most casual television viewers, I had an eyewitness available to answer my questions. Mom described to me how her hospital had once been assigned to . . . *clean up Buchenwald,* how the female medical personnel were barred from participating, how she had chosen to tour the camp anyway.

In 1969, the Holocaust again became the topic of family conversation. It was my younger brother Bob's senior year at his high school. He had joined the school's thespian club, which was staging a production of *The Diary of Ann Frank.* Bob himself was cast as Ann Frank's father Otto. At one of the show's performances, I remember being pleasantly surprised that my little brother was quite a good actor. Bob would later recall Mom coming back stage afterward. To his surprise, instead of Mom offering her routine congratulations for his performance, she was in tears. The play had brought back memories of what she had seen for real 24 years earlier.

***

By 1975 Jane and I were both married and living on our own. Bob was still single. But he was only one year from graduation at the Rush Presbyterian Medical School in Chicago. With fewer expenses, my parents decided that Dad could close down his medical practice and return to a salaried position with the Michigan Department of Mental Health, this time in the remote Upper Peninsula town of Newberry. [It was this point that Mom entrusted me with her Army footlocker.]

For the first few years back in Michigan, both of my parents seemed happy. Dad talked about working until he was 70, the State's mandatory retirement age. However, in 1981, at the age of 63, new health issues emerged that brought his professional career to an abrupt end. First, he began suffering from reduced vision resulting from ruptured blood vessels inside his right eye. Laser treatments at the hospital in Marquette, a college town two hours drive west of Newberry, brought only temporary relief. Eventually, a trip to see an ophthalmological specialist in Chicago led to a failed surgical procedure, which in turn resulted in the loss of the eye. Later that same year Dad was diagnosed with leukemia. Upon learning of this diagnosis, both Mom and Bob and were immediately suspicious that this condition was the result of Dad's wartime exposure to radar.[lxxxii] Whatever the cause, each successive attack resulted in his being re-hospitalized in Marquette. During each of these episodes, Dad would rally following his chemotherapy. The cancer would go into remission. But each episode weakened him. Soon he was no longer able to work. He lost weight. He lost his teeth. But worst of all, he lost hope. A physician himself, he had no illusions about how this was going to end. For the first time in his life, my father seemed clinically depressed.

***

By November of 1985 Dad was again back in the hospital at Marquette. His condition was grave. Bob, who was now a surgeon with his own private practice here in Illinois, had become familiar with an experimental new procedure that offered the hope of actually curing this type of cancer: a bone marrow transplant. Nowadays, these transplants are a fairly common medical procedure. Back in 1985, however, this was not yet the case. When Bob inquired about its availability, he was informed that the procedure Dad needed was being performed at only one hospital in the entire country. And this hospital was located in Oregon, about four days' journey from Michigan by car. Bob suggested that we rent a large van. His plan was that I would drive while he served as Dad's medical caregiver. To our surprise, Dad himself expressed no particular interest in such extraordinary measures on his behalf. His attitude seemed to be that his time had come. As it turned out, he was not eligible for this surgery anyway. To Bob's chagrin, when he contacted the Oregon hospital directly, he was told that the procedure was available only to patients younger than 45. Being 67, Dad did not qualify. When Bob protested that Dad's military service to his country-- not to mention his postwar contributions to the medical profession-- entitled him to special consideration, his plea fell on deaf ears.

Over that year's Thanksgiving weekend, Bob and I drove from Chicago up to Marquette to see Dad. Nothing specific was said in the car. But we were both fearful that this might be the end. Our sister Jane, who had been in Marquette since this most recent hospitalization began, was with Mom when we arrived at the hospital. Dad himself seemed at peace. During my last visit with him, he said . . . *I did the best I could.*

Capt. Charles W. Dunn, Jr. died early on the early morning on December 17, 1985. Both Bob and I were back at work in Chicago when we got the news. There was a wake at a funeral home up in Newberry. But it was Dad's wish that his remains be cremated. Bob thinks this was because Dad knew that any actual burial in the frozen Upper Peninsula might be delayed until the spring thaw. If so, he did not want to inconvenience the rest of us with another trip up north for the actual interment.

Dad's ashes were of course given to Mom. Two years later Jane persuaded Mom to move into a retirement home near her in Illinois. At this point Jane took possession of the ashes and kept them for an additional 16 years. When Mom passed away in 2003, Jane arranged for both of our parents' remains to be buried side-by-side at the Abraham Lincoln National Cemetery near Joliet, Illinois.

The nine o'clock news is coming over the address system, and the announcer is talking about an atomic bomb being used against the Japanese. All I can make out is that it's terrific.

From Dad aboard the *RMS Queen Elizabeth* [on the Atlantic],
To Mom in Mitchel Field AAF station hospital in Hempstead, NY [recovering from her miscarriage], August 6, 1945

Epilogue
HIROSHIMA

In the fall of 1968 the Illinois Board of Education issued me a teaching certificate. In preparation for the certificate, Northwestern University's College of Education had required a social studies methods course over that summer. This class was taught by Daniel Powell, an experienced social studies instructor with the Chicago Public School System and editor of *Ideas in Conflict*, a then widely used anthology of primary source documents on American History. Mr. Powell, his course, and his anthology were my first introduction to what was then called the "New Social Studies." This more inductive approach to teaching history and other curricula had been developed with funds provided by U.S. Office of Education as part of a blanket Federal initiative to improve the quality of secondary school instruction, an initiative motivated by post-*Sputnik* Cold War fears that American students were falling behind their Soviet peers in such subjects as "rocket science."

According to this pedagogical view, the purpose of teaching history is not to disseminate trivia, foster patriotism, or even acquaint students with the instructor's political biases. Rather, since history is about understanding different points of view, the teacher's goal-- like the midwife in Socrates' metaphor-- is to assist students in the birth of their own informed opinions. Students reach this goal by examining historical evidence for themselves, not hearsay evidence from textbooks, but the direct testimony to be found in the primary source materials written by those who actually witnessed major events.

For we Americans, our national experience is rife with questions that stirred great controversy at the time they were raised. Should the Continental Congress declare independence? Should state conventions ratify the second constitution? Should voters support Alexander Hamilton's new Federalist Party or Thomas Jefferson's new Democratic-Republicans? Should the Cherokee Nation be evicted from Georgia? Should Congress fund President Polk's war on Mexico? Should slavery be abolished? Should the market economy be regulated, or even replaced with socialism? Should the Philippines be annexed? Should the United States give up its tradition of isolationism to join the war against fascism? Should persons of Japanese ancestry, as a military necessity, be relocated from the Pacific Coast? Should atomic bombs be dropped on Japan? Should the goal of the Civil Rights movement be racial integration or separatism?

Should its method be that of civil disobedience or "black power?" Should the United States assume a "hawk" or "dove" posture toward the Soviet Union? Should Congress approve of the Gulf of Tonkin resolution against North Vietnam? And, were I still teaching, should Operation Iraqi Freedom be launched?

Moreover, at the highest affective levels, history is about critical thinking; it is about trying to win arguments. Of course the best way to achieve the latter is by presenting evidence in support of one's positions. As a high school instructor [in Maine Township northwest Chicago], I-- and my teaching colleagues Janet Conway and Fred A. Franz-- began the practice of concluding various topics in our U.S. History "team" program with the requirement that students take sides in a series of class debates on issues appropriate to these topics. It was Jan who first proposed adding these debates. To prepare, each student was assigned to one or the other side of the question. Both sides were then provided with alternate reading lists of relevant primary source documents. On the day of the debate, the two sides would sit along opposite walls of the classroom. They were then directed to role-play as if it really was the time when the question was a public issue. Students were not to speak in the past tense about what others had once said, but in the present tense about what "we" currently believe to be true. In an effort to keep the number of students on both sides of the classroom roughly equal, students were sometimes assigned to a position with which they personally disagreed. However, these students were told that they would not be graded for what they assume to be true, but only on how well they play their roles-- like actors cast to portray characters in a drama or public defenders representing indigent defendants in court. My goal was not to change anyone's opinion. On the other hand, whether an individual student emerged from one of these debates with his/her original viewpoint intact or with an entirely new one, I wanted his/her perspective to be grounded on the best available evidence.

For many of these historic questions, no real consensus has ever been reached. When preparing for these class debates, students would sometimes ask about my own view of the issue at hand. Whenever this came up, I always responded with the concern that, if my views were shared prematurely, this might prejudice the proceedings. But I always promised to "fess up" immediately afterward. And I always did. However, for the debate about whether President Truman should order the use nuclear weapons against the Japanese near the end of World War II, I had no unequivocal opinion of my own. Up until 2005 this uncertainty was merely academic. However, after reading my parents' letters, especially those in which they expressed real concern about the possibility of being redeployed to the Far East, the dilemma became more personal.

***

My wife Usha's family is from India. Six of her seven siblings have immigrated to the United States. The youngest is my brother-in-law Rakesh Ahuja who, after earning an MBA at Drexel University in Philadelphia, became a manager at IBM. In 2000 he was transferred to that company's Tokyo office. In December of 2005, Usha and I accepted an invitation to visit him and his family who were then residing in Tokyo's Roppongi district. While our stay in Japan was brief, we did make one very memorable excursion beyond Tokyo. This side trip included stopovers in Kyoto and Hiroshima.

***

By the time of our Japan trip, it had been had been nearly two years since Mom's passing had released me from the promise not to investigate her footlocker's contents. But it had only been a few months since I had completed a preliminary reading of my parents' correspondence. By now I was feeling called to write something. But neither a theme for the manuscript nor an outline of its form had yet come into focus. Hiroshima changed that. In particular, its Peace Memorial Museum displays an array of exhibits documenting the suffering of the victims. On August 6, 1945 about 70,000 people were incinerated where they stood. In the months and years that followed, however, many thousands more who had survived the initial blast were stricken with radiation poisoning, ultimately doubling the total number of fatalities. A statue in the park outside the museum was particularly moving. This memorial is dedicated to a little girl named Sadako Sasaki. She was two years old when the bomb exploded about a mile and a half from her family home. Nine years later she was diagnosed with leukemia. When she was hospitalized in February of 1955, a friend suggested that she fold 1000 pieces of paper into origami cranes. This advice corresponded to a local belief that the gods will grant any wish to the person who does so. Sadako continued to fold paper into cranes until her own death that October.

I felt conflicted. If no atomic weapons were used, would the war have gone on for another year as was being predicted at the time? Would one or even both of my parents then have been redeployed to the Pacific Theatre? Would Dad have been required to

Me at Ground Zero in Hiroshima, December, 2005.

to resume his combat flying? Would he have then become one of the war's last casualties? Was it necessary that so many innocent people at Hiroshima-- and three days later at Nagasaki-- be either killed outright or condemned to a slow death from radiation poisoning in order for my siblings and me to be born? Only God can answer such questions. But I do know that, if little Sadako had lived, she would have had the possibility of a full life. She might be alive today. After all, she would be only three years older than I am now. As Usha and I departed the museum and wandered about near

223

the epicenter of the explosion, I felt somehow complicit in what had occurred at this place.

_____

ENDNOTES

Prologue

[i] Tom Brokaw, *The Greatest Generation* [New York; Random House, 1998], p. 382.

[ii] Within the privacy of their relationship, Dad always called Mom *Gina*.

[iii] During the War, *Ricky Gallagher* was Mom's nickname for Dad.

Chapter 1

[iv] Rob Morris, *Untold Valor: Forgotten Stories of American Bomber Crews Over Europe in WW II*, Kindle ed. [Washington, D.C: Potomac Books Inc., 2006], location 41.

[v] Bill Yenne, *Big Week; Six Days That Changed the Course of WWII*, Kindle ed. [New York: Berkley Caliber, 2013], location 1844.

Chapter 2

[vi] Morris, Kindle ed., location 38.

[vii] By October of 1942, Dad was among flying 1,098 officers who had been detached from the 8th AAF in England to support the impending American invasion of North Africa. See Yenne, Kindle ed., location 1030.

[viii] For this claim, there is some corroboration. According to Gen. J Kemp McLaughlin's memoir, "The 92nd had also sent twenty-five navigators to North Africa . . . to guide fighter groups there . . . on the initial invasion." See J Kemp McLaughlin, *The Mighty Eighth in WWII; A Memoir,* Kindle ed., [Lexington KY: University of Kentucky Press, 2006], p. 48.

[ix] Dr. Robert N. Dunn, email to the author, November 14, 2008. For an additional account of this mishap, see McLaughlin, p. 53.

[x] Dr. Robert N. Dunn, email to the author, August 23, 2013.

Chapter 3

[xi] Robert Roberts, *A Medic's Story: An Autobiography of Experiences During World War II* [Bloomington, IN: 1sr Books Library, 2002], p. 14.

[xii] Ibid., p. 15.

[xiii] Jean Ambers, letter to the author, October 22, 2007.

[xiv] Ibid.

[xv] Roberts, p. 23.

[xvi] Ibid., p. 22.

[xvii] Ibid., p. 29.

[xviii] Jean Ambers, letter to the author, October 22, 2007.

Chapter 4

[xix] Hyman Lebson, "The Forty Fifth Evacuation Hospital in World War II, 1942-1945" [Randallstown, MD, unpublished paper, 1995], p. 71.

[xx] Ibid., p. 70.

[xxi] Jean Ambers, letter to the author, January 20, 2008.

[xxii] Ibid.

[xxiii] Ibid.

Chapter 5

[xxiv] John J. O'Neil in Marshall J. Thixton, et. al., *Bombs Away: Pathfinders of the Eighth Air Force* [Trumball, Connecticut: FNP Military Division, 1998], p. 63

[xxv] Donald L. Miller, *Masters of the Air: America's Bomber Boys Who Fought the Air War Against Nazi Germany,* [New York: Simon & Schuster, 2006], p. 235.

[xxvi] O'Neil in Thixton, et. al., pp. 69-70.

[xxvii] Robert E. Doherty and Geoffrey D. Ward, *Snetterton Falcons: the 96th Bomb Group in World War II* [Dallas: Taylor Publishing Company., 1989], p. 126.

[xxviii] John V. Croul, "Teen-Age Navigator: the Wartime Diary of John V. Croul, Navigator of a B-17 Flying Fortress Bomber in the European Theater of Operations During 1944" [Newport Beach, CA: unpublished binder, 2005], p. 11.

[xxix] Dr. Robert N. Dunn, email to the author, November 24, 2008.

Chapter 7

[xxx] Croul, p. 16.

[xxxi] Ibid.

[xxxii] Ibid.

[xxxiii] Roberts, p. 32.

[xxxiv] Lebson, p. 95.

[xxxv] Maj. Philip S. Wagner, "Activity Under Fire" in Irving Glucoft and Eric Fleischmann, *Medical Services in Combat: the 45th Evacuation Hospital, D+10 to V-E Day* [Baden, Germany: n. p., 1945], p. 33.

[xxxvi] Roberts, pp. 32,34.

[xxxvii] Ibid.

Chapter 8

[xxxviii] Lebson, p. 92.

Chapter 9

[xxxix] Doherty and Ward, p. 158.

[xl] Ibid, p.183.

[xli] Ibid., pp. 191-192.

[xlii] Ibid.

Chapter 10

[xliii] Wagner in Glucoft and Fleischmann, p. 34.

[xliv] Wagner's description asserts that only POW patients were evacuated prior to the retreat into the school basement, with the remaining patients—166 of them—being obliged to temporarily share that basement with the medical personnel of the 45th. See Wagner in Glucoft and Fleischmann, p. 34.

[xlv] Mom's account had given me the impression that 45th's medical personnel had sought shelter in the local high school only after the German paratroopers were spotted. On the contrary, all three histories of the 45th make it clear that the high school had been converted into a hospital back in September when the 45th first arrived in Eupen. All three written accounts also describe the medical staff's evacuation as having been disrupted, but each views this event as an orderly change in plans-- not the panicked retreat into the basement that Mom's later account had led me to visualize. See Lebson, pp. 141-147; Roberts, pp. 63-67; Wagner in Glucoft and Fleischmann, p. 34.

[xlvi] Ibid.

[xlvii] Roberts, p. 81.

[xlviii] Lebson, p. 165.

[xlix] Ibid.

[l] Roberts, p. 90. However, while both the Roberts and Lebson accounts assert that their 45th Evacuation Hospital was the first Allied medical unit to cross the Rhine at Remagen, Lebson does not repeat Roberts' claim that it was the first to provide medical services in central Germany. In fact, both the Lebson and Roberts accounts report that another Evacuation Hospital, the 50th, was already at Bad Honnef---at least briefly-- when their own 45th arrived to take over. See Roberts p. 84 and Lebson p. 166. The Roberts narrative offers no explanation for this apparent discrepancy.

Chapter 12

[li] Sidney Scheinberg, *Join the Air Corps and Become a Flying Officer in the U.S. Army: A Memoir of My War Years* [Lexington, KY: n. p., 2010], pp. 56-57.

[lii] Croul, p. 14

[liii] Ibid., pp. 11-12.

[liv] Ibid., p.18.

[lv] Roberts, p. 61.

[lvi] Morris, Kindle ed., location 36.

[lvii] Ibid.

[lviii] Croul, p. 15.

[lix] This was probably Sgt. J. J. Palmer, a waist gunner on the B-17 piloted by a Capt. Martin. Doherty and Ward, p. 196.

Chapter 13

[lx] Lebson, pp. 88-89.

[lxi] "District Weddings; Lieut. R. E. Fulton and Second Lieut. E. C. Dean at Wotton-under-Edge," *Gloucester County Gazette*, May 13, 1944, n.p.

[lxii] Ruth Blake, letter to the author, August 2, 2007.

[lxiii] Croul, p. 20.

Chapter 14

[lxiv] Truman Smith, *The Wrong Stuff: The Adventures and Misadventures of an 8ᵗʰ Air Force Aviator,* Kindle ed. [Norman OK, University Oklahoma Press, 2002], p. 13.

[lxv] CherylAnne Williams, letter to the author, November 1, 2007.

Chapter 16

[lxvi] Scheinberg, p.64.

[lxvii] Ibid., p.65.

[lxviii] Charles Alling, *A Mighty Fortress: Lead Bomber Over Europe*, Kindle ed. [Philadelphia: Casemate, 2006], location 1570.

Chapter 17

[lxix] Jean Ambers, letter to the author, September 9, 2008.

[lxx] Lebson, p. 150

[lxxi] Ibid., p.151.

Chapter 19

[lxxii] Lebson, p. 175.

[lxxiii] Roberts, p. 94.

[lxxiv] Lebson, p. 176.

[lxxv] Roberts, p. 95.

[lxxvi] Lebson, p. 178.

[lxxvii] Roberts, p. 95.

[lxxviii] "Fighter Pilot Peter Vicary [sic] Killed," *Croydon Advertiser*, n.d. Photocopy forwarded to the author by Joy Gadsby, All Saints Church Historian, June 12, 2008.

Chapter 22

[lxxix] Dr. Robert N. Dunn, email to the author, August 2, 2011.

[lxxx] Translated by Michael Carlberg, email to the author, January 28, 2005.

Chapter 23

[lxxxi] Brokaw, p. 15

[lxxxii] Eventually, Bob located a medical journal report suggesting that prolonged exposure to radar increases the risk of non-lymphocytic leukemia. See Daniel Groves, et. al., "Cancer in Korean War Navy Technicians; Mortality Survey After 40 Years, *American Journal of Epidemiology,* Vol. 55, No. 9, p. 710.

ACKNOWLEDGEMENTS

Many, many people have assisted with this project. Regarding Dad's late brother Dr. Benjamin A. Moeller, Jr., his daughter Marilyn Mason supplied additional information about her father's experiences as a medical student at the University of Tennessee.

A vast amount of information about Dad's flying career originated with my younger brother Dr. Robert N. Dunn, who had previously conducted his own research. Beyond that, Bob made many useful suggestions about where additional information might be obtained. And while he did not serve in any of the same units as Dad, Kenneth Drinnon is an 8th AAF veteran who graciously answered a number of questions about what everyday life was like for American airmen stationed in England.

Mom's wartime English neighbor Jean Ambers shared many stories about Mom's relationship with the Breadman-Sims extended family in Wotton-under-Edge. Jean's son Jason Ambers forwarded family photographs and assisted with the research in England. Jean's niece Karen Anstice supplied some additional Breadman family photographs. Ruth Blake of the Wotton-under-Edge Heritage Center and local resident Geraldine Cook helped place me in contact with Jean Ambers to begin with. Norah Barnes, whose parents had also billeted American nurses in their Wotton-under-Edge home, added information about Mom's nursing colleagues Julia Ramacciotti and Jane Kreitz. My longtime friend Dan Shields added his own post-war photos and recollections. David Baird of the Heritage Center later proofread the Wotton-under-Edge chapter.

For the time that Dad served with the 96th Bomb Group, three of his fellow airmen-- Jack Croul, Stanley Hand and the late Sidney Scheinberg-- provided copies of their own respective memoirs. While Lawrence Witt, another airman who served with the 96th had passed away before I had the opportunity to contact him, his daughter Laura Edge has written a WWII memoir like mine from the postwar generation's perspective. Her book *On the Wings of Dawn* and her critique of my manuscript's USAAF-related chapters were both very helpful. Dale Budde, editor of the *96th Bomb Group Newsletter*, added some further information about the 8th AAF's "Mickey" program.

For the activities of Mom's unit, the 45th Evacuation Hospital, the family of the late Hyman Lebson provided a complimentary copy of his unpublished memoir. Robert Roberts' published account of his own experiences with the 45th was also very informative. Marian Elcano, nee Seabring, offered reminiscences of her own life as a nurse in the unit. And Susan Hankey Webb provided some additional information about her mother, nurse Julia Ramacciotti.

Regarding Mom's Army friends, it was difficult to locate information beyond what was available in her correspondence. Mom's chaplain Rev. George W. Zinz was the one exception. His daughter CherylAnne Williams answered all of my questions about her father and volunteered her own anecdotes and photographs.

Regarding RAF Reserves Flt. Lt. Peter Vickery, a number of people helped me track down his story. In the United States, Dr. Gilbert Guinn, Emeritus Professor at Lander University, placed me in contact with John Clark who had been a cadet in the same pilot training program as Peter. In England, Peter's military service records were obtained with the help of Diane Allum at RAF Cranwell. Anne Martin of the Archifdy Ceredigion Archives forwarded a local Welsh newspaper account of Peter's tragic Spitfire crash. The late Joy Gadsby, volunteer historian for the All Saints Church in Sanderstead where Peter is buried, provided invaluable service by hunting down and forwarding several materials that were available only locally.

Frances Guthrie of the Walter de la Mare Society in London provided a helpful clarification about a poem by that author quoted in Mom's correspondence.

My cousin Michael Carlberg translated from the original Swedish our Uncle Knut North's impressions of my parents as newlyweds just back from the war. My late paternal aunts, Dr. Maryon Schnepfe and Marguerite Elliott, provided much information about the Moeller family. Cousin Marilyn Mason added her own insights about the Moellers. Cousin Geraldine Flynn did the same for the Norths.

Of all in the extended family, I am most indebted to Mom's late sister Louise Oppenhagen, who passed away in 2013. Aunt Louise provided much insight into both Mom's childhood and the early years of my parents' marriage. She also must be acknowledged for her information about Mom's medical history, as should my sister-in-law Dr. Anna Martinazzo Dunn.

If civilization is the process of bringing order out of chaos, then it was the manuscript's first editor, Susan Nordlinger, who began the process of civilizing what I was trying to write. To the second editor, Michael Denneny, I am grateful for helping to round the manuscript into its final shape. I am grateful, too, for the recent manuscript overviews provided by Katherine Don, Nili Yelin, and David Smith. In addition, both Catharine Dockery and Dan Fallon played leading roles in getting this book printed.

Most of all, I want to thank my immediate family: my wife Usha, our daughter Monica Royer, and our son Andy. Monica shared childhood memories of her "Nana" and "Dada." Andy gave much strategic advice about what should be included in the manuscript. Usha's love, patience and encouragement over an extended period of time were the most important contributions of all.

To everyone who contributed to creation of this narrative, I am very grateful. I would not have been able to complete my task without them. If I have failed to acknowledge anyone who made a contribution the process, the omission was not intentional. Whatever errors remain in the narrative are mine alone.

BIBLIOGRAPHY

Allday, Jack Stuart. *Warrior General: The Legend and Legacy of Archie J. Old, Jr.* Dallas: n.p., 2011.

Alling, Charles. *A Mighty Fortress: Lead Bomber Over Europe*, Kindle ed. Philadelphia: Casemate, 2006.

Baylis, Charles D. [ed.]. *Gunter Field: Southeast Army Air Force Training Center.* Baton Rouge, Louisiana: Army and Navy Publishing Company, 1942.

Bowman, Martin. *B-17 Flying Fortress Units of the Eighth Air Force (Part 2).* Oxford [U.K.]: Osprey Publishing, 2002.

Brokaw, Tom. *The Greatest Generation.* New York: Random House, 1998.

Brown, Candy Kyler. *What I Never Told You: A Daughter Traces the Wartime Imprisonment of Her Father.* Bloomington, IN: AuthorHouse, 2010.

Croul, John V. "Teen-Age Navigator: The Wartime Diary of John V. Croul: Navigator of a B-17 Flying Fortress Bomber in the European Theater of Operations During 1944." Newport Beach, CA: unpublished binder, 2005.

Doherty, Robert E. and Geoffrey D. Ward. *Snetterton Falcons: The 96th Bomb Group in World War II.* Dallas: Taylor Publishing Company, 1989.

Drinnon, Kenneth C. *Wings of Tru Love: A WWII Ball-Turret Gunner Memoir,* Kindle ed. [Bloomington, IN]: Xlibris Corporation, 2011.

Edge, Laura. *On the Wings of Dawn: American Airmen as German Prisoners.* [Ann Arbor, MI]: n.p., 2012.

Glucoft, Irving and Eric Fleischmann. *Medical Service in Combat: The 45th Evacuation Hospital, D+10 to V-E Day.* Baden, Germany: n.p., 1945.

Groves, Daniel, et. al., "Cancer in Korean War Navy Technicians; Mortality Survey After 40 Years. *American Journal of Epidemiology,* Vol. 55, No. 9, p. 710.

Guinn, Gilbert. *The Arnold Scheme: British Pilots, the American South and the Allies Daring Plan.* Charleston, SC: The History Press, 2007.

Hansen, Randall. *Fire and Fury: The Allied Bombing of Germany, 1942-1945,* Kindle ed. New York: NAL Caliber, 2009.

Kiernan, Denise. *The Girls of Atomic City: The Untold Story of the Women Who Helped Win World War II.* New York: Simon & Schuster, 2013.

Kozak, Warren. *LeMay: The Life and Wars of Curtis LeMay,* Kindle ed. Washington, D.C.: Regnery History, 2009.

Lebson, Hyman. "The Forty Fifth Evacuation Hospital in Word War II, 1942-1945." [Randallstown, MD]: unpublished paper, 1995.

Listermann, Phil H. *Allied Wings No. 1: Supermarine Spitfire Mk. XII.* Boe Cedex, France: Graphic Sud, 2007.

McCollum, John W. [ed]. *The Best of War Stories of the National Capital Area Chapter: 8th Air Force Historical Society.* Washington, D.C.: National Capital Area Chapter, Air Force Historical Society, 1996.

McLaughlin, J. Kemp. *The Mighty Eighth in WWII: A Memoir,* Kindle, ed. Lexington, KY: University Press of Kentucky, 2006.

Makos, Adam. *A Higher Call: An Incredible True Story of Combat and Chivalry in the War-Torn Skies of World War II,* Kindle ed. New York: Berkley Caliber, 2013.

Miller, Donald L. *Masters of the Air: America's Bomber Boys Who Fought the Air War Against Nazi Germany.* New York: Simon & Schuster, 2006.

"Mission 25: Col. Stanley I Hand." N.p.: unpublished booklet, [2013].

Morris, Rob. *Untold Valor: Forgotten Stories of American Bomber Crews Over Europe in WW II,* Kindle ed. Washington, D.C: Potomac Books Inc., 2006.

Muller, Richard R. "Blowout at Poltava: A Plan To Encircle Berlin Sent American Bombers into a Luftwaffe Ambush," *World War II,* January-February, 2015, pp. 36-43.

Novey, Jack. *The Cold Blue Sky: A B-17 Gunner in World War Two.* Charlottesville, VA: Howell Press, 1997.

Offutt, Carol Rose. *For This Marvelous Country: Counting on Me to Get Them Back Home,* Kindle ed. N.p.: n.p., 2009.

Olson, Lynne. *Citizens of London: The American Who Stood with Britain in Its Darkest, Finest Hour,* Kindle ed. [New York]: Random House, 2010.

O'Neil, John J., II and John J. O'Neil, III. "How 'Mickey' Got Its Name," *96th Bomb Group Newsletter,* April, 2014, pp. 8-10.

Peterson, Stanley A. *"The Saint": Stories by the Navigator of a B-17.* N.p.: n.p., 2014.

Roberts, Robert. *A Medic's Story: an Autobiography of Experiences During World War II.* Bloomington, IN: 1st Books Library, 2002

Saunders, Andy. *No 43 "Fighting Cocks" Squadron.* Oxford [U.K.]: Osprey Publishing, 2003.

Scheinberg, Sidney. *Join the Air Corps and Become a Flying Officer in the U.S. Army: A Memoir of My War Years.* Lexington, KY: n.p., 2010.

Smith, Truman. *The Wrong Stuff: The Adventures and Misadventures of an 8th Air Force Aviator,* Kindle ed. Norman, OK: University of Oklahoma Press, 2002.

Snyder, Steve. *Shot Down: The True Story of a Pilot and the Crew of the B-17 Susan Ruth,* Kindle ed. Seal Beach CA: Sea Breeze Publishing, 2015.

Steele, Earle E. *"Beauty is Therapy:" Memories of the Traverse City State Hospital.* Traverse City, MI: Denali and Co., 2001.

Thixton, Marshall J, George E. Moffat, and John J. O'Neil. *Bombs Away by Pathfinders of the Eighth Air Force.* Trumball, CN: FNP Military Division, 1998.

Thomas, Andrew. *Griffon Spitfire Aces.* Oxford [U.K.]: Osprey Publishing, 2008.

Walter, John C. *My War: The True Experiences of a U.S. Army Air Force Pilot,* Kindle ed. Bloomington, IN: AuthorHouse, 2004.

Yenne, Bill. *Big Week: Six Days That Changed the Course of WWII,* Kindle ed. New York: Berkley Caliber, 2013.

Yenne, Bill. *Hit the Target: Eight Men Who Led the Eighth Air Force to Victory Over the Luftwaffe,* Kindle ed. New York: NAL Caliber, 2015.

WWII TIMELINE

1941

May 11 — Mom graduates from the nursing program at West Suburban Hospital in Oak Park Illinois.

July 24 — Dad enlists in the USAAF to train as a radio operator.

Aug. 22 — After passing the required exam, Mom receives her certificate of registration to practice nursing in Illinois.

Dec. 14 — Dad is transferred to Maxwell Field AAF base in Montgomery, AL for pre-flight training.

Dec. 27 — Dad attends college football game in Montgomery, AL with his brother Benjamin Moeller, Jr.

1942

Feb. [?] — Dad is transferred to Turner Field Army Air Force base in Albany, Georgia for advanced navigation training.

May 23 — Dad graduates, earns his wings, is commissioned as a 2nd Lieutenant, and is assigned to the 92nd BG at Dow Field AAF base in Bangor, Maine.

June 20 — Dad is assigned to fly anti-submarine patrol missions from Sarasota Florida.

Aug. 18 — Dad's 325th Squadron of the 92nd BG becomes the third operational unit of the 8th AAF to arrive in the United Kingdom, specifically at Bovingdon in Hertfordshire.

Aug. [?] — Dad flies on at least one of the 8th AAF's first bombing missions. [This mission or missions occurred on Aug. 19, Aug. 20, August 21, August 24 and/or September 6.]

Aug. 27 — Dad is transferred to the 11th Combat Crew Replacement Center, also located at Bovingdon. While with this unit, he provides navigational services for aircraft being ferried from England to Gibraltar. After the U.S. invades Morocco, he serves as navigator on a B-25.

Oct. 26 — Dad is promoted to 1st Lieutenant.

1943

Jan. 6 — Dad returns to the 325th Squadron of 92nd BG, which was being relocated at Alconbury in Cambridgeshire.

Apr. 7 — Mom enlists in the U. S. Army, is commissioned as a 2nd lieutenant, and is immediately assigned to the Station Hospital at Selfridge Field Army Air Force base near Detroit, Michigan.

May 27 — Dad witnesses the destruction of one B-17 and damage to several others when a bomb explodes accidentally at Alconbury.

June 21 — After her return from a three-day leave, Mom is caught up in the Detroit race riot.

Aug. 27 — Dad is transferred to the 813th Squadron of 482nd BG, which had been formed at Alconbury a week earlier to provide pathfinding, that is, radar-targeting services to other groups.

N.d. — Dad applies for a temporary transfer to a training program back in the United States.

N.d. — Dad breaks his leg.

N.d. — Dad flies training missions at an AAF base in Maryland.

Sept. 8 — Mom receives a 10-day leave of absence.

Sept. 18 — Mom is transferred to Grenier Field AAF base near Manchester, New Hampshire.

Sept. [?] — Mom and Dad first meet in a surgical recovery ward of the Station Hospital at Grenier Field.

Nov. 7 — Mom is relieved of her nursing duties at Grenier Field and ordered to New York City for reassignment.

Nov. 8 — Mom is transferred to Camp Kilmer in New Jersey.

Nov. 15 — Mom is officially assigned to the 45th Evacuation Hospital.

Nov. 16 — Mom's 45th Evacuation Hospital boards the RMS *Aquitania* in New York City.

Nov. 24 — The 45th Evacuation Hospital disembarks near Glasgow in Scotland.

Nov. 25 — Mom's 45th Evacuation Hospital arrives in Wotton-under-Edge in Gloucestershire, and is billeted in the home of Mr. & Mrs. Reginald Sims at 46 Long Street.

Dec. 17 — Mom receives a two-day leave. Quite possibly she tours London and meets RAF Flt. Lt. John Peter Vickery.

1944

Jan. 3   Dad returns by air to the United Kingdom.

Jan. 31   Mom receives a second two-day leave.

Feb. 1   Both Mom and Dad know that the other is in England.

Feb. 2 or 3   Peter Vickery visits Mom in Wotton.

Feb. 10   Dad visits Mom in Snetterton Heath for the first time.

Mar. 9   Dad serves as pathfinder to the 40th BG on a mission to Berlin.

Mar. 11   Dad is commended for his pathfinding role March 9.

Mar. 19   Dad is transferred to the 96th BG at Snetterton Heath in Norfolk and is specifically assigned to its 413th squadron specializing in pathfinding.

Mar. 20   Mom receives a third two-day leave in the United Kingdom.

Mar. 30   Dad makes a presentation at the 8th AAF's 3rd Division headquarters where he meets Gen. Curtis LeMay.

May 2   Mom attends the marriage of fellow nurse Elizabeth Dean in Wotton.

May 12   Dad flies a particularly difficult mission to Zwickau in Czechoslovakia.

May 18   Dad is promoted to captain.

May [?]   Dad is awarded the DFC for his role in the mission on March 9.

May 24   Dad wears Mom's knit scarf for the first time on a bombing mission to Berlin.

June 1   Dad provides first aid to a mechanic who is injured while working an airplane and is unusually troubled by the incident.

June 1   Dad receives the sweater that Mom had knit.

June 2   Dad again wears Mom's knit scarf on a mission, this time against targets in northern France.

June 6   On D-Day, Dad's pathfinding bomber leads two attacks against German positions in the Normandy area of France: in the early morning at St. Aubin-Sur-Mer and in the afternoon at Pont l'Eveque.

June 11	Dad flies a difficult mission to Pontabault, France.
June 13	Mom's 45th Evacuation Hospital departs Wotton-under-Edge for Hursley Hants.
June 15	The 45th Evacuation Hospital arrives in Southhampton.
June 16	The 45th Evacuation Hospital boards the HMS *Glenearn* in Southhampton. Later that day it disembarks at Omaha Beach in Normandy.
June 21	Dad's 96th BG is sent on the first shuttle mission from England, an effort that bombs a synthetic oil refinery at Ruhland in Germany and lands at Poltava in the Soviet Union.
June 21	That night the *Luftwaffe* launches a counterattack that destroys or damages most of the American planes at Poltava.
Jun. 22	Dad begins his return from Poltava with a stop in Teheran in Iran.
June 24	Mom's 45th Evacuation Hospital, located at La Cambe in Normandy, begins functioning independently of other hospitals.
July 8	After an additional stopovers in Egypt, Libya, Algeria and probably Gibraltar, Dad completes his return from Poltava to England.
July 18	Mom receives confirmation that Dad has returned safely from the Soviet Union.
July 18	After his return from a mission, probably to Kiel, Dad is photographed by *The Stars and Stripes,* the U.S. military's independent news source, for an upcoming issue of that newspaper.
July 24	Mom's 45th Evacuation Hospital departs La Cambe for Airel, France.
July 26	Dad is hospitalized for stress at Snetterton Heath AAF base.
Aug. 6	Dad flies a mission, probably to bomb a tank factory in northern Germany.
Aug. 7	Mom's 45th Evacuation Hospital departs Airel for Torigni in France.
Aug. 8	Dad flies a mission that unsuccessfully attempts to bomb a German battalion headquarters near Caen.
Aug. 8	Mom's 45th Evacuation Hospital departs Torigni for St. Sever in France.

Aug. 8	Dad flies a mission that unsuccessfully attempts to bomb a German battalion headquarters near Caen.
Aug. 14	Dad flies a mission, probably to bomb a factory at Ludwigshafen in Germany.
Aug. 21.	Mom's 45th Evacuation Hospital departs St. Sever for Senonches in France.
Sept. 1	Dad tries unsuccessfully to rendezvous with Mom in Normandy by posing as the copilot of an ambulance plane flying wounded soldiers out of France.
Sept. 3	Dad makes his first visit to Wotton in Mom's absence.
Sept. 5	Mom's 45th Evacuation Hospital departs Senonches for La Capelle in France.
Sept. 11	Dad's 96th BG departs England on another shuttle mission, bombs an oil refinery at Chemnitz in Germany and lands at Mirgorod in the Soviet Union.
Sept. 13	Dad's 96th BG departs from the Mirgorod, bombs a steel mill in at Diosgyor in Hungary, and lands at Foggia in Italy.
Sept. 14	Mom's 45th Evacuation Hospital departs La Capelle in France for Ouffet in Belgium.
Sept. 15	Mom's 45th Evacuation Hospital departs Ouffet for Baelen in Belgium.
Sept. 17	Dad returns to England from Foggia.
Sept. 25-27	Dad flies bombing missions on three consecutive days.
Sept. 27	Mom's 45th Evacuation Hospital departs Baelen for Eupen in Belgium and begins operating in an abandoned high school.
Oct. 2	Dad sees a crew chief [mechanic] wounded when a machine gun fires accidentally from a B-17 parked at the air base.
Oct. 3	Dad flies his final combat mission to bomb a factory near Nuremburg.
Oct. 18	Mom is promoted to 1st Lieutenant.
Dec. 1	Dad makes a second solo visit to Wotton where he purchases an engagement ring for Mom from a local jeweler.

Dec. 16	The Battle of the Bulge begins.
Dec. 16	Dad is again hospitalized for stress at Snetterton Heath AAF base.
Dec. 19	In the midst of the Battle of the Bulge, the hospital's location is encircled by the enemy and forced to delay its planned withdrawal.
Dec. 24	Dad is transferred to 96th BG Headquarters, also located at Snetterton Heath.
Dec. 30	Mom's 45th Evacuation Hospital finally does withdraw from Eupen to Jodoigne in Belgium.

1945

Jan. 1	Dad is re-assigned to 45th CBW Headquarters, also located at Snetterton Heath.
Jan. 4	Dad learns that Mom has survived the Battle of the Bulge.
Jan. 12	An Oak Leaf is added to Dad's DFC.
Jan. 14	Dad is again hospitalized for stress at Snetterton Heath AAF base.
Jan. 17	Mom's 45th Evacuation Hospital departs from Jodoigne to Spa in Belgium. The unit is now located at an old Belgian army cavalry equestrian training facility. Surgeries are soon performed in a converted stable.
Jan. 22	Dad writes the poem *"Ten O'Clock."*
Jan. 24	Mom and three other nurses-- at a publicity event staged by the Army Signal Corps-- are photographed skiing in Belgium. These pictures are syndicated throughout the United States.
Jan 26	Mom belatedly receives the engagement ring from Dad.
Jan. 29	Mom departs with two other nurses for a three-day leave in Paris.
Jan. 30	Dad is again hospitalized for stress at Snetterton Heath.
Jan. 31	Mom hires a sidewalk artist to do a charcoal sketch of Dad.
Feb. 21	Dad makes a third solo visit to Wotton.
Feb. 26	In Brussels with a group of visiting 8th AAF senior officers, Dad sneaks away from his traveling party to spend a twelve-hour rendezvous with

Mom in nearby Spa.

Feb. 27	Dad returns to England with his traveling party.
Mar. 3	Gen. Courtney Hodges, commander of the U.S. 1st Army, issues written permission for Mom to marry.
Mar. 3	Mom's 45th Evacuation Hospital departs Spa in Belgium, for Eschweiler in Germany.
Mar 17	Bob Harnish agrees to become Dad's best man.
Mar. 23	Mom's 45th Evacuation Hospital departs from Eschweiler for Bad Neuenahr in Germany.
Mar. 24	After departing from Bad Neuenahr, Mom's 45th Evacuation Hospital is the first Allied medical unit to cross the Rhine River at Remagen into central Germany.
Mar. 25	At Bad Honnef in Germany, the 45th Evacuation Hospital begins receiving patients east of the Rhine.
N.d.	Dad writes an untitled poem that begins *Now is a time for greatness* . . . .
Apr. 2	Mom's 45th Evacuation Hospital departs from Bad Honnef for Bad Wildungen in Germany.
Apr. 5	Peter Vickery is killed in a flying accident at Aberporth in Wales.
Apr. 21	Mom flies by military air transport to the RAF base at Biggin Hill near London. Here Dad meets her. They fly together on the final leg back to Snetterton Heath AAF base.
Apr. 21	In Mom's absence, the 45th Evacuation Hospital departs Bad Wildungen for Nohra in Germany, near the Buchenwald concentration camp.
Apr. 24	Mom and Dad are married in the Airmen's Chapel of St. Andrew's, the Anglican Church in Quidenham near Snetterton Heath.
Apr. 27	The male personnel of 45th Evacuation Hospital are assigned to provide medical services to the survivors at Buchenwald. The female nursing personnel are held back at Weimar.
May 2	Mom returns from her English honeymoon to her fellow nurses who are billeted in Weimar.

May 6	Mom tours the Nazi concentration camp at Buchenwald.
May 7	Mom receives a letter informing her of Peter's death.
May 10	The wedding dress Mom ordered from a shop in Chicago is belatedly delivered to her in Weimar.
May 11	Male personnel of the 45th Evacuation Hospital return to Nohra from Buchenwald.
May 12	Mom is photographed in her wedding gown.
May 23	Dad writes the poem "Perseverance."
June 4	Mom's 45th Evacuation Hospital departs for St. Wendel in Germany.
June 8	Dad is again assigned to 96th BG Headquarters.
June 10	Mom meets Dad's brother, Dr. Benjamin Moeller, for the first time when he visits her in St. Wendel.
June 22	Mom is granted a seven-day leave that she spends with Dad and Uncle Benjy in England.
June 25	The Army finally grants Mom's request to change her name from North to Dunn.
July 12	Dad writes an untitled poem that begins with *Pale blossoms we* . . . .
July 14	Mom's 45th Evacuation Hospital departs St. Wendel for Schwabisch Hall in Germany.
July 15	Mom writes Dad to inform him that she is pregnant.
July 22	Mom's 45th Evacuation Hospital departs Schwabisch Hall for Bretten in Germany.
July 25	Dad learns that Mom might be pregnant.
July 26	Mom writes Dad to confirm that she is pregnant.
July 27	The Army orders Mom to a Paris Hospital to confirm her pregnancy.
July 29	Dad tries unsuccessfully to rendezvous with Mom, whom he believes is still at Schwabisch Hall, by sneaking away from an official 8th AAF officer's visit to Wurzburg. Using a small liaison plane, he looks for Mom

in Schwabisch Hall.

Aug. 3   Mom is sent home from Paris by military transport plane. She miscarries en route.

Aug. 4   Dad learns that his bride is [was] pregnant.

Aug. 6   Dad embarks from Scotland for home aboard the RMS *Queen Elizabeth*.

Aug. 6   Dad hears over the ship's public address system that an atomic bomb has been used against Japan.

Aug. 10   Dad disembarks in Norfolk Virginia and learns that Mom has miscarried.

Aug. 11   Dad visits Mom, who is now a patient in the station hospital at Mitchel Field AAF base near Hempstead, New York.

Aug. 14   Dad is granted an extended leave on the date that is both his 27th birthday and V-J Day.

Aug. 16   Mom is granted a 21-day leave, much of which she and Dad spend visiting with her new mother-in-law, Helen Dunn, in Danvers, Massachusetts.

Sept. [?] Mom returns to Chicago and resumes residence with her parents and younger sister Louise.

Sept. [?] Dad returns to active duty at Sioux Falls AAF base in South Dakota.

Oct. 3   Dad is discharged from active duty with the AAF and boards a train for Chicago.

GLOSSARY

190: The FW 190 was as a German single-engine, single-seat fighter plane manufactured by Focke Wulf and extensively used by the *Luftwaffe* to intercept 8th AAF bombing formations. Sometimes called "the butcher bird" by the Germans themselves, it was much feared by American airmen.

4-F: Unfit for military service.

8th AAF: The United States' Eighth Army Air Force was sent to England to bomb strategic targets in Germany from high altitudes using four-engine "heavy" bombers.

9th AAF: The United States' Ninth Army Air Force was sent to England to attack German targets in France and the Low Countries from low and medium altitudes using twin-engine "medium" bombers.

1/11th CCRC: Eleventh Combat Crew Replacement Center was a unit spun off from the 92nd Bomb Group at Bovingdon. The new unit's primary purpose was to provide additional training for new crews arriving in England. It also loaned flying personnel for Operation Torch, the American invasion of North Africa.

A-20: The Havoc [known in British service as the Boston] was a twin- engine attack plane manufactured in the United States by Douglas and widely used by both the AAF and RAF.

"Ack-ack": Anti-aircraft fire.

Air Division: In the Army Air Force, this was an organization consisting of several wings. In the 8th AAF there were three such air divisions, each consisting of at least four bomber wings plus one escort fighter wing.

ANC: Army Nurse Corps.

A of O: Army of Occupation

APC: A tablet containing aspirin, phenactin and caffeine.

APO: Army Post Office.

AWOL: Absent without leave.

B-17: The Flying Fortress was a four-engine heavy bomber manufactured in the United States by Boeing and widely used by the 8th Army Air Force in England. Its crew usually consisted of ten: two pilots, a navigator, a flight engineer, a radio operator, and four additional gunners.

B-18: The Bolo was a twin-engine bomber manufactured in the United States by Douglas, which had adapted it from the prewar DC-2 commercial airliner. The Army Air Force regarded it as obsolete and therefore did not use it operationally beyond the Western Hemisphere. However, beginning in 1942, some B-18's were modified for anti-submarine warfare with the addition of British-developed airborne radar for the detection of submarines on the ocean surface and deployed for that purpose along the Eastern Seaboard.

B-24: The Liberator was a four-engine heavy bomber manufactured in the United State by Consolidated and also used by the 8th USAAF in England, although not as extensively as the B-17. Normally, a crew of nine manned it.

B-25: The Mitchell, named in honor of controversial prewar Air Corps advocate General "Billy" Mitchell, was a successful twin-engine medium bomber manufactured in the United States by North American and deployed by the Allies in every theatre of war. Typically, it was manned by a crew of five.

B-29: The Superfortress was the most advanced heavy bomber to go into widespread service during WWII. Designed for the specific purpose of bombing Japan from ultra long distances, its use was limited to the Pacific Theatre. Like the B-17, it was made in the United States by Boeing and powered by four piston engines. But unlike the B-17, it had a pressurized cabin to provide a comfortable crew environment even at high altitude and a modern tricycle-type landing gear.

BG: Bomb group.

Bomb Group: In the 8th Army Air Force, a bomb group usually consisted of four squadrons of about seven planes each.

The Bulge: The last German offensive of the war, it began on December 16, 1944 when the Germans tried to drive a salient, or "bulge," between American and British Armies in Belgium. While the Allies ultimately turned the Germans back, it cost the United States more casualties than any other battle of World War II.

CBI: China, Burma, India theatre of war.

CBW: Combat wing.

CO: Commanding officer.

Combat Wing: In the 8th Air Force, a combat wing usually consisted of three bomb groups.

DO: Duty officer.

D-Day: June 6, 1944, the day that the Anglo-American Allies crossed English Channel to liberate France beginning with the province of Normandy. It was the largest amphibious assault in the history of warfare. This reopening of a Western Front relieved pressure on the Soviet Army, which had been fighting against Nazi Germany in eastern Europe since June of 1941.

ETO: European theatre of operations.

Fort: A B-17 Flying Fortress.

Fortress Europe: A term coined by Adolph Hitler referring to all European countries then under German occupation. According to the Nazis, occupied Europe was militarily impervious to any Allied attempt at liberation. Hitler's aide Herman Goering, *Reich* Minister of Aviation and *Luftwaffe* commander, once boasted that no Allied plane would be able to successfully bomb Germany itself.

GI: General infantry in the U.S. Army. More commonly, it referred to all American enlisted men regardless of job description.

GI Bill: Legislation passed by Congress in 1944 to provided financial assistance to returning WWII veterans opting to resume their educations.

Group: Same as a bomb group, or BG.

H2S: Airborne radar first developed by the British for use on RAF night bombers.

H2X: Developed from British H2S technology, it was airborne radar installed on American bombers.

HQ: headquarters.

Intruder: This was a warplane that, at night, attacked enemy aircraft that were either taking off from or landing on their own runway. The intruder avoided detection by appearing to be a friendly plane in the landing pattern.

"Jerry": American slang for a German soldier.

Ju-88: A twin-engine medium bomber manufactured in Germany by Junkers and also sometimes used as a nocturnal intruder.

KP: "Kitchen Police," i.e., cafeteria workers.

LCI: Landing craft infantry. This was a boat with an unloading ramp in the bow that, during an amphibious assault, carried soldiers from troopships to the beach.

Lend-Lease: A foreign aid program approved by Congress in mid-1941 to provide weapons and other military supplies to the United Kingdom and other countries fighting to stop the spread of fascism.

LSI: Landing Ship Infantry. The was a freighter converted to carry LCIs close enough to the beach so that the military personnel aboard could come ashore.

Luftwaffe: The WWII name for the German air force.

Mickey navigator: The second navigator on a Pathfinder Force [PFF] bomber. The Mickey navigator used H2X radar to survey the ground, thus locating the target.

NCO: Non-commissioned officer, that is, an enlisted man.

Normandy: The province of northwestern France where the Allies came ashore on D-Day.

OAF: Occupational Air Force, i.e., that component of the USAAF that would remain in Europe after V-E Day.

Oak Leaf: A second award of the same medal.

Operation Dragoon: Allied code for the invasion of southern France.

Operation Overlord: Allied code for the invasion or northern France.

Operation Torch: Allied code for the invasion of North Africa.

P-38: The Lightning was a twin-engine, single-seat fighter manufactured in the United States by Lockheed and widely used by in every theatre of war in which the AAF was deployed.

P-39: The Airacrobra was a single-engine, single-seat fighter manufactured in the United States by Bell. The AAF used it only in the early stages of the war. [However, it was used successfully by the Soviet Union on the Eastern Front, having been provided to that country by the thousands under the Lend-Lease program.]

P-51: The Mustang was a single-engine, single-seat fighter manufactured in the United States by North American. In Europe, the P-51 was employed by the 8th AAF as an escort fighter and is widely credited with salvaging the strategic bombing campaign against Germany by effectively protecting AAF formations from *Luftwaffe* interception.

Pathfinder: In the 8th AAF, a pathfinder was a bombing plane equipped with an American version of the RAF's H2S airborne radar, usually located where the ventral gun turret would normally be. A second navigator, informally referred to as the Mickey navigator, operated this equipment.

"Petty Girls": George Petty was a popular artist who drew illustrations of pin-up girls for *Esquire* magazine, among other publications. During WWII, some of these Petty Girls re-appeared as decorations on various AAF planes.

PFF: Pathfinder Force.

POE: Port of entry.

POW: Prisoner of war.

PRO: Public Relations Office.

PTO: Pacific theatre of operations.

PX: Military canteen.

R&R: Rest and recuperation.

RAF: Royal Air Force.

RAFVR: Royal Air Force Volunteer Reserves.

S-2: The Office of Military Intelligence within the Army Air Force.

S & S: The *Stars and Stripes.*

SAC: The Strategic Air Command of the post-war United States Air Force. During the early days of the Cold War, SAC evolved from the old USAAF's wartime 8th Air Force for the purpose of delivering a nuclear counterattack against the Soviet Union, if necessary.

Sad Sack: In *Yank* magazine, it was a popular WWII cartoon strip created by George Baker about a depressed enlisted man.

Section 8: Discharge from the Army because of mental unfitness.

"Short snorter": Anyone who crossed an ocean by air rather than by ship. In WWII this was still such a novelty that the passengers would ask that the pilot to autograph a one dollar bill, thus conferring "short snorter" status on them.

Shuttle mission: From the point-of-view of the 8th Army Air Force in England, it was any bombing mission in which the attacking force did not plan to return directly to its own base. Instead, after the attacking force bombed a target within Fortress Europe, it would continue on to land in an alternate location under Allied control such as the Soviet Union or Italy.

Spitfire: A single-engine, single-seat fighter manufactured in England by Supermarine and widely used in every theater of war in which the RAF was deployed.

***Stars and Stripes*:** The U.S. Army's official newspaper.

TCC: [AAF] Troop Carrier Command.

U-boat: A German submarine, or *Unterseeboot.*

UK: The United Kingdom, which includes England, Wales, Scotland and Northern Ireland.

USAAF: The United States Army Air Force.

USAF: The United States Air Force. It was created in 1947 out of the older USAAF when that military branch became completely independent of the Army.

USMC: United States Marine Corps.

USO: United Service Organizations, an organization that continues to provide recreational, welfare, and morale boosting services for young Americans who are away from home and in the military.

V-1: Nicknamed "doodlebug" by the British and "buzz-bomb" by the Americans, this small, unmanned aircraft was first deployed by the Germans in June of 1944. Operating much like today's cruise missiles, but without precision accuracy, these weapons were aimed toward targets in both southeastern England and Allied-controlled areas of western Europe.

V-2: This was an early ballistic missile deployed by the Germans. V-2 attacks began in September of 1944, primarily against targets in southeastern England Because V-2s traveled well beyond the speed of sound, there was generally little or no warning before they impacted the ground.

V-E Day: The day that Germany surrendered and European hostilities in WWII ended. Various sources give this date as either May 7 or May 8,1945.

V-J Day: The day that Japan surrendered, August 14,1945, although the official surrender ceremony was not held until September 2 of that year.

V-Mail: Personal letters that were photocopied and miniaturized to save weight for air mail delivery.

WAC: A United States Army enlisted woman in the Women's Army Auxiliary Corps.

***Waffen SS*:** The military, or weaponized arm of the SS, the organization of storm troopers commanded by the fanatical Nazi Heinrich Himmler. Moreover, the *Waffen SS* often operated independently of the German Army 's normal command structure. Indeed, it was the *Waffen SS* rather than the regular German Army that was responsible for many of the Nazi regime's war crimes.

Wehrmacht: The WWII German army.

Wing: Same as a combat wing or CBW.

Yank: A magazine published during WWII by the U.S. Army.

Z of I: Zone of the Interior, i.e., the United States.

APPENDIX A
CELEBRITIES

Both Dad and Mom occasionally made connection with celebrities within the military. For example, Curtis LeMay was the first AAF general who Dad mentioned by name in his correspondence. At that time Gen. LeMay did not yet enjoy the same public stature as Douglas MacArthur or George M. Patton. In early 1944 he was merely an obscure division commander within the 8th AAF in England. But his reputation would grow. In August of 1944 Gen. LeMay would be transferred to the Pacific Theatre. Up until then both the 8th AAF in Europe and the 20th AAF in the Pacific were attempting to bomb military targets with conventional explosives from high altitudes, and to do this during daylight hours for the purpose of maximizing accuracy. In the Pacific, the 20th AAF introduced the new B-29 "Superfortress" bomber which featured a pressurized cabin to increase crew comfort at high altitudes. But the extreme distance to Japan from the nearest Allied controlled islands was causing the entire 20th AAF program to founder. Gen. LeMay would be tasked with transforming the bombing of Japan into a more effective effort. His solution was to direct the new B-29s to begin attacking from low altitude at night with incendiary bombs. This change in tactics increased the size of the bomb loads that could be carried. On the other hand, it also meant that precision targets such as factories, railroad terminals, naval bases, and army barracks would be harder to locate. For LeMay this was acceptable. The goal was no longer to destroy Japan's industrial and military capability but rather to demoralize Japan's civilian population by burning out its wooden cities. Putting aside the question of whether or not this tactic was within the bounds of military ethics, it did prove effective.

What was Dad's connection to this man? On March 30, 1944 Gen. LeMay was still in England as commander of the 8th AAF's 3rd Air Division. For Dad's part, he had been transferred less than two weeks earlier to the 413nd Squadron of the 96th Bomb Group at Snetterton Heath. The 413th was a component of the 96th Group, which was part of in the 45th Combat Wing, which, in turn, was part of the 3rd Division. By early 1944 the 8th AAF as a whole had become an immense force. Its 3rd Air Division alone controlled more than 500 bombers. Dad's letter that day indicates that he was among a group of navigators invited to 3rd Division headquarters.

> *The* [other] *navigators and I had to go there to attend a critique. The first speaker was Maj. Gen. LeMay, & the next one was me. 'They all laughed------.' No-- of course they didn't, but I had to speak for nearly half an hour; & although impromptu, I was complimented very highly when it was over. Made me think of you again-- remember the evening you said I could hold my own anywhere? I felt really good indeed & nearly grinned in front of all when it popped in my head.*
> Yours,
> *Porgie*

[Porgie was the title character from the 1935 George Gershwin opera *Porgy and Bess.*]

With the coming of peace, the USAAF would be partitioned away from the Army and become an independent service, the United States Air Force, or USAF. Within the new USAF, Dad's old 8th AAF was renamed the Strategic Air Command, commonly referred to as "SAC." During the Cold War it was SAC's responsibility to deter the Soviet Union from launching a surprise attack against the United States by being itself poised to deliver a massive retaliatory thermonuclear strike against that nation. Gen LeMay was responsible for planning much of this. Moreover, in private, he is even said to have advocated for a preemptive strike against the Soviet Union under certain circumstances. Following his retirement from the military in 1965, Gen. LeMay publically called for a more hawkish policy toward the Soviet Union. In 1968 Alabama Governor George Wallace, who in the early sixties had made his political reputation by opposing racial integration in that state's public schools, invited Gen. LeMay to join him as running mate for his own presidential bid on the new American Independent Party ticket. As it turned out, however, the Republican ticket of Richard Nixon and Spiro Agnew was victorious that year. Further, some film critics have suggested that Gen. LeMay was the inspiration for the Buck Turgidson character in Stanley Kubrick's 1964 satirical movie *Dr. Strangelove: Or How I Learned Stopped Worrying and Love the Bomb.*

***

Another military celebrity of the time that Dad happened to mention was a B-17. By the end of the War, the Boeing Aviation Corporation of Seattle, Washington manufactured well over 8000 of these large airplanes. [Thousands more were manufactured under license by the Douglas and Vega aviation companies.] When, in mid-1944, the 5000th Flying Fortress rolled off Boeing's assembly line in Seattle, this milestone received considerable media attention-- no doubt both to bolster public support for the war and to encourage war bond sales. To generate this publicity, not only was this particular plane nicknamed the *5 Grand*, but also its unpainted aluminum skin was covered with the signatures of the 35,000 Boeing employees who had played a role in creating it.

This very plane was then assigned to the 96th Bomb Group at Snetterton Heath. Dad's letter of July 24, 1944 noted the *5 Grand's* arrival.

> *Did you see the picture of the 5000th B-17 turned out at the Boeing plants? It was in a Life* [Magazine] *not too far back. Anyway, it's covered completely with autographs; and we have it on the field. It's attracting lots of attention.*

By the very next day, however, Dad had an update. *Remember the 5000th plane I wrote of? Well it cracked up. An ignominious end to a much-publicized plane.* What Dad might have later added, however, is that the *5 Grand* was eventually salvaged. There are numerous reports that it survived the War and then flew back to the United States.

***

The *Memphis Belle* was another a celebrity airplane. Indeed, it was the title character in a documentary film directed by William Wyler, produced as a joint venture by Paramount Pictures and the Government's Office of War Information, and released in April of 1944. The *Memphis Belle* itself was a B-17 piloted by Lt. Robert Morgan who had named it in honor of his girlfriend back in Tennessee. The documentary follows the plane on its 25th mission, thus making its crew among the first to survive an 8th AAF combat tour and earn the right to return home.

Dad himself had started out with the 92nd Bomb Group while Lt. Morgan was in the

91st. Nonetheless, Dad once told me that he had at some point been part of the same crew as Lt. Morgan. His letter to Mom of August 27, 1944, makes the same claim.

> *Dearest Gina:*
>   *Didn't write last night-- was so moved by 'The Memphis Belle.' It is a Technicolor picture of a raid on Germany-- did I tell you? The raid is a real one, and so are the flyers and planes. I used to fly with the pilot, and some of the scenes show a lot of fellows in my old group. I walked out feeling very humble somehow.*

After completing the requisite 25 missions, The AAF sent both the plane itself and its crew on a national tour promoting the sale of government war bonds. Following the War, the airplane spent decades on outdoor display in the Memphis area. In 2005 it was sent to the Air Force Museum in Dayton Ohio for restoration.

***

Billy Conn once was one of America's most successful prizefighters. In 1939 he won the light heavyweight boxing championship by defeating Melio Bettina. Two years later he attempted to move up in class by challenging the reigning heavyweight champ, the immortal Joe Lewis. For the first twelve rounds of the fight, which was held in front of nearly 55,000 people at the Polo Grounds in New York City, Conn outmaneuvered his larger opponent. Indeed, according to virtually everyone present that evening, he was well on his way to winning a decision based on points awarded by the three ringside judges. But Mr. Conn would not be satisfied with such an outcome. In the thirteenth round he moved in closer to finish Joe Lewis off. However, when he did so, it was the bigger, stronger Louis who knocked him out instead. During the war, Billy Conn-- like most other professional athletes in the United States-- was inducted into the Army. The induction of such sports celebrities generally was not for the purpose of sending them into combat. Rather, the Government wanted them to entertain the troops by stage sporting exhibitions during tours of overseas bases. On August 7, 1944 Mr. Conn's tour came to Snetterton Heath.

The Dad I later came to know possessed virtually no interest in any kind of sports. Nor did he later provide much encouragement for his children to take steps in that direction. Consequently, it came as no surprise to read in one of his letters that he had no interest in meeting the great Billy Conn. *Billy Conn is here this evening to put on an exhibition bout, and in contrast I am going to read the teachings of Epictetus* [an ancient Greek philosopher.]

***

Next to Edward R. Murrow, who provided live radio coverage of major European events even before America entered the War, perhaps the most admired American journalist of that time was Ernie Pyle. Once the United States entered the war, Mr. Pyle traveled to remote battlefields where he shared the hardships of ordinary GIs. Back in the States, his syndicated newspaper column generated widespread public sympathy for their suffering.

Mom never claimed to have run into Ernie Pyle during any of the military campaigns in which she participated. However, given her own admiration for the grievously wounded young men for whom she was providing nursing care each day, it did not surprise me to learn that Mr. Pyle's brand of journalism had caught her attention. On October 21, 1944 she wrote from Belgium that

> *A few officers have drifted in and are listening to the news; the news from the S. Pacific seemed encouraging and another step closer to the end . . . . By this time many of our patients will be back in the States, and I wonder how well they are making the necessary adjustments. An article by Ernie Pyle made me think of this yesterday.*

The next year, Mr. Pyle was killed by machine gun fire on the Japanese-held island of Ie Shima.

***

Marlene Dietrich was a famous German film actress who, during the inter-war years, had made several excellent European films, including the 1930 classic *Blue Angel*. Although she originally moved to the U.S. during the early thirties to take advantage of the film opportunities offered by Hollywood, she was, at the same time, vehemently opposed to the rise of the Nazi Party back in Germany. Although not Jewish herself, she was particularly offended by the Party's anti-Semitic rhetoric. When Hitler rose to power in 1933, she refused to return to her homeland. Instead, when the United States entered WWII, she volunteered to help the Allied war effort by encouraging war bond sales and entertaining American troops overseas.

On December 11, 1944 Mom reported that Ms. Dietrich was part of a touring USO entertainment troupe that visited the 45th Evacuation Hospital then stationed in Eupen in Belgium. Mom further observed that Ms. Dietrich, who then was 43, was something less to look at in the flesh than expected, given her sultry on-screen persona.

> *Marlene Dietrich is making an appearance around here, but oh the disappointed groans from the GIs; she doesn't quite meet their expectations. This is the first time we have had a famous female in these parts; it must be that the* [front] *line is getting ahead of us.*

Mom would later tell me much the same about another well-known film actress, the American Loretta Young, who also visited her unit. But no mention of Ms. Young is made in her wartime correspondence.

***

Mom would later claim that, back during the War, Dad was often complimented for looking rather like a particular Hollywood leading man of that era, Van Johnson. The real Van Johnson was just two years older than Dad, having had first broken into Hollywood films in 1935, the same year that Dad started college. During the war years, Mr. Johnson's most memorable film role-- at least in my opinion-- was his portrayal of Lt. Ted Lawson in *Thirty Seconds Over Tokyo*. The real Ted Lawson was a young AAF officer who participated in the first bombing raid against Japan, a 1942 mission proposed and led by the celebrated AAF Col. Jimmie Doolittle. Lt. Lawson himself lost a leg when his plane ran short of fuel and was obliged to crash land along the Chinese coast. Nonetheless, he eventually managed to escape back to the West. Upon his return to the States, Lt. Lawson published a best selling account of his adventure. The story was immediately brought to the Hollywood screen. For his role as Lt. Lawson, Van Johnson donned the same brown-over-tan AAF officer's uniform that Dad was required to wear every day. Moreover, Mr. Johnson's on screen physical appearance matched Dad's own description at the time: 6 feet tall, 180 pounds, athletic physique, strawberry blond hair.

On March 21, 1945 Dad's upcoming marriage to Mom was still in the planning stages. On that evening he watched *Thirty Seconds Over Tokyo*, which had been released back in the States the previous year. He found it . . . *a little gooey once or twice but really good.* Further, Dad opined . . . *Van Johnson does look quite a bit like me at that.* On May 14 it had been a full week since the Germans surrendered. At the AAF base at Snetterton Heath things were relaxed. That evening Dad and his buddies happened to attend another Hollywood film. *. . . we discovered there was a Van Johnson show* [movie] *at a nearby base, so we chased over and saw that. The resemblance is there, alright.*

Dad's sister Dr. Maryon Schnepfe later agreed. In 2008 I happened to be sharing with her a couple of old wartime snapshots of Dad. Although she was then not yet aware of this manuscript's contents, her reaction to seeing these old photos of him was appropriate. She wrote

> Truly, your father was a good-looking dude. Van Johnson reminded Mama [Dad's birth mother] of Mickey [Dad], who stared in a film: <u>A Guy Named Joe.</u> Probably, Mickey was better looking than Van Johnson.

By June 12, many AAF units in England were already packing up to leave. On that day the correspondence reveals a real-world connection between Dad and the 1942 bombing mission dramatized in the movie *Thirty Seconds Over Tokyo*. On that particular day, Dad wrote to Mom . . .

> *Yesterday afternoon Col. Powell and I flew to a base that is scheduled to leave today. All the crews were loading their baggage, people rushing around tidying up the millions of ends that pop up at such times. A happy spot. I had been to this field two or three times in 1942, but never since until yesterday. Some of the gang there had been with Doolittle on the first Tokyo raid. I* [previously] *met a few in Africa. . . .*

***

By mid-January of 1945 the Battle of the Bulge had ended. This last enemy offensive of the War had been pushed back. The German heartland lay open to the Allies. It was now apparent that European hostilities were near an end. On January 24, 1945 Mom wrote from Belgium

> *I was called off duty (and three other nurses) to go skiing; it seemed very strange, but when we got out it was to pose for a Signal Corps photographer— how about that?*

As previously mentioned, this "photo op" was for a staged publicity event. To the best of my knowledge, Mom had never previously skied. Nor would she ever do so again. Nonetheless, the same print media that had circulated many images of President Roosevelt-- who was a paraplegic-- seeming to walk, now published photographs of Mom appearing to ski. In the un-retouched image below, Mom is peering down at her feet as if to steady herself rather than surveying the terrain ahead of her as would an experienced cross-country skier.

Mom "skiing" in Belgium, January 24, 1945

A month later, on February 21 she reported to Dad back in England that she *Had a letter from home tonight that said the skiing pictures were in the* [Chicago] *newspapers. Mom, kiddingly, said I should be ashamed of the notoriety.* [The family back in Chicago had forwarded the clipping below, but did not indicate which Chicago newspaper-- there were at least four dailies at the time-- it was taken from.]

THE SNOWBOUND LIEUTENANTS. In a respite from war's cares and travails, Lts. Clara Hubbard, Lisbon, N. H.; Hazel Skinnell, Pembroke, Va., and Alva North, Chicago, enjoy the skiing in a resort town in Belgium. They're with evacuation hospital.

Only three of the four nurses are named in the caption.
Mom is second from the right.

***

In a letter written months later, on July 27, Dad described an occasion where he and Mom had been in the presence of royalty. At a time when commercial television did not yet exit, a movie at the cinema was often preceded by a short newsreel of significant events from the previous few weeks. In this particular letter Dad mentioned having just seen a newsreel that must have been filmed while they were together in London, either during their honeymoon or their more recent week with Uncle Benjy.

> *At the last show, the newsreel showed the Queen* [Elizabeth, the wife of King George VI] *& the two princesses* [now Queen Elizabeth II and her late younger Princess Margaret] *at the children's institution; they . . . drove by us on the way to Forest Row.*

The letter does not claim that the faces of Mom or Dad are visible in the crowd. However, it does suggest that this newsreel might have shown . . . *we two calling Wotton from a wayside telephone, chatting with a lonely but cheerful bobby* [uniformed policeman], *strolling together hand in hand, heart in heart, singing 'Make Believe.'* Such sentiments do sound like those of honeymooners.

APPENDIX B
POETS

The father who lives on in my own memory is middle aged and stodgy. But the *Ricky Gallagher* who drafted the many wartime love letters to *Gina* seems to share the sensibilities of a 19th century English Romantic poet, or perhaps those of an American Transcendentalist from that same era. *Ricky* was keenly aware of the natural world around him. On the spring day of April 25, 1944, he wrote . . . *the country tells secrets, & all are vibrant. I was thinking today how much living there is if only you can give yourself up to it.* A postscript to this same letter, added the next morning, observes . . . *It's 7:30, and everything is gloriously green & bright. I love you.*

In mid-1944 Dad participated in two AAF shuttle missions launched from England. These operations included landings in Allied controlled areas on the other side of Hitler's Fortress Europe. The exotic scenery in these countries further inspired his prose. On his way back from the Soviet Union on June 22, 1944, for instance, his plane laid over in Iran in Central Asia, a part of the world he had never seen. A letter that he wrote on July 9, 1944 describes the landscape.

> *Some of the things that you would like to have seen were silent things. In Teheran, where we stayed one night, there is a peace that is somewhat akin to the rolling landscape of Southwestern England.*
>
> *We arrived late in the afternoon dirty as pigs & all fagged out. Our camp was above the city and the mountains were behind us-- some of them snow capped. It was very hot. Over the desert the heat waves danced and dust was a haze all over.*
>
> *Yet at sunset there was an incredible sense of detachment and peace. The little plot . . . was verdant and the* [illegible] *of all that was not. I felt like the shepherds must have felt.*

Before making it back to England, Dad's plane also made stopovers in the Middle East and North Africa. Much of the letter that he wrote to Mom on the day after his return reads like a travelogue. He describes a harbor in Libya.

> *Tripoli was a spot of brilliant heat, too. Hardly anyone moves around in the daytime. There was absolutely no wind. The harbor lifeless & calm. All the appearance of a busy place, and yet there was no screaming of birds or rattle of chains* [from ships' anchors] *or whistles. Just heat and dead ships.*

In September, on his way back from the second shuttle mission, Dad's plane stopped over on the Adriatic side of the Italian peninsula. While there, he and his crewmates went sightseeing. On September 13 he described his initial reaction to that country.

> *The dust is swishing all around making a wonderful sunset and grating your teeth at the same time.*
> *All about are those little plumes and spindle shaped trees you see pictures of in Latin books with pictures of Roman roads and aqueducts.*
> *In the distance are mountains, and in a way it is very much like Oran or Teheran. You must see this sometime. There is a peace to it that in undefinable. And yet the country is more desolate than beautiful. It calls attention more to the sky and its thoughts than the earth.*

The next day, he and his flying buddies went sightseeing.

> *One of the towns is on a hill overlooking the surrounding plain with a magnificent vista. One of the kids in our crew is from Arizona, and it made him feel a bit homesick-- the first time he had seen mountains since joining the Army* [AAF].
> *The most impressive thing on our tour was the church which was the most ornate & be-gilded I've yet been in.*

When he wanted to, Dad could turn a phrase. Before dawn on New Year's morning in 1945, for instance, he was waiting for definitive word that Mom had survived the horrific Battle of the Bulge. Yet, even under these circumstances, he could tell her that he felt her presence near him.

> *You should see it outside-- low clouds, a benevolent moon, translucent fleece, a touch of a breeze, and every star an unblinking dot--* [the constellation] *Orion a broach above you. Yes-- I saw the year in with you. I am not lonely except to feel the interstices of your heart.*

A motoring trip to headquarters on March 30, 1945 inspired similar observations. At bedtime that evening he wrote

> *It had just rained and everything was sparkling in the sun. Best scene-- a rolling field, green as only and English field can be, with daffodils curtsying in the*

breeze. Now to hold wings of love around you-- 'night!

Two days later he wrote

Dearest Gina:
About seven this morning it was wonderfully pastoral around here. The smoke was floating from the chimneys & drifting into a haze making the grass and shadows of the woods more noticeable. Everything was still, the sky with light clouds turning baby pink. It gives a lot of down to earth feeling in just a few moments to take in all of a sense of place.

On June 13 Dad described an early morning walk through the local English countryside.

There were special places where the sweep of the surf across the wheat & poppies, with a line of trees measuring the greater tempo was arresting enough to make the ebb & flow breeze [into] purposeful music. There were cathedral arches of trees with flying buttresses of bough and leaf attesting to the easy burden of their dignity.
I had to stop several times to soak it all in. The sunshine was glorious; and it seemed that I must drink it in for you, too. Imagining that you were with me or that I was able to see for both of us-- looking at it through your eyes. The things that are best & beautiful always put your hand in mine.

I love you
Ricky

A week later, while impatiently for the mail to be delivered, Dad turned this small experience into a metaphor.

The mail is at flood tide; and, since it came, I have been one of the rocks on which it beats. Have you watched the sea gather itself, heavy and green to begin its surge-- and striking the rocks is flung into diamonds? The rock, its catalyst, cannot pay tribute to such glory in kind yet is he always waiting.

On July 15 Dad described what he could see-- and imagine-- merely by looking out the open doorway of his barracks room on a Sunday morning.

Sitting here, I can watch the sea of light & changing shade the leaves make and watch their curtsies and obeisances to the cadent breeze passing through them. It is cooler after the night's showers, and the birds are very happy about it. I think of 'The Clock' sitting here-- listening to all the sounds, a jeep, distant planes, a GI whistling, somehow harmonizing (probably crating some stuff). Then, on the other side of my mind, I can see we two in the theater look at each other, finding love mirrored on our faces more wonderfully than on the screen-- looking back to our little house.

[This is probably a reference to a movie entitled *The Clock* that had been released a couple of months earlier. In this wartime romance, the Judy Garland character marries a soldier she has just met only 48 hours before he must return to active duty.]

On July 30, Dad described the afternoon sky.

Sitting outside in the sun. Way up high are a few cirrus clouds, the scene is very blue but it is not warm-- simply bright. The leaves of the little shrubs and the big trees make sharp patterns and dull noises as these sheets of paper rifle in the breeze.

***

In one sense, given his liberal arts background, it is not surprising that Dad's wartime letters reveal a more extensive literary awareness than do Mom's. However, except for occasional endorsements of Lebanese-American poet Kahlil Gibran's *The Prophet* and French aviation pioneer Antoine de Saint Xupery's *Wind, Sand and Stars*, I do not recall him later expressing any particular admiration for literature. So, when first reading through his wartime letters, the breadth of his onetime poetic interest astonished me.

In an undated letter written early in 1944, Dad passed along to Mom a poem that had been recommended by an AAF acquaintance. Dad's letter does not specifically name this poet, but does acknowledge that it is translated from its original Sanskrit. In fact, the poet is the 5th century Indian Kalidasa. In English, his poem is usually titled as either "Exhortation to the Dawn" or "Embrace the Day." In his letter to Mom, Dad wrote

I was looking thru my orders for my discharge [a joke] *& came across this. It was given to me by a Lt. Ahlquist who sent 3000 letters home in 9 months and who lived for some time in India. From the ancient Sanscrit*[sic]:--

'Listen to the Exhortation of the Dawn!
Look to this Day!
For it is Life, the very Life of Life.
In its Brief Course lie all the Verities and
Realities of your Existence.
The Bliss of Growth,
The Glory of Action,
The Splendor of Beauty;
For Yesterday was but a Dream,
And Tomorrow only a Vision
But today well lived
Makes Every Yesterday a Dream of Happiness,
And Every Tomorrow a Vision of Hope.
Look well, therefore, to this Day!
Such is the Salutation of the Dawn!'

Making every moment count must have seemed a very appropriate theme to a young man who was being awakened at 3 o'clock each morning without knowing whether or not he would be flying another bombing mission 700 miles into enemy territory that day.

Strangely, Dad closed his Kalidasa letter by adding the post-scripted admission that he was . . . *a self-centered, selfish, stupid ass! Kick me-- please.* This expression of humbled self-awareness was from a man who I later found to be remote. Indeed, people who did not really know him well sometimes mistook this aloofness for arrogance. Perhaps the uncertainty about whether or not he would actually survive the war had evoked an introspectiveness that he would put aside in peacetime.

In a second undated letter apparently written shortly thereafter, Dad added that he was hoping the Kalidasa poem would become a conversation piece within their relationship.

> *'Salutation to the Dawn'-- I thought you'd enjoy it. And don't forget to ask me about some things in my letter. It was too late to ask then. I'm curious and besides a conversation by mail is a very nice thing.*

On May 2, 1944, just after his departure from Wotton-under-Edge for the return to Snetterton Heath at the end of a leave, Mom wrote a letter reminiscing about a recent . . . *bicycle ride . . .* in . . . *the ethereal woods . . . .* This experience with nature had brought to mind the . . . *Exhortation of the Dawn . . . .*

***

In the spring of 1944, both Dad and Mom still were living amidst the rustic English countryside, although not in close proximity. On April 26 he wrote

> *Dear Gina:*
> *Found the words that best describes how the light on the trees was early this morning.*
>
> > 'Earth's full of heaven
> > And every bush aflame with God'
>
> *Can you imagine who wrote it-- Elizabeth Barrett Browning. Try to read her poetry and about the lives of she and her husband.*

[This passage is from Browning's "Aurora Leigh." Dad had not transcribed it quite correctly. Ms. Browning's original words are "Earth's crammed with heaven, and every common bush afire with God . . . ."]

By the end of October of 1944 Dad had reason to believe that he would no longer be required to fly any further combat missions. Consequently his letters during this time were often about non-military topics. For instance, on October 30 he described a visit to his base's barbershop.

> *Had a haircut today and while waiting read part of a biography of Walt Whitman and 'Sonnets from the Portuguese' by Elizabeth Barrett Browning. They are very lovely beautiful things. I shall try to borrow the book until I can buy it myself.*

***

Knowing of Dad's youthful ambition to become an operatic tenor, it came as no surprise that he also quoted from the lyrics of arias. On May 10, 1944 he recalled a scene from the story of Manon Lescaut It originated as an 18th century French novel by Antoine Francois Prevost. However, the passage Dad's quote is possibly from Giacomo Puccini's later Italian opera.

> 'When I close my eyes, my spirit sees a sweet lowly dwelling
> Placid past all telling standing white amid the trees.
> Beneath their green leafy branches bubbles a limped spring
> Where each mirrored leaflet dances, & the birds sweet carols sing.
> It is Paradise! Ah no! All is sad and dark and drear.
> For there lacks one thing so dear, and that is you, Manon.
> Come-- there let us live our lives. If you will come
> Oh-- Manon!'
>
> <u>The Dream</u>

***

When I knew him, Dad did own an old copy of Kahlil Gibran's *The Prophet*. But I do not recall him ever reading it in my presence, much less quoting from it. Back in March of 1944 when he was being transferred from the 482nd Bomb Group at Alconbury to the 92nd Group at Snetterton Heath, he had placed his copy of Gibran's volume in a footlocker to be shipped separately. However, there was a delay in its arrival at Snetterton. So he had written to his adoptive mother, Helen Dunn back in Massachusetts requesting that she mail him a second copy. On May 26 he reported . . . *Mother is sending me 'The Prophet,' so it should be here in two weeks or so.* In the meantime, Dad had also promised Mom that he would provide her with a copy of the Gibran volume prior to the widely anticipated Allied invasion of the Continent. By June 9, Operation Overlord was into its third day with Mom's Evacuation Hospital about to embark for France. However, Dad still had received neither the footlocker from Alconbury nor that second copy his adoptive mother was shipping from Massachusetts. This being the case, Dad was unable to keep his promise. In an effort to compensate, he concluded that evening's letter to Mom by quoting from memory the last three lines from Gibran's poem "Beauty."

***

By January of 1945 Dad had not flown into combat since the previous October. Instead, he was now assigned to a desk job with the 45th Combat Wing. This new position placed him closer to the 8th AAF's strategic planning process, but the new responsibilities did not prevent him from daydreaming. His letter on January 24 begins with a description of a planning session at headquarters.

> *Dearest:*
> *In the war room while the poop pours in for tomorrow's effort. Pins are being popped into maps and strings and tapes are drawn across. Then it finishes up with pointers, and you really have a sight.*

This same letter then goes on to describe his interest in a contemporary English poet.

This noon I read more of Walter de la Mare, which I hadn't read for days. I felt sort of dreamy with your letters beside me. It is always like this when there has been little eventful during the day . . . .

It may have been Dad's correspondence that was first to discuss de la Mare. But it was Mom who was first to quote passages from him. On February 17 she was in a particularly dreamy mood. . . .

> . . . 'our' memories surpass all others and so dearly realized in the quiet of this *hour. Once again the feeling of wonder, awe, and thanksgiving blend together. It's as nothing I've ever experienced before we met.*

Then, without further introduction, she quoted from de la Mares poem "Quiet." She closed the body of her letter by adding . . . *Sometimes it* [is] *hard to believe; it seems so perfect, you and I.*

On March 6 Dad followed up.

> *Today I just am completely off the ball. One of those days when you can't seem to buckle down to anything. I decided it was just the time to either practice* [singing] *or take a bath, so I did both.*
> *Tonight I'm all wrapped up in poetry and a visit to the hospital.*

In this same letter Dad described having just visited Snetterton's base hospital where a fellow airman, a Lt. Faulkner, was being treated for pneumonia rather than a battle wound. However, this airman was more concerned that his wife back home had just divorced him. According to Dad's letter, Lt. Faulkner . . . *says he will always be in love with his wife.* This conversation moved Dad to quote from de la Mare's poem "Silence."

***

All this verse had its effect on Mom. As early as May 2, 1944, Mom was promising . . . *I shall endeavor to read more of Eliz. B. Browning.* On July 20, 1945 during the hectic days just prior to her return to the United States, she reported

> *While glancing through a magazine, I found a page called Memory Lane; and there was Eliz. Browning's Sonnet* [No. 43].

> How do I love thee? Let me count the ways.
> I love thee to the depth and breadth and height
> My soul can reach, when feeling out of sight
> For the ends of Being and ideal Grace.

***

On July 31, the eve of my parents' respective redeployments back to the States, Dad offered Mom an introduction to an American poet, this time accompanied by a bit of literary analysis.

I've buried myself with an anthology of poems by Carl Sandburg. Most of his poems are surface echoes as realistic as the reality itself; & his song is often a shout; but this one is all tenderness-- oh how well it speaks of today.

While Dad's letter omits the title, it is Sandburg's "Home Thoughts."

'The sea rocks have a green moss.
The pine rocks have red berries.
I have memories of you.

Speak to me of how you miss me.
Tell me the hours go long and slow.

Speak to me of the drag on your heart,
The iron drag of the long days.

I know hours empty as a beggar's tin cup on a rainy day, empty as a soldier's sleeve with an arm lost.'

Speak to me . . .

Yet truly I need no invocation-- only a moment of silence to listen to my heart's voice-- you.

***

In retrospect, Dad did later share a wartime anecdote hinting at a one-time poetic interest. In particular, he described an early flight to Gibraltar, the large British military base guarding the entrance to the Mediterranean. My recollection of the conversation is that Dad claimed to be on the first American plane to land in Gibraltar. Perhaps what he really said was that his was the first 8th AAF B-17 to reach that British bastion. In any event, a B-17 crew of ten typically included four officers: pilot, copilot, navigator and bombardier. According to Dad, while laying over in Gibraltar he and the three other commissioned officers among this particular plane's crew were invited aboard an unnamed British battleship. While Alexandria in Egypt was the Royal Navy's Mediterranean headquarters, it also maintained a large presence at Gibraltar. So there is no reason to doubt Dad's recollection that he and the other three young American officers actually boarded a battleship. Following their tour, the four young Americans were then asked to join the Captain for lunch in his cabin.

While Dad's wartime correspondence does not corroborate this story, he was very specific about one detail. Seagoing vessels designed before the introduction of radar were usually configured with a "crow's nest," that is, an observation platform atop the ship's highest mast. From this crow's nest, which on a battleship was usually enclosed, lookouts could provide the earliest possible sighting of any enemy vessel approaching from over the horizon. Dad remembered climbing up the mast to this crow's nest, looking down from his high perch, and experiencing the feeling that the battleship-- which would have displaced at least 30,000 tons-- seemed so small beneath him that he could capsize it merely by shifting his own weight from one railing of the crow's nest to the other.

Afterward, while sitting for lunch in the captain's cabin with the all of the ship's officers, each Englishman at the table took turns reciting a favorite poetic verse. Dad remembered being embarrassed that none of other three Americans present were capable of doing the same. If I had then known about Dad what I do now, I would have asked if he, at least, had spoken up for the United States with a passage or two.